AGAINST THE WIND

MEMORIES OF CLARE HURLING

AGAINST THE WIND

MEMORIES
OF
CLARE HURLING

OLLIE BYRNES

MERCIER PRESS

MERCIER PRESS
PO Box 5, 5 French Church Street, Cork
and
16 Hume Street, Dublin

10 9 8 7 6 5 4 3 2 1

A CIP record for this book is available from the British Library.

DEDICATED TO MY PARENTS
BRIDIE BYRNES AND THE LATE MARTIN BYRNES

Printed in Ireland by Colour Books Ltd.

CONTENTS

FOREWORD

JIMMY SMYTH

Against the Wind is the first book on hurling in the county of Clare. It ranges from the hurling exploits of Thomas O'Gorman, Tullycrine, in 1718, up to and including the under twenty-one Munster championship in 1996. It includes accounts of hurling in the county prior to the foundation of the GAA in 1884; the barefoot All-Ireland final of 1889, the periods leading up to Clare's first All-Ireland win in 1914; the All-Ireland final of 1932, the first National Hurling League win of 1946, the Oireachtas win in 1954: the never to be forgotten loss to Limerick in the 1955 Munster final; the two National League wins of 1977 and 1978, five All-Ireland camogie wins and finally, the glorious ascent into heaven, the winning of the All-Ireland senior hurling title in 1995.

The pages abound with stories of good and bad days in colleges, camogie, club and county – hurling stories, that come either orally from players and devoted followers or from the printed reports of Clare GAA activities of the time. They paint the stories of saints and heroes worshipped down the years and tell of the great passion for hurling that exists in the county. They resurrect and vividly bring to mind through painstaking research, the names of those who have worn club or county colours down the years. The book weaves many dreams and lights the lamp of memory on many grand and glorious incidents and games.

When Anthony Daly raised the McCarthy Cup in 1995, I realised that the win was bigger than any one person. It was more than the preservation of honour, glory and reputations; more than self-fulfilment, more than the joy of mastering an art, more than the satisfaction of beating an opponent, more than the thrill of seeing the net shaking, and more than the exuberance of fitness and health. It was on a plane far higher than this. It was a totality, the merging of a collective spirit, a unification of minds that included every man, woman and child of a county unit at home and abroad. It brought life into the people and it was good to be alive. This book reinforces this realisation.

It is with pleasure that I write this foreword. I congratulate the author Ollie Byrnes and commend the enthusiasm that prompted him to fill this long-standing void – the writing of a factual account of hurling and camogie in the county down the years. I am certain that every son and daughter, young and old, will get great enjoyment from what he has written.

Ollie Byrnes – pictured in Merchant's Square, Ennis

PREFACE

The idea of writing something on Clare hurling first occurred to me around 1988, when several well-known hurlers were interviewed on a local radio station which I operated at the time, West Coast Radio. The station itself disappeared with the advent of licensed local broadcasting, but I still had some tapes of interviews which I felt might serve as a starting point for a book.

I acquired a general love for history during my schooldays in Ennis CBS, and for this I am very grateful to my teachers, Brother Power, Cyril Brennan and Seán O'Brien, who brought the subject to life for me. Other influences include a history of local Ennis club *Éire Óg (1952–1967)*, written by John McCarthy and Michael Brennan, and the first ever *Clare G.A.A. Yearbook*, produced by John Cronin; both appeared around 1967. When I was thirteen, a neighbour of ours, Raymond Kelly, was emigrating and left me his hurling scrapbook, which was a real treasure trove and ignited a huge interest in sport.

The primary object of the book is to trace the history of Clare hurling from earliest times and to attempt to give an overall view of how it has developed over the years. As well as dealing with the sport on a county level, I have included pieces on club and colleges hurling, the nurseries for all great county teams, and I have attempted to base their inclusion on their degree of involvement with county teams, admittedly not an exact science. Some clubs have therefore received far greater attention than others, but this should in no way be interpreted as any reflection on the less prominent clubs. It has more to do with the limitations of writing a reasonably concise history rather than one which would extend to several volumes!

Rather than give a year-by-year account of events, I have divided the book into different eras in an attempt to give the story more coherence, although these periods are not always strictly adhered to in the case of club hurling. Some periods are dealt with in some detail while others are not. To some degree, this is a reflection of success and lack of success at county championship level, but is more to do with what I considered to be of interest or not. I have no doubt that somebody else would select differently, but I hope that I have been able to make a reasonable attempt to paint what would be a similar overall picture.

Many fine club histories have been written over the years, some of which are indeed significantly longer than this particular book and have given me invaluable assistance in putting this story together. Likewise, thanks to all of the newspapers, which have also been a great source of information and are quoted from extensively, particularly *The Clare Champion*.

There are many people who contributed in one way or another to the realisation of this project and I sincerely thank them all for their goodwill and assistance. However, a few people in particular deserve special mention. I am greatly indebted to my family for their steadfast support over the years. To my late father Martin and my mother Bridie a special thanks for encouraging me to have a go at this, and for giving me a love for the game as a child by buying me my first hurley when I was three. I would also like to thank my brother Paul and my sister Mary for their practical help and support through good days and bad.

Another person who helped me greatly is Jimmy Smyth. Apart from doing me the honour of writing the foreword, he has given me some invaluable advice over the past couple of years and has been a very positive influence. Thanks to Michael O'Sullivan for allowing me access to his entire video collection, made in collaboration with the late Aidan Tuttle, which was a major help; to Jim and Kitty McNicholas for the material on camogie; to Máirín Elliott and Róisín Ní Dhonnchadha for help with translation; to Tom Butler for organising interviews with the Cork hurlers; to Seamus O'Reilly of *The County Express* for access to his scrapbooks and photo library, and for his great encouragement; to Gerard Colleran of *The Banner* magazine for help with publicity; to Pat McCabe for the tape recorder; to Frankie O'Gorman for his help with securing a publisher and for his help and advice in relation to photographs; to Anne McBride for her valuable help; to the staff of the De Valera Library and the Manse local study centre for their assistance; to the staff of *The Clare Champion*; to Seán Spellissy of The Book Gallery for sourcing several valuable reference books and leaving me some of them on very long-term loan!

I wish to acknowledge the contribution of all hurling people who gave their time generously, and without whom the book would be merely a recitation of facts and statistics. It was a great pleasure to visit the homes of so many of my hurling heroes and I will always cherish the experience. Their hospitality, warmth and positive attitude gave me tremendous encouragement and made the work involved very satisfying. A passionate love of hurling usually overcame shyness and led to many wonderful evenings of debate. Unfortunately, I could only include a fraction of the material on this occasion and I had to omit a few colourful stories!

I would like to stress that the selection of contributors to the book was done on the basis of trying to gather the widest possible cross-section of accounts and opinions while maintaining some continuity throughout the book. Some of those requested were unavailable for comment, and I have no doubt that there are many more out there who would have been just as capable of airing their views, as nearly everyone has an opinion when it comes to sport, especially hurling. For those of you who might fall into this category, I hope that the book will at least act as a source for further lively debate.

In order to avoid the necessity of making lengthy introductions throughout the book, there is an A–Z of contributors at the back, with some additional biographical information on each of them. Some are well known figures in Clare hurling, but other names may not be that familiar – yet.

There are a couple of people who worked closely with me on this project and to whom I am greatly indebted. Firstly, I would like to thank Gerry Quinn for his invaluable help in arranging interviews with many of the people featured in the book and driving me around the county to meet them during the dark winter nights. I would also particularly like to thank my editor Michael Garry for the many hours which he has given to the composition and layout of the book, and for his patience with the numerous re-writes, additions and alterations which were necessary as the work evolved. Without his enormous contribution, it would still probably be lying in the bottom drawer! Finally, I would like to thank my publishers Mercier Press for taking a chance with a first-time author.

No history book can come anywhere near re-creating the excitement of a good hurling match. I hope, however, that the memories of those included here will rekindle the memories of some and provoke the interest and curiosity of others in what has been a very proud hurling past.

OLLIE BYRNES

HURLING THROUGH THE FIELDS

It is a fine manly exercise with sufficient of danger to produce excitement.
S. C. HALL
Hurling is a game played by wild Irishmen with sticks.
DR SAMUEL JOHNSON

The above definitions, both of which were written by Englishmen, display different attitudes towards the game of hurling which have existed through the ages. Regular readers of Gaelic games histories will be familiar with the limited amount of documentary evidence which is available on the evolution of hurling. Earliest references suggest that it is an ancient game and was played throughout the country. However, most of the best written accounts come from English travellers, who reported on their various impressions of the game and the different traditions which were peculiar to different areas.

For those who are not so familiar with either the legends or the known origins of hurling, the following is a brief attempt to show that the game existed in different forms long before the founding of the GAA. Legend has it that the Battle of Moytura, Co. Mayo, which took place about 1300 BC, was preceded by a hurling match played by warriors in the rival armies of the Fir Bolg and the Tuatha De Danann. The origin of the present day Poc Fada competition, held annually in the Cooley mountains of Co. Louth, goes back to the legend of Setanta, who hurled his way from Cooley to the palace of his uncle King Conor MacNessa at Eamhain Mhaca. When he reached the palace he was attacked by the hound of Culann and killed him by hurling a silver ball at him.

COLONIAL HURLERS
The Normans made several attempts to suppress hurling and a ban was included in the Statutes of Kilkenny (1367) which were introduced to try and prevent their fellow-settlers from integrating with the native Irish. It was considered that the young men of the time devoted too much of their energies to hurling instead of military exercises:

> It is ordained and established, that the commons of the said land of Ireland, who are in divers marches of war, use not henceforth the games which men call hurlings, with great clubs at ball upon the ground, but that they apply and accustom themselves to use and draw bows and throw lances, and other gentle games which appertain to arms whereby the Irish enemies may be better checked by the liege commons of these parts; and if do or practice the contrary, and this be attaint, that he will be taken and imprisoned, and fined at the will of our lord the king.

Fortunately, it seems that this attempt to force the youth of the time away from hurling towards 'other gentle games' also failed. In 1550 Thomond writer Lochlann Ó Dálaigh referred to the fact that the young nobility of Clare liked to use the camán. Hurling certainly seems to have been prominent in the region around that time as it was banned by the Statutes of Galway in 1527 which stated: 'It is ordered that at no time to engage in the hurling of the little ball with hockey sticks or staves'. The Church also weighed in behind the authorities and Archbishop Colton of Armagh threatened excommunication on those who played hurling as it resulted in 'mortal sins, beatings and homicides'.

In spite of all efforts at prohibition, hurling persisted as a popular sport and was even patronised by the descendants of the Cromwellian settlers. In the eighteenth century, they became very involved with teams, both as playing and non-playing captains, and enormous bets of up to a thousand pounds were laid on the outcome of games. This period ushered in a more formal and regulated approach to the game, with teams wearing coloured caps and sashes and travelling in uniforms provided by their landlord. It was also common for teams to parade behind a band before the game, not too unlike what happens in the present day. The playing area was roped off and the landlord and his men ensured that the large crowds who attended were kept under control.

Inter-county and even inter-provincial games also took place around this time. Clare and Galway played against each other at Turloughmore near Gort in October 1759. The teams marched from Gort preceded by a 'band of musick, a French horn, a running footman and a fellow in a harlequin dress' according to a description in an eighteenth century newspaper *Pue's Occurrences*, which goes on to state:

> The above procession closed with many carriages and horsemen, the numerous company at the fixture made a fine impression. None of the hurlers were in the least hurt, the greatest harmony having subsisted. The Clare hurlers were elegantly entertained the following night and a hundred guineas was proposed to be hurled for at a re-match.

As regards inter-provincial competition, Finn's *Leinster Journal* of 1768 contained the following notice:

> The grandest match that was ever hurled in Ireland will be played on Thursday, the 8th of Sept., between the provinces of Leinster and Munster for 68 guineas at the noted green of Lisduff near Urlingford.

THE BANNER COUNTY

After the Treaty of Limerick in 1691 thousands of Irishmen, often referred to as 'The Wild Geese', sailed with Patrick Sarsfield to the continent to form the Irish Brigade in the service of France. The most famous regiment in the Brigade was Clare's Dragoons, formed by Daniel O'Brien, Viscount Clare. It was a cavalry regiment and went on to glory in many battles, including Blenheim (1704), Ramillies (1706) and Fontenoy (1745). The men and officers of the regiment were mostly Clare-born. They were initiated at Carrigaholt where the O'Briens had a stronghold and transported from there to France.

At the battle of Ramillies, they routed a Scottish regiment in the service of the Dutch and also defeated an English regiment, capturing the regimental banners of both, which were then left with the Irish Benedictine nuns at Ypres by Murrough O'Brien, Lieutenant-Colonel of the Clare regiment. This is believed to be the origin of terms like *Up the Banner* which are usually invoked nowadays to urge on Clare's representatives to glory on the sports field. The original incident is mentioned by Thomas Davis in his rousing poem *Clare Dragoons*:

When on Ramillies' Bloody field

The baffled French were forced to yield
And the victor Saxon backward reeled
Before the charge of Clare's Dragoons.
The flags, we conquered in that fray
Look lone in Ypres' choir, they say,
We'll win them company today,
Or bravely die like Clare's Dragoons.

A more sympathetic look is given to the plight of the exiled Clare soldier in a poem by Emily Lawless (1845–1913) entitled *Before and after the Battle, Fontenoy, 1745*:

Oh, bad the march, the weary march, beneath these alien skies,
But good the night, the friendly night, that soothes our tired eyes,
And bad the war, the tedious war, that keeps us sweltering here,
But good the hour, the friendly hour, that brings the battle near.
That brings us on the battle, that summons to their share
The homeless troops, the banished men, the exiled sons of Clare.

HURLING IN PARIS

Hurling was played throughout Clare around this time, including West Clare, where it is less prevalent today. One hurling legend from the west was Thomas O'Gorman from Tullycrine* in the parish of Kilmurray-McMahon whose exploits were famous. He was born about 1718 into a wealthy Catholic family and grew to be an imposing figure, standing at six feet six. He emigrated to Paris in the mid-eighteenth century to escape the hardships of the Penal Laws and immediately set about organising hurling matches among the large number of Irishmen there. They played exhibition matches in one of the city's parks, which attracted huge crowds of curious Parisians. Word of his prowess on the hurling field reached the court of King Louis XV and O'Gorman became such a celebrity that the king decided to come and see him play.

Fascinated by his hurling talent and impressive physique, the king arranged a commission for him in the Irish Brigade where his courage and skill on the battle-field earned him the title of Chevalier. He also married a wealthy French woman and this in turn led him to become a prominent figure in the French wine business. Another of his interests was genealogy and he was particularly interested in tracing links between French and Irish culture in the city's libraries. His researches uncovered a great deal of information and many of his manuscripts are now to be found in Dublin libraries, including the National Library. At the outbreak of the French Revolution, Paris was not the safest of places for somebody like O'Gorman who had close associations with the French aristocracy. So, discretion being the better part of valour, he returned to his native Clare and was given shelter by the O'Brien family of Drummellihy where he lived until his death in 1813. He is buried in Kilmacduane Churchyard near Tullycrine.*

COLLAPSE OF PATRONAGE SYSTEM

There has always been a neighbourly rivalry between the hurlers of Clare and Galway which ensures that both counties take a keen interest in each other's hurling affairs. This was even true in 1828 and the following delightfully descriptive piece appeared in the *Ennis Chronicle and Clare Advertiser* on Saturday 19 April of that year:

---

* Then Tullycreene

The rural fete given by Lord Clonbrack at Ahascragh in Co. Galway last week, in attaining his majority, was not one of an ordinary kind. One hundred and fifty pipers and fiddlers were assembled on the lawn, and upward of 20,000 persons collected to enjoy the privilege. Horse and foot furnished the highest amusements while forty large tables groaned under barrels of porter and dishes of beef – a temporary whiskey shop was erected free of access and fireworks concluded the entertainment. We have been favoured with an account of a hurling match, which was strongly contested by fifty-four men, neatly dressed. A handsome prize given by his lordship was the stimulus to this manly exertion which gave great delight to a numerous and respectable concourse. The contest lasted several hours. Six puncheons of whiskey and forty-four hogsheads of porter were drunk on the occasion and not a single broken head or aching heart.

It certainly was not an event 'of an ordinary kind' in any sense of the word! In fact, it would seem to have been a rare occurrence at that time, as most landlords withdrew their patronage from hurling following the rising of 1798 and the subsequent Act of Union in 1800. The political and social conditions of the nineteenth century were not conducive to the promotion of native games. The gentry became more wary of any involvements which might leave them open to accusations of collaboration with those suspected of trying to undermine the authorities, and clergy of all denominations were determined to suppress what they considered to be wild behaviour. Also the English language became much more prevalent due to the combined influences of the famine, the church and the education system; so it seemed that the next logical step was to embrace English pastimes also.

Cricket and rugby became the sports favoured by the ruling classes. This led to all kinds of difficulties for those who wanted to continue playing hurling. One practical problem was the availability of ash to manufacture the hurleys themselves. Under the landlord's patronage a good supply of ash was assured, but now hurlers had to resort to stealing ash from the landlord's estate on windy nights, when the noise from the saw could not be heard.

Accounts of the game around this period are mixed. In many reports it is associated with faction fights and indeed mostly came to attention in this context. It is incorrect however to assume that hurling *originated* in faction fights, a mistake which is often made. A less than complimentary report on hurling is contained in Hely Dutton's *Statistical Survey of the County of Clare*, written in 1808. 'The hurling matches called goals are very injurious to the morals and industry of the younger classes; after performing feats of activity that would astonish a bread and cheese Englishman, they too often adjourn to the whiskey house, both men and women, and spend the night in dancing, singing and drinking until perhaps morning, and too often quarrels and broken heads are the result of this inebriety.'

However, English writers have left what are, for the most part, complimentary accounts of the game. While touring the south of Ireland in 1812, Edward Wakefield wrote: 'Hurling is a prevalent amusement. Children, as soon as they are able to walk, follow each other about in bands of a dozen or more, with balls and hurls, eagerly contending for victory.' S. C. Hall described the hurling which he witnessed around 1843–1844 as 'a fine manly game, with sufficient of danger to produce excitement, and is indeed par excellence the game of the peasantry of Ireland. To be an expert hurler, one must possess athletic powers of no ordinary character – he must have a quick eye, a ready hand, a strong arm and be a good runner.'

As in sports such as cricket and rugby, coloured caps were part of the hurling attire in East Clare and East Galway in the nineteenth century, the only part of the country where this was prevalent at the time. The sport itself appears to have been as popular in West Clare as in East Clare and the following is a description of a game played around 1800 in Rhynanna (near the site of the present Shannon Airport) between teams from east and west. It is taken from a contemporary manuscript:

> The westerners came in large fleets across the Fergus, embarking at every quay from Ballynacally to Labasheeda. The contest was of short duration. Tradaree produced the ablest and most expert hurlers and the men of the west could not cope with the Tradaree men. The meeting ended peaceably, and so rapidly did the westerners re-embark that in twenty minutes their vast fleet disappeared out of the waters of Rhynanna.

Records show that the game was also very popular in Kilkee before the famine. On Sunday afternoons, the men from the neighbourhood gathered on the green near the Catholic church for a game of hurling, beginning at 2.30 and continuing until 7.00 when Fr Comyn the parish priest arrived on the scene and took up the ball. Exhibition games were put on for summer visitors to Kilkee.

Pádraig Ó hEithir was born in Miltown Malbay in 1902 and told me what he had heard about hurling from his father as a child: 'My father was reared in a place called Dunsallagh. He told me that in his time back around 1860, when winter came, they couldn't kick football very well and they used to play "spaic"* as they called it. There wasn't a tree in West Clare you could cut so they played with a twisted stick, rounded at the end, and a sort of hurling ball. They played in a "curragh" which was a place with unused ground. That time land was precious and they used to take the surface off and shake hayseed on it and it would be grand in the summertime.'

In his book *Sceál na hIomána* Br Ó Caithnia tells us that there are very few long, accurate accounts of hurling in Clare after the famine. Seán McMahon from Doolin gathered accounts of hurling from old people around 1942. They remember hurling as a rough game in the period around 1880. Some people thought that the object of the game was to push your opponent. They had two types of teams, one with seven men and one with fifteen, and the sliotar was three times as big as it is today. There were no written rules and the only sideline they had was the fence surrounding the field. But there seems to have been a great love of hurling. They even brought their hurleys with them to mass and left them outside the door so that they could have a game before going home. There was a playing field near the Cliffs of Moher called 'Páirc na Croise.'

A different, more cross-country type of hurling was played in Clonlara. The two opposing teams, each consisting of all the young men of a certain district, met mid-way between the two districts. They lined up, perhaps forty aside, equipped with heavy sticks turned up at the end which they used for hurleys. The side that succeeded in getting the ball home to its own locality was declared the winner, an opposite rule to that which applied in other parts of the country, where the object was to hurl the ball towards the opposing team's district. These games were often played at Mack's field near Cappakea Hill. The ball would be thrown in and the game would start over ditches and hedges, through bogs and marshes, each team trying to bring the ball home. It might take a whole summer to decide one of the

---

*The origin is believed to be 'spaic aitinn', a furze or whin root used to make a hurley.

matches, as night would fall before the game ended. Kieran Sheedy, in his book *Feakle*, describes a similar game called 'caid' played in the Feakle area. This cross-country hurling was very undisciplined.

However, apart from isolated areas where people's love of hurling kept the game alive, the fun of the hurling fields was more or less stilled with the Famine of 1845–51. This great game, along with other popular native pastimes, went into decline and very few matches were played until the founding of the GAA on 1 November 1884.

MICHAEL CUSACK

Clare people are very proud of the fact that the founder of the Gaelic Athletic Association was a Clareman. He was born at the height of the Famine in Carron near the heart of the Burren on 20 September 1847, the son of Matthew Cusack a native of Rath and Bridget Flannery from Ennis. He saw hurling played in North Clare and South Galway during his youth, but he was also keenly interested in other sports such as rugby, cricket and athletics. His job as a teacher brought him to different parts of the country, including Dublin, where he founded the Metropolitan Hurling Club in 1882. Around this time he refereed a hurling game between Tipperary and South Galway, said to be the first inter-county game seen in Dublin since the first decade of the nineteenth century, and on Easter Monday 1884, he brought the Metropolitan's to Ballinasloe to take on Killimor. It was probably at this venue that the rules of hurling were first tested by Cusack.

Cusack's vision was to bring sport back into the hands of the so-called 'ordinary people', and this vision prompted him to form the GAA, an organisation which he hoped would cross the sectarian divide. He later secured the patronage of Dr Croke of Cashel, Michael Davitt and Charles Stewart Parnell. Michael Cusack was also a fluent Irish speaker and pioneer of the Irish language movement as well as being a founder-member of the Gaelic League.

His love of hurling can be seen from his many letters, an example being the following comment in a letter published by *The Clare Journal* of 23 January 1904. 'To me personally, it matters little what team wins. I am content that Ireland's game of hurling is as safe as it was when the Milesians took it over from the glorious Tuatha De Danann race'.

The Early GAA Years (1886–1914)

The Turnpike was the bedrock of athletics.

JIMMY MAHONY

Kilnamona won the medals and we mean to wear them.

MICHAEL 'CURK' LYONS

The earliest official GAA championships date from 1887, but hurling games were played in Clare prior to that. *The Clare Journal* of 2 September 1886 records a game at Kilfenora:

> On Sunday a very pleasing sight was witnessed at Kilfenora. The Lisdoonvarna hurling club was invited by the Kilfenora hurling club to play a match of this old and interesting Irish game. About one o'clock a procession was formed, when upwards of one hundred stalwart young men and about an equal number from Lisdoonvarna, with the Kilfenora Brass Band playing national music, marched to Ballykeel demesne, to the delight of the elders to whose memories it brought back fond memories of the good old times when they too could wield a hurley, before gaunt famine and the emigrant ship deprived us of a bold peasantry, our country's pride.

Throughout the autumn of 1886 *The Clare Journal* reports in a similar tone on hurling matches played throughout the county. Another example went as follows:

> Hurling, that once popular pastime, much appreciated some time ago by the Irish people, but which for a long time past seemed vanished, is once more about awaking from its lethargy amongst the people of Dysart.

It is interesting to take a look at the names of some of the earliest clubs affiliated in Clare after the great work of Michael Cusack – Lámh Láidir Abú (Dysart), Brian Boru's (Crusheen), Lord Edward's (Barefield), Faugh a Ballagh (Ennis), Fireball McNamara's (O'Callaghan's Mills), Wolfe Tone's (Bodyke), Daniel O'Connell's (Feakle), John Clune's (Carrahan), William O'Brien's (Killanena) and Robert Emmet's (Tulla).

Such was the response to Cusack's call that the parish of Kilmaley fielded three strong teams in the early years of the GAA, Inch fielded a team under the name Michael Davitt's, Kilmaley went under Wolfe Tone's and Connolly also had an independent club. In February 1887 a huge crowd turned out at Slaveen Hill to see Inch Davitt's playing Crusheen. The Crusheen men were met at Slaveen Cross and led to the playing field, where they received a great reception from hundreds of spectators. Inch were captained by Pat Halpin and organised by James O'Duffy who later did great work for the GAA in New York.

The Kilmaley team of this era was backboned by the Fitzpatricks, Mungovans, McGuanes and Caseys, with John Casey regarded as their most outstanding player. This team had great encounters with Crusheen, Ruan and Clooney and, according to a contemporary account, these games generated 'feverish but healthy excitement'.

An interesting account of a game between A. M. Sullivan's (Ennis) and Lord Edward's (Barefield) is given in *The Clare Journal* of 23 March 1887:

> The Ennis men presented a very neat and smart appearance – dressed in a suit of green and yellow jerseys with white pants. The A. M. Sullivan's play was universally admired for its coolness and calmness. However, with the sides deadlocked at half-time, Lord Edward's prevailed by 2–1 to nil in an entertaining contest.

Tremendous goodwill existed towards the game of hurling at a time when the GAA didn't have pitches of their own. Many farmers in different areas gave permission to play games on their land, e.g., Con Cearney's field (Carrahan), Danny McGann's (Ruan) and Carmody's field (Quin). If the local team had not prepared the field properly it would have to be marked out before the game. Two sticks were used as uprights and the crossbar was usually a rope.

TOURNAMENTS

Apart from official championships, many inter-club tournaments took place during the early days of the GAA. One of the earliest recorded was at Fushagh in the townland of Kilcross near Ennis. Seven teams competed, including Ennis Faugh's, Corofin, Barefield, A. M. Sullivan's, Kilmaley, Dysart and Kilnamona. The winners were Kilnamona who received a prize of a fat sheep!

An example of the solidarity that existed between the GAA and the Nationalist movement is demonstrated by the ultimate fate of the fat sheep. A dispute had arisen between the RIC and the Clarecastle carters, a number of whom were jailed for refusing to hire out their carts to the RIC to carry out evictions at Bodyke and Kildysart. The fat sheep was donated to the dependants of the carters by the Kilnamona hurlers.

Pat 'The Kippen' McTigue was a member of the Kilnamona team. He was the father of the celebrated world light-heavyweight boxing champion Mike McTigue, who won glory for Kilnamona and Clare on St Patrick's Day 1923 at the La Scala Theatre, Dublin, defeating Louis Fawl ('Battling Siki') from Senegal on points after twenty rounds! He went on to fight a further two light-heavyweight title fights and also fought heavyweight.

Ruan was a major centre of hurling activity at that time and organised an open tournament in 1887. Entrants included the hosts Ruan, Kilnamona, Ennis Faughs, Kilmaley, Dysart, Corofin, Clooney, Killanena, Crusheen and Barefield. The prize on this occasion was a pony. Contemporary reports describe every match in the series as a 'grueller' but none equalled the final between Ennis Faughs and Killanena.

After normal time the sides were level, so thirty minutes of extra time was played to decide ownership of the pony. The Faughs were victorious after what was described as 'fierce and terrible rushes by both sides'. The Ennis team included Martin Moloney, Jack Casey, Stephen Kenny, Harry Moloney and Matt Ryan, while 'Old Boy' Moloney, Davey Moloney, Jim Hayes and Jimmy 'Jamesy' Moloney were prominent for Killanena.

Garranboy (now Smith O'Brien's) from the parish of Killaloe took part in many tournaments around this time. In 1887 they won the Castleconnell tournament in

Limerick, beating the hosts, and were finalists in the Templekelly festival in Tipperary – they were beaten by one point in a replay of this game at Nenagh.

One of the most famous tournaments held in these years was the Carrahan tournament. The prize was a banner five feet by four feet depicting a hurler, which became known as the Carrahan Flag. Once again several teams took part including Quin and Clooney. The final was due to be played in 1888 but, due to the shooting of Arthur Creagh a local landlord, it was postponed until 18 May 1889.

Robert Emmet's (Tulla) and Feakle were finalists, but Tulla proved superior on the day winning by 2–3 to 1–2. The Tulla team included Patrick Nihill, John McKenna, Michael Kinnirey, Daniel Quigney and James King. An article written many years later (1946) by a writer styling himself 'Old Timer' recalls the Carrahan Flag:

> I remember at Newmarket about the turn of the century Tulla had a Fife and Drum Band which paraded the streets prior to a match. At the head of the band marched two men carrying an oil-painted banner depicting a hurler in a rural setting. At the bottom in bold letters was the inscription 'Won at Carrahan 1888'. Such trophies were usually used to instil fire and zeal.

The Carrahan Flag was restored to its former glory in 1974 by Tulla man Eugene McCarthy.

OGONNELLOE

The first ever county final took place in Broadford on 17 July 1887 between Ogonelloe and Garranboy, and Garranboy won by 0–3 to 0–1. Garranboy were captained by Matthew Crowe and other team members included Patrick Smyth, John Hayes, Michael Ryan, James Niall, Michael Crowe and Pat Vaughan.

The Ogonnelloe club, formed around 1884, is regarded as the oldest in Clare. They are the holders of an enviable record; from 1884 to 1888 they played eighty-three games and only lost one! Their march to greatness was interrupted by a tour of major American cities in 1888, the so-called 'American Invasion'. According to a contemporary account from Jack O'Rourke of Kilbane, who travelled with them to the United States, 'the Ogonnelloe twenty-one were the best men that ever donned jerseys'. One of their greatest hurlers was John Fitzgibbon, who later won fame as an athlete in the United States. Apparently he had few equals over the mile.

Ogonnelloe's progress to victory in the 1888 county championships was reported in a highly lyrical manner by the *Munster News*. Firstly, the semi-final is described:

> Thousands of spectators were present to see renowned teams of O'Gonnelloe and Kilbane at play. Mr Peter Scanlan's field kindly lent on the occasion, commanded a splendid view of the magnificent hills and charming vales of Tipperary. The day was beautifully fine and the purple-tinged peak of Keeper stood out in sunlit splendour to the sky. Language would fail to convey the deep-seated enthusiasm of the multitudes who came from long distances to view the two crack hurling teams of the county. Like mountain deer, the respective Gaels dashed into the field, their coloured jerseys sparkling in the April sunbeams, and it would be difficult to witness a neater collection of athletic manhood, ready to meet in a friendly competence for the championship of the historic county.

Ogonnelloe emerged victorious on a score line of 3–1 to 0–1 and went on to win the final against Tulla. According to *The Munster News*, it was 'a decisive victory for the celebrated Gaels of O'Gonnelloe who now wear the bright smiling laurels of the county championship upon their victorious brows.'

GAA SPLIT

The GAA almost met an early death in 1891 due to a split in the association which evolved out of the Charles Stewart Parnell/Katharine O'Shea affair. It seems that no area of Irish life remained unaffected by the ripples from this famous episode. An ostensibly adulterous relationship, albeit a lengthy and stable one, became enmeshed in a web of British political opportunism, hypocrisy and outrage. The affair split the Irish Party and ultimately the whole of Ireland. Marcus de Búrca takes up the story in his book *The GAA:*

> To find an explanation of the almost total eclipse of the GAA in 1891 one has to return to the political arena. Ironically, when neither the Fenians with their intriguing nor the clergy with their boycotting and verbal onslaughts managed between them to kill the association, the Home Rule Party (Irish Party) nearly succeeded in doing so, when early in 1891 it broke into two bitterly opposed sections. Many county boards were dissolved – in Clare no official county championships took place from 1891 to 1895.

Parnell, the champion of Home Rule, saw his power and achievements dwindle away before his early death in 1891 aged 45. His funeral in Dublin turned into a legendary demonstration of people power and was one of the largest ever witnessed in the city. Marcus de Búrca continues:

> Occupying a prominent place in the vast cortege were the men of the GAA – said by some to number as many as 2,000 – who walked, each carrying a hurley draped in black and held in reverse to resemble a rifle, through the city to Glasnevin cemetery.

In 1896 a county board was re-established in Clare, with Pat O'Neill of Tulla as secretary, and the county took part once again in championship hurling. Other Munster counties such as Tipperary, Cork, Limerick and Kerry had continued with their participation during the Parnell split.

CROKE CUP

County teams around this time were comprised mostly of the winning county championship teams and the championship resembled more the present All-Ireland club series than the All-Ireland as we know it today. In 1896 the Croke cup competition came into being. Most Rev. Dr Croke, Bishop of Cashel and Emly, presented two silver cups to the GAA in that year, one for Gaelic football and the other for hurling. Clare became the first holders of the hurling trophy.

Tulla had the pick of the county team in 1896 as a result of being county champions, but they selected some players from other neighbouring parishes. The seventeen-man team included twelve players from Tulla, two from O'Callaghan's Mills and one each from Feakle, Bodyke and Broadford. They defeated Tipperary on New Year's Day 1897 in the 1896 Croke cup at Mallow. (It was common for competitions to overlap into the next year). Tipperary were represented by Tubberadora, a townland three miles from Holycross. In the semi-final, they had an easy victory over Connaught champions Ardrahan.

The final against Crosstown of Wexford took place at Jones' Road on 27 June 1897. The Clare team travelled up the day before and stayed overnight at O'Doherty's Hotel in Bridge Street. After what must have been a good night's rest they journeyed on to Jones' Road the next day, and won a decisive 6–16 to 0–2 victory over Wexford. The celebrated Pat O'Neill kept a clean sheet in goal while Tom 'Feather' Henchy of Feakle caught the eye at wing-forward. (Tom Henchy is reputed to have earned the nickname 'Feather' from his habit of sticking a feather in the ground a certain distance from the goal-posts so that, when racing out from his wing-forward position, he could take aim without looking to where the posts were!) There were seventeen players on each team with the Clare side lining out as follows:

Pat O'Neill (captain)
Pat O'Dea
John Kelly, John Larkin, Jack Coughlan
Tom Coughlan, Pat King, Matt Ryan
John Conway, Jim Corry
Martin Corry, Michael Cooney, Ned Corry
John Moloney, Michael Meehan, Tom Henchy
Pat McMahon

The Independent stated that 'the Wexford players were fairly outpaced by the Banner County men, whose dexterity was simply marvellous and whose speed was sustained to the end'. Their reporter went on to say that 'the winners scored goals and points with machine-like regularity'. *The Clare Journal* also reported on the match:

> The event, though not largely advertised, drew a crowd of over 2,000 people to the well-known grounds and the weather was beautifully fine without being too oppressive. The sturdy Claremen arrived on Saturday evening and to the casual observer, appeared in the pink of condition.
>
> A considerable delay occurred due to the late arrival of the Wexfordians, who travelled up by special train on Sunday morning. A further delay occurred in choosing a referee as Wexford objected to Mr Deering (Cork), but the parties eventually settled on Mr Stephen Holland (Dublin).
>
> On the Monday after the Croke Cup Final, the Clare team visited Glasnevin Cemetery and offered up prayers for the repose of the soul of the Manchester Martyrs, Allen, Larkin and O'Brien.

The homecoming celebrations are described in the Tulla club history *The Claret and Gold*:

> The victorious team reached Ardsollus at 8 o'clock on Monday evening. They received a great reception at Limerick and Cratloe. The Quin and Tulla bands were in attendance at Ardsollus and a procession was formed and marched into Quin. From Quin to Tulla bonfires blazed and every crossroads helped to swell the crowd. In Tulla a large crowd turned out and scenes of great enthusiasm were witnessed.

Tipperary (Tubberadora) exacted revenge when they defeated Clare by 5–1 to 0–1 at Kilmallock on 24 May 1897 in the 1896 championship. During these years Tubberadora were one of the greatest hurling combinations, winning All-Ireland titles in 1895, 1896 and 1898, with all teams captained by Mikey Maher.

Clare had mixed luck in the 1896–1901 championships. In the 1897 championship, played at Limerick on 19 June 1898, they lost to Limerick (Kilfinnane) by 2–5 to 2–3. However, they had a good win over Cork (St Finbarr's) in the 1899 championship played on 13 May 1900, but were then decisively beaten by Tipperary, 5–16 to 0–8 in the Munster final at the Market's Field.

KILNAMONA

Kilnamona were among the elite of Clare senior hurling clubs in the first decade of the twentieth century, other strong clubs being O'Callaghan's Mills and Tulla. Kilnamona won their first senior championship in 1902, defeating Barefield decisively by 1–17 to 2–2. Controversy raged afterwards and was carried in the local papers with Barefield demanding a re-match.

The Barefield club alleged that Kilnamona had the pick of four parishes and challenged Kilnamona to a re-match for the medals. Kilnamona were very hurt by this allegation and their captain Michael 'Curk' Lyons replied in the *Saturday Record* of 1 November, 1902 on behalf of his club: 'Kilnamona won the medals and we mean to wear them', although he did propose playing an alternative challenge match involving a wager of £17 a side, the money to be lodged with the editor of *The Clareman*. Some of this money would be used to pay the referee's expenses and the rest would be used to purchase two cups which the winning team would present to the county board for competitions. It seems, however, that this match never took place.

Kilnamona proved their worth by retaining the senior championship of 1903, played on 5 January 1904. They destroyed the challenge of Thomond's on a score of 4–14 to nil. Kilnamona won another senior championship against O'Callaghan's Mills in 1908 in what was a glorious decade for them. Emigration was a major factor in their decline as a hurling power within Clare; Mick McDonnell and Mick Brody left for the States. This powerful Kilnamona team also included Mick 'Curk' Lyons, Dan Leary, John Rynne, Denis Rynne (Snr), John McTigue and Rory O'Sullivan. Many of these men were all-round athletes. Denis Rynne (Snr) was a champion Munster sprinter and Johnny Rynne was a renowned high-jumper.

Clare Croke Cup Champions, 1908
Back row: B. Lynch, J. O'Regan, John Shalloo, John Rodgers, Ed Grace, Paddy Kenny, M. Lynch; Centre row: William 'Dodger' Considine, Amby Power, W. O'Halloran, T. Boyce, J. O'Halloran, P. Culloo, James Cullinan; Seated: P. J. Floyd, P. Brody, Jack Kelly, Tom McGrath, Denis 'Dunny' O'Callaghan, Michael Moroney, Thomas McInerney, F. Power, D. Roughan [secretary of county board]

O'CALLAGHAN'S MILLS

O'Callaghan's Mills were very successful from 1904 to 1914, contesting at least eight county finals and winning four. They were founded in 1886 but did not come to prominence until a decade later when they reached a tournament final, losing to Kilbane (in the parish of Broadford) by two points. They also lost the county finals of 1896 and 1897 to Tulla. An indication of their strength is the fact that they fielded two senior teams at one stage, St Patrick's and Fireballs. The Fireballs defeated St Patrick's in the county final of 1909.

In 1908 the Mills also annexed the county cup from rivals Kilnamona by twenty-five points to fifteen, but lost the delayed 1908 county final by the narrowest of margins to Kilnamona. This county cup is not to be confused with the William Redmond cup which was also played for at this time. The successful Clare team which won the Croke cup in 1908 included seven players from O'Callaghan's Mills, Ed Grace, Jack Kelly, Michael Moroney, Tom McInerney, Tom McGrath, Denis 'Dunny' O'Callaghan and John Shalloo. The team also included Amby Power (Quin), Paddy Kenny (Ennis), Mick Brody and James Cullinan (Kilnamona). It is interesting to note that Clare's defeat to Kerry in the championship of 1908 by 4–9 to 3–6 did not prevent them from representing Munster in the prestigious Croke Cup, beating Antrim 2–9 to 0–2 in the semi-final, and Galway by 3–14 to 1–4 in the final.

CHAMPIONSHIP

The first senior hurling championship under GAA rules took place in 1887 and was played on an open-draw system. Clare, represented by Smith O'Brien's, were drawn against Wicklow at Athlone on 19 July 1887, but the Bannermen received a walkover. In the second round, they travelled to Nenagh where they went under to Tipperary by 1–7 to 0–2.

The senior championships of 1888 were unfinished due to the fact that a large number of hurlers went to the United States to play exhibition games in various cities. In 1889 Tulla Emmets won the county championship, beating neighbours Feakle by 2–3 to 0–6 in the final at Con Cearney's Field in Carrahan, thus giving the Tullamen the right to represent Clare in the All-Ireland championship.

Tulla's opening game in Newport was against South Liberties (Limerick), with the Clare representatives winning by 5–1 to 2–2. Unfortunately, Tulla lost to Moycarkey (Tipperary) in the second round by 3–0 to 2–2. Tulla were given the game on an objection, as it was ruled that one of Tipperary's goals was scored after the ball had gone wide.

Kerry overcame Cork on the other side of the Munster championship but, surprisingly, didn't travel for the Munster final. So Clare were declared champions of Munster for 1889 and qualified to contest their first ever All-Ireland final against Kickham's (Dublin) at Inchicore. They were captained by non-playing captain John Considine. This was a fairly common practice at the time as non-playing captains were selected for their influence in keeping teams together and making them train. The Clare team (twenty-one a side) was as follows:

John Considine
Thomas Coughlan, Denis McKenna, Daniel McNamara
John McNamara, Daniel Quigney, Daniel Moroney
Matthew O'Dea, William Moroney, Michael Corry
Ned Corry, Pat O'Neill (goal),Timothy O'Connell

Michael Flynn, Patrick Vaughan, John McKenna
Martin Russell, Patrick McGrath, Timothy Donnellan
John Moloney, James King, Michael Kinnirey

'The match,' wrote P. P. Sutton in his GAA notes in *Sport*, a contemporary publication, 'was by a long chalk the finest display of our national pastime I have ever witnessed, and the Kickham's covered themselves from head to foot with honours by hurling with the most extreme pluck and brilliancy. Though beaten by such a big score, 5–1 to 1–6, the Claremen are really skilled hurlers, but their discipline and staying powers were inferior to the Dubliners.' For Kickham's, W. J. Spain scored three goals.

William Moloney of Tulla was vice-president of the Clare county board at the time and stated that a number of their players were injured going into the final, including Patrick Liddy who, though present at the game, was unable to take part. Clare were also at a great disadvantage because of the fact that they played in their bare feet on ground that was so slippery that sawdust had to be laid on several portions of it.

The GAA organisation was having teething problems with championship competitions running on to the following year and causing confusion. In the 1901 championship Limerick defeated Clare 6–9 to 3–13 but lost the game on an objection. Clare trounced Limerick in the re-match by 2–10 to 0–1 to qualify for another Munster final, this time against Cork in the Market's Field. However, this fixture wasn't played until 26 April 1903! Admission cost three old pence and gate receipts came to £56. *The Clare Journal*'s report of the game tells us that there was an important last-minute substitution due to unforeseen circumstances:

> The appointed official Mr Matt McGrath was unable to referee due to the fact that he was unable to gain admission to the grounds but Limerick's Mr Denis Spencer Lyons proved an admirable deputy.

That 1901 Munster final was considered to be one of the finest since the association was founded. Skill and sportsmanship abounded and the teams were level at the interval, but Cork (Redmond's) pulled away in the second half to win 3–10 to 2–6. Incidentally, London Irish won the All-Ireland final that year, 1–5 to 0–4, with a team which included three Claremen and nine Corkmen. J. J. Coughlan, Paddy and Jack King from Rannagh, Tulla were described by GAA historian Thomas F. O'Sullivan as 'fine defensive hurlers with long accurate drives'.

Clare's Munster championship record in the first decade of the twentieth century was fairly dismal, with many first-round defeats, including two defeats to Kerry in 1907 and 1908. However, by this stage a strong combination had developed, with Amby and Joe Power, Edward Grace, Thomas McGrath, John Shalloo and Willie 'Dodger' Considine amongst others gracing the scene. All of these would play leading roles in the years to come.

In the 1909 championship, Clare defeated Limerick by 5–7 to 1–14 but failed to Tipperary, 4–10 to 2–9 in Limerick. Typical of the rivalry between Limerick and Clare, the Shannonsiders gained revenge the following year, winning narrowly by 3–10 to 4–5. Clare and Waterford drew 1–1 to 1–1 in the 1911 championship at Fermoy and, with Waterford failing to muster a team for the replay, the Bannermen got a walkover. Limerick subsequently defeated them by 10–5 to 6–1 in the semi-final of the 1911 Munster championship.

Ennis Hurling Club won the county championship in 1911. In the following season, Ennis (now known as the Dalcassians) and O'Callaghan's Mills dominated the county selection with Pako 'Brophy' Malone (goal-keeper), Martin 'Handsome' Moloney, Paddy Kenny and Willie 'Dodger' Considine (Ennis), Edward Grace and Thomas McGrath (O'Callaghan's Mills) and Amby Power (Quin) in the line-up. In the first round of the Munster championship Tipperary just about held out to win 3–3 to 2–3 with Clare missing many chances. However, it was the beginning of a new era, though Clare again failed narrowly to Tipperary at the semi-final stage in 1913.

Jimmy Mahony, a native of the Old Mill Street area of Ennis, was born in 1900, emigrated to the United States in 1928, and died in New York in 1995. Jimmy was a frequent visitor to his beloved Ennis and in 1988 he recounted to me in some detail what town life was like in the early years of the century. 'The town was very quiet; the only excitement was looking forward to the passage of the Home Rule Bill. We had the Clare Militia in the Military Barracks; they had Sunday parades with a band which put on quite a show. Apart from that, the big interest was Gaelic games. Gaelic football was very strong in Ennis and there were a lot of street leagues in hurling which produced some of the successful senior and junior players of 1914.

'They practised every evening and many of them learned how to handle a stick from the old-timers in the Turnpike. The Turnpike was the bedrock of athletics. You had great families like the Considines – Tull, Brendan and Willie 'Dodger', the Spellissys at the top of Gaol Street [now O'Connell Street] – Jack, James ('Sham') and Michael ('Beezer'). Old Mill Street also had a hurling team; the most prominent players were Steve Miller, Martin Moloney and Paddy Kenny.'

1914 ALL-IRELAND

Clare opened their 1914 Munster championship campaign with an away win over Kerry 7–3 to 4–1 at Listowel in May 1914. Limerick, who had earlier defeated Tipperary by fourteen points, fell to Clare by 4–2 to 0–2 at Mallow. This game was originally fixed for the Market's Field but the British Forces occupied the Limerick grounds while mobilising for the Great War. 'Sham' Spelissy was the top scorer at Mallow notching up two goals. In a preview to the subsequent Munster final against Cork at Thurles on 20 September 1914, *The Clare Journal* devoted a column of twenty lines to the game.

The team was made up of players from Ennis Dalcassians, O'Callaghan's Mills, Quin and Newmarket-on-Fergus. Jim 'Bawn' Clancy of Moohane, Newmarket was a team member and was interviewed by *Gaelic Sport* magazine in 1970. The panel of twenty were brought to Lisdoonvarna for training during the week before the All-Ireland. Morning training seems to have been popular in Clare even then, although the pace might have been a bit slower. 'We had to tog out and walk from Lisdoonvarna to Liscannor and walk back again each morning before breakfast. Jim Guerin was one of the best men of his time; he out-played the great John 'Tyler' Mackey in the first round of the championship against Limerick in 1914'.

Because the Munster final was delayed, Cork had already been nominated to represent Munster in the All-Ireland semi-final and defeated Galway 6–6 to nil. Boosted by the junior and senior hurling victories at Mallow, the training fund committee launched an appeal in September in preparation for the Munster final.

Thomas McGrath opened the scoring for Clare with a goal after five minutes. However, Cork fought back to lead by 1–1 to 1–0 at the interval. The second half was equally close and hard-fought with Clare emerging winners by the narrowest of margins, 3–2 to 3–1. Clare's second Munster championship victory was celebrated in verse and can by found in *Ballads of County Clare* by Seán P. Ó Cillín:

> When the starting whistle sounded,
> Oh the ball was quickly grounded,
> The hurlers gathered round it,
> They rallied and they reeled,
> You have seldom seen such slashing,
> And scores of hurley's smashing,
> No one could cut a tanner on the field,
>
> Now they're back in Co. Clare,
> And there's music everywhere,
> The boys are full of frolics and of fun,
> The Banner County bred them,
> And Maria Reddin fed them,
> And Amby Power led them,
> Like a father with his son,
> He led the gallant hurlers all the way to Thurles,
> And the Munster Final Championship they won.

Clare continued their preparation for All-Ireland honours with a challenge game against Toomevara. On 8 October *The Clare Journal* carried a front page appeal from the training fund committee. This request for financial contributions was prefaced by the claim that 'hitherto untrained men have invariably gone down before the products of scientific training'. The team was brought together for collective training at Lisdoonvarna under the watchful eye of trainer Jim O'Hehir from Ballynacally, father of the famous sports commentator Micheál O'Hehir.

In the lead-up to the final against Laois, *The Clare Journal* gave extensive coverage to the game, including pen pictures of the players. Laois, the Leinster champions, had overcome tough opposition, including Dublin, and later Kilkenny in the Leinster final. They beat the famed Kilkenny men in both 1914 and 1915. Most of the Laois team came from Kilcotton and Rathdowney.

The Clare team was a seasoned side, with Amby and Joe Power, Edward Grace, Thomas McGrath and Willie 'Dodger' Considine, all seasoned players with eight to ten years service on the senior team. Relative newcomers included Rob Doherty, James Clancy and seventeen year-old Brendan Considine.

The bulk of the Clare supporters travelled up by train on the Sunday morning. *The Clare Journal* described the crowd as 'the largest ever to leave Ennis'. Elizabeth Crimmins from Newmarket-on-Fergus was an eighteen year-old girl at the time. She told me about her trip to the match. 'I went to every hurling match, especially when Newmarket were playing; I knew John Fox, Rob Doherty, Jim Clancy and Jim Guerin. We went by train from Ballycar to Dublin. Many of us had never been on a train before and when we got out at Kingsbridge, as it was then, we got into the first tram and got off when it stopped; we thought we were in Jones' Road!' (Croke Park).

Clare came on to the pitch accompanied by Mr William Redmond MP for East Clare. They were greeted by terrific cheering from the estimated attendance of 15,000 who paid a total of £475 at the gate. Clare built up an interval lead of 10 points, 3–1 to nil, with a goal from Jim Clancy after seven minutes, two from Jim Guerin and a point from Brendan Considine. Laois fought back with an early second-half goal but, with the Clare backs playing soundly, the Clare forwards went on to score two more goals from Jim Guerin and Martin 'Handsome' Moloney to leave Clare comfortable winners, 5–1 to 1–0 against a disappointing Laois team.

Clare's win was reported in the following day's *Irish Independent*. 'They excelled in both science and dash. Not only in attack did they demonstrate marked superiority, but their backs gave a grand display which was generally admired.' Referring to the level of support, the paper went on to add: 'Clare appeared to have the majority of adherents'. The victorious Clare team collected the Great Southern Challenge Cup and the after-match celebrations took place in Wynne's Hotel. They returned home the following day to a heroes' welcome.

The 1914 team was backboned by Joe Power at centre-field, who was described as a 'wonderful overhead hurler' by *The Clare Journal*. 'Sham' Spellissy was described as 'a fine athlete and a scientific hurler'. The goa-lkeeper was Pat 'Fowler' McInerney; he preferred to play outfield in the thick of the fray and later distinguished himself at full-back in a long career. The majority of the team were approximately six feet tall with Amby Power standing at 6ft 4ins and built accordingly.

Brendan Considine hurled for Clare at different times during the period from 1914 to 1930. He described the 1914 team to Brendan Fullam in *Giants of the Ash:*

> The 1914 team were a fine body of men. Many of them were highly-skilled in the art of doubling on a ball. Tom McGrath from O'Callaghan's Mills was a fine full forward. He had great drive and speed. Bob Doherty of Newmarket always played with determination and distinction. Martin Moloney was a beautiful player and a lovely striker of the ball, and my brother 'Dodger' Considine played a wonderful game in the final. He had strength and courage above the ordinary. The full-forward line were known as the forwards machine.

Clare All-Ireland Senior Champions, 1914
Team management: Dr T. P. Fitzgerald, James O'Regan, Jim O'Hehir; Back [extreme]: John Rodgers, Patrick McDermott, Patrick Moloney; Back [l/r]: Thomas McGrath, John Fox, Rob Doherty, M. Flanagan, Jim Clancy, Joe Power; Seated: Jim Guerin, Pat 'Fowler' McInerney, Willie 'Dodger' Considine, Amby Power, Martin 'Handsome' Moloney, Ed Grace, John Shalloo; Front: Brendan Considine, James 'Sham' Spellissy

Brendan later won an All-Ireland medal with Dublin and a Munster championship medal with Cork; he also played for Waterford but returned to the Clare colours in the late 1920s.

Tom 'Fowler' McInerney, now living in Nenagh, was interviewed by Liam Ryan in *The Irish Times* of 28 August 1995. Tom spoke about the difficulties which his brother Pat 'Fowler' encountered before the 1914 All-Ireland. Their father was not keen to see hurling interfere with his sons other duties around the farm and this proved a major impediment to pre-match training. A letter arrived from Clare captain Amby Power saying that if Pat wasn't in Quin to train he'd get another man.

According to Tom: 'He couldn't tell his father because he wouldn't let him go; there was too much work to be done. He came in to his dinner, went upstairs, put his best suit in a bag and threw it out the back window. He went out the back, changed, put his working clothes in a shed, walked to Quin and joined the team for two weeks collective training. He came home the Monday evening after the match, said nothing, changed into his working clothes, and went back working as if he'd never been away. A neighbour helping us out at the time whispered to me that they had won.'

1914 JUNIOR ALL-IRELAND

Clare was the first county to win the senior and junior hurling championship double. The exploits of the successful junior team are often dismissed, but contemporary accounts would indicate that this team was a highly-talented side. At least six members of the team played in a senior trial at Quin on 31 May 1914. Dan Flannery and Simon Minogue lined out for East Clare, while Paddy Gordon, Dan Minogue, Jack Spellissy and Jim Marrinan represented Ennis Dalcassians, who were the hurling backbone of Mid-Clare at the time.

The entire panel for the 1914 final included the following:

Dan Minogue, Ennis Dalcassians
M. J. Baker, Ennis Dalcassians
Paddy Gordon, Ennis Dalcassians
Edward Lucid, Ennis Dalcassians
Fred Garrihy, Ennis Dalcassians
Jack Spellissy, Ennis Dalcassians
Johnny 'Joker' Coote, Ennis Dalcassians
James Marrinan, Ennis Dalcassians
Dan Crowe, Clonlara
Dan Flannery, Scariff
Simon Minogue, Feakle
P. Rodgers, Feakle
Paddy Connell, Tulla
Jim Quinn, Tulla
Paddy Quinn, Tulla
Tommy Daly, Tulla
Michael Bolton, Tulla
A. Gleeson, Bodyke

Match reports in the newspapers of the day were short and erratic. Reporters went in for flowery English rather than match content, so we have very sketchy accounts of games. The coronation of King George V and Queen Mary on 22 June 1911 was described as a brilliant spectacle and received almost a full page of coverage in *The Clare Journal*, while reports of sporting events, even major ones, were relegated to a few paragraphs.

The Clare juniors opened their campaign against Tipperary in Mallow on 7 September 1914. A feature of the play was the work of the Clare goal-keeper Tommy Daly. 'His saving performances were most praiseworthy and it is no exaggeration that his performance was invaluable to the side' according to *The Clare Journal*. Clare led Tipperary by eight points at half-time and eventually won by twelve points, 4–4 to 1–1.

In the Munster final, the team emulated the success of their senior colleagues with an exciting 6–2 to 5–2 win over Cork. While Clare led by 5–1 to 1–2 at the interval, it took sterling displays from Dan Crowe, Dan Minogue, Simon Minogue, Paddy Gordon and Dan Flannery to hold out for a three-point victory. Clare went on to defeat Galway 6–2 to 2–1 in the All-Ireland semi-final, thus qualifying to meet Laois in the decider at Jones' Road.

The final was not played until March 1915, with the team leaving Ennis the day before at 2.40p.m. and arriving in Dublin at 10.40p.m. They made their headquarters at the Royal College Hotel, where a huge gathering were on hand to meet them. The match was timed for 2.15 the following day and about 1,700 turned up. Once again, Tommy Daly's saves in the first half proved vital. Clare were trailing 0–1 to 1–0 when Ned Lucid made a solo run from mid-field in the twenty-eighth minute and crashed the ball to the net. Clare pulled away in the second half with another goal from Lucid and two from Minogue. They ran out easy winners at 6–5 to 1–1.

According to Jimmy Mahony, 'The winning of the 1914 double was a nine-day wonder. Obviously people were jubilant and the local pubs were packed with people celebrating. M. J. Baker, a member of the Clare junior team, had a pub in Lifford which was packed.'

In 1934, the GAA celebrated its fiftieth anniversary and a jubilee year souvenir booklet was published by Cumann Dal gCais, Ennis. The same M. J. Baker called on his poetic skills when he took out an advertisement in this publication, giving his own reasons for the 1914 successes:

The Clare team won the double in 1914,
They were quick and fast to clear,
For they trained at M. J. Baker's,
Who supplied the best of beer.

TULL'S GOT IT!
(1915–1932)

It went from end to end and it was beautiful to watch.

ESTHER GILLIGAN

A car stopped and four lads got out and they were like madmen: 'Clare won, Clare won' they shouted.

JOE MCNAMARA

Due to the delay in playing the 1915 Munster final, Clare were nominated to represent Munster in the All-Ireland semi-final against Galway; they overcame the tribesmen by 2–1 to 1–1. Clare had earlier opened the defence of their championship on 13 June 1915 when they defeated Waterford by 10–4 to 2–1 at Limerick. The Clare line-out was very similar to the previous year, so expectations were great. Cork, Clare's victims in the 1914 Munster final, qualified for the southern decider again, overcoming Tipperary in Limerick.

The 1915 Munster final drew a capacity attendance to Limerick on 26 September with *The Clare Journal* describing the grounds as 'thronged with a section of the crowd having to climb on to the top of the corrugated roof of the stand to get a better view'. The Cork team proved superior on the day, with their forward line of Jim Barry-Murphy, James Kennedy and Nagle on top. Martin Moloney and Rob Doherty were magnificent for Clare, with newcomer Hannon doing well to notch a goal in the first half. The St John's brass band entertained the masses at the interval, by which time Cork had built up a big lead of 6–2 to 1–1. The expected fight-back never materialised and Cork added to their lead to win very easily by 8–2 to 2–1.

The Clare juniors found themselves defending their All-Ireland title only two months after they had won it. They successfully defended it in the opening round when they trounced Waterford by 13–4 to 5–5 at Fermoy on 23 May 1915, but surrendered to Tipperary by 9–2 to 2–1 at Tipperary on 5 December 1915.

Joe McNamara of Newmarket-on-Fergus remembers hearing that things were very bad behind the scenes in 1915. '1915 is a sad story; they picked two teams, a Quin selection and a county board team; something was wrong. Laois easily disposed of Cork in the 1915 All-Ireland final. If Clare needed new players, they had the juniors of 1914 – Jack Spellissy and his crowd – to fall back on.'

Limerick narrowly defeated Clare in the 1916 senior championship. The complete report of the game in *The Saturday Record* of 16 July read as follows: 'Limerick had a double victory over Clare in senior hurling and junior football in ties for the Munster championship. In the former game, Clare lost by 3–3 to 3–0.'

In spite of the turbulent period 1916–1922, championship competition continued. Clare contested without much success during these years. In 1918 they reached the Munster final but were very heavily defeated by 11–3 to 1–2 by Limerick.

TWO COUNTY BOARDS
The War of Independence and subsequent Civil War disrupted GAA activity throughout the country. Only Limerick and Cork participated in the Munster cham-

pionship of 1921. In 1923 a serious split occurred in GAA circles in Clare (the only county of the thirty-two) due to the executions of two prominent hurlers, Con McMahon and Paddy Hennessy, both attached to the first battalion of the Mid-Clare Brigade. Con McMahon had been an active member of the flying column and a member of the volunteers since 1917. He participated in the disarming of British soldiers in Ennis in 1921 and was commandant of the first battalion at the time of his execution. Likewise, Paddy Hennessy's record during the Black and Tan war was commendable.

Hennessy and McMahon were found in possession of ammunition without proper authority and being implicated in the destruction of the railway line at Ard Sollus station on 14 January 1923, and also of being in possession of articles taken from Ard Sollus station. They were investigated and tried by committee, and were executed at Limerick gaol on 20 January 1923. On the eve of the execution, Paddy Hennessy wrote to his comrades: 'I am in the best of spirit and expect to face death like a soldier and true Irishman. I forgive my enemies. I forgive them from the bottom of my heart'. They were buried in Clooney cemetery with Joe Considine who was killed in action at the Four Courts. Annie O'Loughlin (nee Conheady) from Clooney was a young girl then and remembers the funeral. 'I remember the shots fired over the grave'.

There were resignations from the Clare county board when a meeting failed to carry a motion of protest against the executions. The county board split and, shortly afterwards, an anti-treaty board representing about twenty-five clubs was established to rival the existing one. For some time each board ran separate competitions and objections were the norm, especially if it could be proved that a player had played in a game run by the rival board.

Due to the split the county team suffered and were easily disposed of in the Munster championships of 1923 and 1924. Tipperary annihilated an obviously weakened county selection at Clonmel in 1923 by 11–2 to 1–4 and Clare lost to Limerick in 1924 by 5–9 to 4–0. [Per Munster GAA history. *The Clare Champion* gave the score as 8–9 to 4–0.] Then Fr Michael Hamilton of Clonlara helped unite the two factions. (He later became chairman of the county board and worked closely with another great Clare GAA man Mick Hennessy, a brother of the executed Paddy Hennessy). The two groups came together in 1925–26 and Clare won the inaugural national league division two title with players of the calibre of Tony Nealon, Mickie Arthur, Paddy 'Boo' Doherty, Jimmy Nelson and 'Brud' White.

Pádraig Ó hEithir also praises the great healing power of the GAA and the game of hurling which was new to him. 'I was about eighteen when I first saw hurling played. It was mysterious to me but it made a great impression. Later I was in the show grounds to see county finals. The pitch was good. Tull, Brendan and Dodger Considine and Larry Blake were special. It was also great to see ex-soldiers and ex-prisoners playing football together in Miltown; the GAA united them.' John Hanly agrees. 'The GAA helped cure the Civil War above any other organisation. They became the great peacemakers'.

ENNIS DALCASSIANS V NEWMARKET

With the exception of 1923, when Kilkishen won the senior championship, Ennis Dalcassians and Newmarket-on-Fergus shared the rest of the titles between them during the 1920s. Ennis re-emerged on the scene in 1924 with a side brimful of talent, including Tull Considine a dual star with Clare, Gerry Cronin, the Fahy brothers Eddie, Bill 'Botch', Mickey and Wally, Jackie Duffy and Joe Madigan. Bill and

Clare Team 1925–26. Division Two League Champions
Front row l/r: Tom O'Halloran, Jackie Duffy, Tom 'Hawker' Blake, Freddie Garrihy; Second row l/r:
?, Mickie Arthur, John Malone, Paddy 'Boo' Doherty, Jack Doherty, 'Brud' White; Third row l/r:
Dan Treacy, Pake Houlihan, Big Jim Burke, George O'Dea, Jim Clancy, Jimmy Nelson, Tony
Nealon; Back row l/r: ?, Fr Michael Hamilton, Paddy McNamara, ?

Eddie Fahy were instrumental in re-organising hurling in Ennis at this time. Later Eddie moved to Dublin and was one of five Claremen to assist the great Dublin team that overwhelmed Cork in the 1927 All-Ireland final by 4–8 to 1–3. The others were Tommy Daly, Pat 'Fowler' McInerney, Jack Gleeson and Tom O'Rourke. Under the rules of the time, the non-resident players could not assist their native county.

Like Ennis, Newmarket too had a great team in the late 1920s, including the likes of Patrick 'The Hound' McNamara and Mickie Arthur. 'Jimbo' Higgins was playing with the Army Metro team in Dublin and Tony Nealon played with Thurles Sarsfields. Nevertheless, even without these great Newmarket players, the 'Blues' had an exceptional team.

'Newmarket had a great team from 1925–1935,' recalls Joe McNamara. 'I remember a Church tournament at the time involving Coolderry of Offaly, Toomevara of Tipperary and Ahane of Limerick, all part of the diocese of Killaloe, and Newmarket won it.' Christy O'Connell of Barefield, a great follower of hurling at the time, recalls county finals at the Ennis show grounds. 'Ennis and Newmarket were the best clubs; Newmarket were exceptional. I'm sure that if the All-Ireland club championship existed, then Newmarket would have won it. They had great players in John Joe Doyle, Tom and Mick O'Rourke, Jimmy and Clement Flanagan,

Georgie O'Dea and Michael "Bocky" Connery. I knew most of them.'

Another famous Newmarket man John Joe 'Goggles' Doyle explains how the famous goggles became part of his hurling attire. 'I had to wear glasses because I was short-sighted and I played a couple of matches wearing glasses which was dangerous. I had more or less decided not to hurl anymore and I was cycling up the Ennis Road when old P. J. Flanagan from Newmarket stopped me and said: "I hear you're giving up hurling. We have to play Ballycar in the semi-final of the junior championship and we'd like to beat them." I was easily persuaded as I was mad for hurling. I came on to the Newmarket senior team as a sub in the 1925 county final against Tulla at the show grounds.

'Having won three titles in a row – 1925, 1926 and 1927 – there was a proposal at the county board that Ennis Dal's and Clarecastle should amalgamate in 1928 and we didn't object. They beat us in the 1928 final. About six Clarecastle men assisted Ennis in that final including Vincent Murphy, Dick Cole and Christy "Swaddie" McMahon.'

The 1929 senior championship was played on a league basis, with Ennis Dalcassian's losing their opening game to Tulla. The Ennis–Clarecastle amalgamation was quickly dissolved, so the Dal's had to find replacements for the six Clarecastle men plus Johnny 'Joker' Coote, who was now resident in Clarecastle and playing with the Magpies. Tull Considine and Rev. Michael Crowe took over training. It is a measure of the respect Tull Considine and Fr Crowe held in Ennis that their players were allowed leave work by their employers at 3.30 each day to go training at the fair green. Further physical training took place at the town hall at 8.00p.m. in preparation for the remainder of the championship.

According to Tom Malone from the Clonbony hurling club in Miltown Malbay, a dispute between Ennis and Clarecastle proved to be an unexpected bonus for Miltown. 'I remember a Clare Cup semi-final game in Miltown involving Ennis Dalcassian's and Clarecastle in 1929. They couldn't agree on a venue so a man here P. J. Hurley, a newsagent, suggested Miltown. It was a tremendous attraction; it gave me a great grá for hurling.'

Unfortunately, the Clare Cup final of 1929 was unfinished. With Ennis leading Newmarket 2–1 to 1–0, a Newmarket player refused to leave the pitch having been dismissed by the referee. On his dismissal the Newmarket player allegedly responded to Canon Hamilton's query 'what happened to you?' with 'it's not a hurley you want out there but a six chamber revolver'. The game had opened at a cracking pace and the superior speed of the Ennis men was evident from the throw-in. According to contemporary newspaper accounts the large crowd was disappointed at the outcome but agreed that Ennis would have won, so the title was awarded to Ennis. The Dalcassian's continued to be a force throughout the 1920s and 1930s but lost a lot of players through emigration. Billy 'Botch' Fahy went to Dublin as did Jim 'Sham' Spellissey, Freddie Garrihy to the United States and Johnny O'Leary to Australia.

1927–1932 RENAISSANCE
Clare defeated Waterford at Dungarvan in the championship of 1927 by 8–1 to 6–5, but lost the Munster final to Cork by 5–3 to 3–4 at the Market's Field. Mick O'Rourke recalled the Clare team going into collective training in Spanish Point around this time. 'I don't think it suited most of us; it was soft living'. Tom Malone also remembers the Clare team in Spanish Point. 'At the time I didn't know enough about it, but it was marvellous to see the Clare team back there; I remember Tom

O'Rourke and Larry Blake.'

On 24 June 1928 Clare travelled to Thurles to take on Tipperary in the championship. John Joe Doyle remembers the journey to the match. 'It was the first time I played in Thurles. We travelled down in seven-seater cars with two small seats which folded into the back of the front seat and could be let down – three of us in the back, two in the small seats and two in front. We went down the evening before and were put up in great style in Hayes' Hotel. That was a common thing in those days. The county board were responsible for it.'

Clare defeated Tipperary 5–5 to 2–5 and qualified for another tilt at Cork. Cork's Eudie Coughlan was moved to centre-back to mark the Clare captain Brendan Considine. The final ended in a draw 2–2 to 2–2 in a game which held excitement and interest to the end. The replay was again held at Thurles on 29 July before 30,000 spectators. It was described as a dour struggle with the issue keenly fought from the start. From a spectator point of view it seems that over-anxiety tended to detract from the hurling. Clare fielded the same team that had beaten Tipperary and drawn with Cork, while Cork made two personnel changes and re-shuffled the team considerably.

Clare were first to score but trailed at the interval by 2–4 to 1–2. In the second half Clare made a few determined rallies but Cork had the upper hand. It was only in the last ten minutes however that Cork pulled away to notch up a final score of 6–4 to 2–2. Best for Clare were George O'Dea in goal, Tony Nealon in defence, Eddie Fahy, Jackie Duffy and Brendan Considine in the attack.

Clare continued to be a major force in championship, league and Thomond Feis competitions during these years, winning the Feis in 1929, but losing the opening championship game to Tipperary the same year by 6–5 to 3–3 at Thurles. *The Clare Champion* described the game as 'a hard strenuous tussle, but it lacked the spectacular features of last year's championship tussles with Cork, as the Claremen did not appear to be tuned to the same standard'.

Tipperary led narrowly at the interval, 2–2 to 1–3, with the Clare defence of John Joe Doyle, Tony Nealon and 'Jimbo' Higgins standing up magnificently to a severe test. After tough exchanges in the Clare goal-mouth, Martin Kennedy had a goal for Tipperary, but Clare replied with a similar score before Kennedy goaled again. Others to shine for the Banner county included Tom and Mick O'Rourke and Larry Blake.

Return of Dr Tommy Daly
Dr Tommy Daly of Tulla is regarded by sports' journalists, especially those who were privileged to see him play, as the greatest goal-keeper of all time. The Tulla man won four All-Ireland senior medals with Dublin from 1917 to 1927. In 1930 he was practising medicine in London and reluctantly signed a non-residents declaration enabling him to play for Clare; his reluctance was due to an unwillingness to displace Clare's usual goalie George O'Dea. It was only when he was assured

Tommy Daly

36

that nobody would welcome him more than O'Dea that he agreed to sign the papers.

George O'Dea of Newmarket had been goal-keeper since about 1918 and had given tremendous service as the Banner's number one custodian during this lengthy period. Referring to Tommy Daly he said: 'By all means bring him back, and when he can't be there I'll be there. Even if Tommy is worth one goal in a game, it might mean an All-Ireland to Clare.' Daly himself said: 'I never felt happy about coming back until the day at the Thomond Feis game in 1930 when George waited at the entrance to accompany me on to the pitch; then I realised I could do something for Clare.' So Tommy Daly stood between the Clare posts for the 1930 championship.

1930 CHAMPIONSHIP
In 1930 Rev. Michael Hamilton, chairman of the county board, Tull Considine, Fr Eamon Murphy of the selection committee and Art McGann (Dublin sub-committee) called on the Clare panel to make every effort to bring honour to Clare. The team of 1930 was a formidable combination and included Mickie White, Larry Blake and Mick Falvey, as well as a strong representation from the Garda and Army Metro clubs based in Dublin.

A Cork newspaper described this clash as 'a game that will live in the annals of hurling'. *The Clare Champion* described it as 'an historic encounter surpassing the best traditions of Munster championship hurling. The tension and excitement were indescribable. Cork, the All-Ireland champions, went down with flying colours after Clare came to level and then scored a goal in the dying moments.' The lead changed hands on several occasions with Clare leading at the interval by 3–5 to 3–4. It was Cork's first championship defeat in four seasons. A huge talking-point was Tommy Daly's point-blank save from 'Balty' Aherne when he denied the Corkman a certain goal from close range. The final score was Clare 6–6 to Cork 5–6.

So Clare qualified to meet Tipperary in the Munster final at Cork on 27 July 1930. Tipperary were aided by a strong breeze in the first half but only led by a point at half-time, 2–3 to 1–5. However, Clare failed to capitalise on the wind advantage in the second half and a much lighter Tipperary team went on to victory by 6–4 to 2–8. One Tipperary player is singled out by John Joe Doyle as the author of Clare's defeat. 'Tommy O'Meara had the game of his life in the 1930 Munster final. Clare might have won the Munster and All-Ireland finals but for the brilliance of O'Meara.' Tull Considine was of the same opinion. 'Tommy O'Meara beat us that day. We were the masters in the second half all the way to the goal posts but we could not get the ball into the net.'

The rule preventing non-residents from playing with their native county was amended and from 1927 to 1932 Clare hurling enjoyed a good deal of success. It's an indication of their strength that Clare contested four senior Munster finals in those six years and were the only team in Munster to beat the powerful Cork team of the same era in the championship. They achieved this on two occasions over a Cork team powered by Dinny Barry-Murphy, Mick 'Gah' Aherne, Paddy 'Balty' Aherne and Eudie Coughlan. Cork captured four All-Ireland titles during these years – 1926, 1928, 1929 and 1931, but they were stopped in 1930 and 1932 by Clare. John Joe Doyle describes the Cork team of this era as exceptional. 'They beat Clare 3–4 to 1–6 at Thurles in 1931. In the All-Ireland final, Cork and Kilkenny played three times to decide it; the second game was the best of the three.'

In an interview given to *The Clare Champion* in 1969 former inter-county player

Mick O'Rourke recalled: 'I first played for Clare in 1926 and we were building a good team. If we had the away-based players we would have won a few All-Irelands. If we had the five Claremen on the Dublin team of 1927 plus John Joe Kinnane who later returned we would hardly have been stopped.' Christy O'Connell said 'Mickie White of Ennis was one of the best Clare hurlers and he was dropped for the 1930 Munster final, even though he outplayed the great Dinny Barry-Murphy of Cork in the previous round.'

MUNSTER CHAMPIONS

In 1932 Clare had an easy victory over Kerry at Limerick before defeating the All-Ireland champions Cork in the Munster final at Thurles on 31 July. Clare had a big lead at the interval which was whittled back by Cork, but Tull Considine snatched a last-minute goal to give victory to Clare. 'Cork Hurlers Find Banner County Too Good For Them' was the headline to an article in *The Irish Press* the following day which went on to describe the match as follows:

> The smashing tactics of Clare made the Cork play in the first half seem puerile. The pace was terrific, the tackling relentless and at times individuals caught the onlooker's breath. Tull Considine was the spearhead of the Clare attack, and to him, in a great measure, was due the successes which clinched the issue for the Banner County. 'Fowler' McInerney held the last line of the Clare defence with splendid resource and determination. Behind him between the posts was the imperturbable Tommy Daly.
>
> Clare led 3–2 to 1–0 at the break. Immediately on the resumption Jim Hurley goaled from a free to reduce the lead and then the rain came down. Cork were playing a determined and masterful game now and their supporters were growing more and more confident. Then Dinny Barry-Murphy goaled. Stormy hurling ensued. Cork were still in the ascendant. Both sides missed good chances before Tull Considine got possession and beat the Cork full-back line for a goal. He followed this with another and Cork hopes sank.

Clare Munster Senior Champions, 1932
Back row l/r: Art McGann, Fr Michael Hamilton, G. McNamara, Robbie Lawlor [trainer], Mick Falvey, Jim Hogan, Jimmy Flanagan, Tull Considine, Tom Burnell, John Joe Doyle, Pat 'Fowler' McInerney, Seán Hurley, Jack Gleeson, Martin 'Bocky' Connery, Tom O'Rourke, Jim Higgins, George O'Dea, Stephen Clune [manager], Paddy McNamara; Front row l/r: Jim Houlihan, Mick O'Rourke, Tommy Daly, Jim Mullane, Larry Blake, Tom 'Fowler' McInerney; Sitting: Art McGann, jnr.

Jim Houlihan's deliveries which gave Clare a couple of goals cannot be overlooked. Tull Considine gave a brilliant performance (with 4–1) worthy of the man who might not unfairly be called the mainspring of Clare hurling.

An article on the game appeared in the magazine *An Camán* of 6 August 1932 under the pseudonym Vigilant. It would seem that Vigilant was also highly impressed by what was described as a sensational Munster final:

> From the very start, the Leesiders seemed to have an unusual want of combination, and Clare went in for strong, bustling, hard-hitting tactics that seemed rather to confuse the Corkmen. Clare played 'a Clare game' no doubt. At all events, it suited Clare, and never allowed the least accommodation for their opponents. But it was a fair, honest, sporting game, and if Cork were not able to counter Clare's tactics it was Cork's loss. Clare were a well-trained team in which the oldest veteran was able to make the pace and make the race with the youngest. It was a treat to watch the old warriors of many hard fights like 'Tull' Considine and McInerney repeating their best form of the days that are gone. There seemed to be a thorough understanding among the Claremen, while Cork, on the whole, and considering their fine record, played very loose and rather unfinished unhurling. Clare's forward line was very good, but I feel that its greatest strength lay in its back division.

Joe McNamara of Newmarket recalls the Clare *v* Galway All-Ireland semi-final vividly. 'I wasn't at the game; it wasn't easy get lifts in those days. A Galway priest stopped on the way back and a group of us asked him "How is it going in Limerick?" He said, "it's not a game at all; Galway are leading by fifteen points at half time." Five minutes passed and another car passed with a Galway crowd and we asked them. "We gave it five minutes in the second half and Galway increased their lead to seventeen points," they said "so we came away."

'The four of us were walking back to Newmarket and I said to Mickie McGrath: "A Clare car didn't pass yet; if it was that bad, wouldn't the Clare crowd be coming back in droves?" Anyway, a car stopped and four lads got out and they were like madmen. "Clare won, Clare won", they shouted.'

Galway started at a ferocious pace and quickly notched up 1–3. Tom Burnell replied with a goal before Galway had another to completely take over and lead at half time by 4–7 to 2–0. John Joe Doyle spoke to John D. Hickey about the game in the *Irish Independent* of 4 January 1956. The following is an abbreviation of his comments:

> The match between Clare and Galway in 1932 provided all the ingredients to qualify for the most memorable match of my career. We appeared to have legs of lead as the Galway forwards sent over point after point not to mention those agonising goals. Undoubtedly the situation was desperate for us, but, despite the atmosphere of despair that was apparent, we knew that we were not as bad as had appeared so far, and that, good as Galway were, they were not in reality so much superior to us.
>
> The second half was in progress for only five minutes when Galway had chalked up two more points, giving them a lead of sixteen points, with about twenty-five minutes playing time left. The sidelines became thronged with spectators leaving, Clare people bewildered, disgusted, perhaps no longer able to look upon the massacre of the team upon which they had placed all their pent-up hopes; while Galway supporters, satisfied that they were home and dried, were anxious to avoid the final rush for the exits so that they could be home early with the good news. Who could blame them?
>
> But during this period of confusion Clare scored a goal by Tull Considine followed by another immediately by Jim Mullane. Then, in a flash, Mick Rourke had another and

a minute later Tull had a beauty of a goal from the left corner. Confusion now played havoc with the Galway defence and the tables were well and truly turned as after goal was recorded on the scoreboard.

The wild cheering of the Clare supporters who had remained brought those leaving the pitch surging back. There was intense excitement, the likes of which is rarely seen in any sports arena, as the two teams were locked in a desperate struggle for mastery. Someone was injured and I took advantage of the short stoppage to wipe a drop of sweat from my glasses. I was seeing better now and feeling better, but I thought that the last five minutes of that match were the toughest I ever experienced.

The final score was Clare 9–4, Galway 4–14.

Esther Gilligan of Ennis is a native of Gowran, Co. Kilkenny. As the young fifteen year-old Esther McGee, she headed off for the 1932 All-Ireland final between Kilkenny and Galway. 'I became interested in hurling at an early age. Bennetsbridge had a great team. I travelled to Croke Park for the final and the fare was five shillings (25p). The hurling was wonderful, great fluency. They hurled the ball first time; there was no rooting or rummaging; it went from end to end and it was beautiful to watch. I can remember the man with the grey hair (Tull Considine). The atmosphere going up on the train was great.

Christy O'Connell, then aged 22, was also at the game. 'It cost 7/6 [37½p]. I followed the Clare team everywhere, to the Mardyke in Cork, to Limerick and Thurles. They were a great team – John Joe Doyle, Tull Considine and Tom Burnell from Tubber; he'd remind you of the present-day Seán McMahon. That was the best Clare team ever, but Lory Meagher and Kilkenny had great craft. I was working, so I had the money to go but many of the lads didn't have the price to get to Croke Park. Things were bad then but people accepted it. The atmosphere at the final was terrific.'

GAA events received only moderate coverage in the newspapers of the 1920s. It was not until *The Irish Press* was launched in 1931 that hurling and Gaelic football received coverage befitting their status and popularity. Eamon de Valera appointed Joe Sherwood as sport's editor of the *Press*. Sherwood was from the north of England and he pioneered exhaustive coverage of GAA events. In fact the 1932 final carried three separate accounts filling most of a page, which was a revolutionary step in Irish journalism at that time. The other major newspapers were eventually forced to follow suit.

Clare opened the scoring after two minutes with a point by Jack Gleeson from the half-way line. Gleeson was described by 'Gael' in *The Irish Press* as 'giving a masterly display at centre-field'. Then, according to the *Press*, 'play proceeded on the most pulsating lines with the pace set a cracker. Not a moment's delay, no dallying with the ball, no "letting up", but full-blooded, first-time driving and a lively missile shooting about – up and down – with electric liveliness.'

Lory Meagher missed a couple of seventies and this reflected a general inability on the part of Kilkenny to get going and come to grips with an unexpectedly resilient Clare team. One of the Kilkenny stars Matty Power 'was held as in a vice by Jim Holohan and Jimbo Higgins, as indeed he continued to be for most of the game'. Neither set of forwards were able to make much progress and 'Fowler' McInerney, Larry Blake and Jim Holohan were described as 'giving early proof of their worth in the Clare defence by bottling up all Kilkenny's dangerous raids and bustling the all too neat and careful Kilkenny raiders off the ball'. John Joe Doyle was also credited with good defensive work and Clare's famous goal-keeper also gave another spectacular performance. 'Dr Tom Daly in the Clare goal "brought down the house" with a wonderful one-hand save of a cannon-ball delivery from "Lowry" – a real gem of a save and a typical "Daly one".' The half-time score was Clare 0–3, Kilkenny 0–2, but things were to change dramatically when play resumed as *The Irish Press* went on to describe:

> It was Kilkenny's dramatic and electric start on the resumption of play in the second half which did the damage – and won the day for them – as inside seven minutes they were three goals up. These goals came about in bewildering – and I might say surprising and somewhat lucky – fashion, and the famous 'Lowry' Meagher, playing now with a new lease of life, was mainly instrumental in bringing all three of them about – actually scoring one.
>
> Most people thought Clare were a well-beaten side then; but these 'men of the West' have great spirit – the old Dalcassian fighting blood and never-say-die spirit are strong in them. Undaunted they fought back by sheer courage and stout-heartedness, and the renowned 'Tull' Considine gave them renewed hopes when in 12 minutes he manoeuvred skilfully and shot a particularly smart goal.

Another *Irish Press* writer J. N. S. gave a graphic and dramatic description of the game's final moments without the benefit of action replay:

> Two minutes from time ... Kilkenny lead by two points. The ball soars in the direction of Dermody ... an arm is thrown up, the ball is snatched from the air ... 'Tull's got it', yell the excited and anxious Clare followers.
>
> ... Yes, Tull's got it ... he's side-stepped Paddy O'Reilly ... swish, the camán comes round and over savagely, yes, venomously ... but, alas, for Clare, Tull Considine, Ireland's far-famed marksman, has lashed the air ... clean missed the ball ... and Dermody (the Kilkenny goalkeeper) not fifteen yards away!
>
> Thus do I, with my humble pen, try to describe what I consider to be the most dramatic of all dramatic episodes in the All-Ireland hurling final, won by Kilkenny by twelve points to nine, at Croke Park yesterday. Kilkenny, I thought, were worthy winners, but to be candid, there was so little between the two teams, that had Clare won, I, too, should have reckoned them worthy winners.

Tull later blamed a push in the back by one of the Kilkenny defenders as the reason why he missed the last-minute shot at goal. The final score was Kilkenny 3–3 to Clare's 2–3. According to Tom Ryall of Kilkenny 'Clare took their defeat sportingly and invited the Kilkenny team and officials to their banquet in Barry's Hotel. Here the players mingled in a friendly atmosphere. This gesture by Clare moulded a great relationship between the counties which still exists.'

Mick O'Rourke said. 'We should have beaten Kilkenny in 1932 though they had powerful backs. Paddy Byrne their centre-back was a huge man and held the whip-hand over Jim Mullane. If Tull Considine was moved out we would have won in my opinion.'

The late Anthony Cusack of Sixmilebridge was a spectator that day and lived long enough to see both his county and club win All-Ireland honours in 1995–96. When I spoke to him about the 1932 All-Ireland he also felt that the wrong tactics were used. 'Jack Gleeson was told to put the ball in low to Tull Considine. Gleeson was a huge, powerful man; he could have scored long-range points. Kilkenny had seen what Tull Considine had done to Cork and Galway, so they shackled him.'

After the 1932 All-Ireland Final
John Joe Doyle [Clare captain], Jimmy Walsh [Kilkenny captain], and centre Seán McCarthy [president of the GAA] and An Taoiseach, Eamonn de Valera

DECLINE IN DAL GCAIS (1933–1947)

Nobody is to rise the ball except Jimmy Smyth.

TULL CONSIDINE

Dalcassianism cursed us for life. We're a small little tribe in Clare and we're the least Normanised and Anglicised county in Ireland.

JOE MCNAMARA

LIMERICK ON THE MARCH

The Clare team that set out to win the Munster championship in 1933 was 'an old team' in the words of Johnny Moloney. 'They were very strong in Munster from 1927 to 1932. Many of the players who were successful in 1932 had spent some years playing with Dublin, so they were at the veteran stage. I remember going to matches in the show grounds in Ennis during that era. Looking back on it, I thought every game was good as long as I was there. I remember the All-Ireland final of 1933 between Kilkenny and Limerick; it was my first final. I was a great Limerick supporter and they were young and glamorous, Mick and John Mackey, Garret Howard, Paddy Clohessy and Jackie Power.'

On 28 May 1933 Clare played Limerick in the first round of the Munster championship at Thurles. One notable feature of this game was that there were some unusual travel arrangements made to bring one of the players, Jim Houlihan, down from Dublin for the game. Jim was then playing his club hurling with Army Metro in Dublin and was given a VIP trip to Thurles. Apparently, Clare had some considerable influence within CIE in the person of P. J. Floyd from Tulla and he chartered a special train for Jim Houlihan, but in spite of his extraordinary efforts, Clare were completely outclassed by Limerick. The train story featured in a newspaper report the following day:

> A little over two hours after they had played on opposite sides in a Dublin championship match at Croke Park Sergeant-Major Jim Houlihan of the Army Metro and Christy O'Brien of the Young Ireland's club opposed each other in the Limerick–Clare championship match. They travelled from Dublin to Thurles on a train specially chartered by the Clare county board for Jim Houlihan.

Seán Clancy from Clonlara, who was born in 1901 and now lives in Dublin, was interviewed by former Clare county board chairman Brendan Vaughan about this unusual episode. Seán was also an army man and remembers approaching Houlihan about the problem after he had received letters requesting his release from Fr Michael Hamilton and Clare county board secretary, Tull Considine, as well as ascertaining from his commandant, General Michael Brennan, that he also wanted to see his team win. Houlihan had a difficult conflict of loyalty to resolve but decided to give the Dublin match priority saying: 'I am making my living from the army

43

and you know as well as I do that we have set our sights on the Dublin championship this year ... I then informed the Clare officials that they could not have
Houlihan for the match in Thurles. Some days elapsed before I received another letter from Fr Hamilton. In it he said that he realised that no car could do the journey
in the interval between the two matches, so the county board arranged with Mr
Floyd the traffic manager of the railway company to provide a fast, non-stop train
to bring Houlihan to Thurles. It was supposed to be the fastest engine in Ireland at
the time.'

'JIMBO' HIGGINS
'Jimbo' Higgins of Newmarket-on-Fergus, sometimes referred to as 'Jumbo', was
regarded by many authorities on the game as probably one of the greatest. Another
Newmarket man Joe McNamara reminded me of his untimely death in 1933. 'Jimbo
gave great service to Clare, the Army Metro and St Finbarr's of Cork, with whom
he won a Cork county championship medal. They asked Jimbo to play with Dublin;
they pleaded with him to play with Cork, but he declined. He was a very tribal
man; you could depend on him. A medal won with any other county would mean
nothing to him.'

MICHAEL CUSACK TOURNAMENT
The Clare team of 1934 once again fell to Mick Mackey's Limerick on a score of 6–4
to 3–2. Later that year, on 16 September, Kilkenny were invited to the Ennis show
grounds to play Clare in the Michael Cusack medals tournament to commemorate
the golden jubilee of the GAA. Good relations existed between the two counties and
Kilkenny, as always, fielded a strong selection which included Mick Larkin, Paddy
Larkin, Paddy 'Nully' Walshe and Peter Blanchfield. John Donoghue of Kilnamona
was a fourteen year-old boy at the time and remembers John Cusack, son of the
founder of the GAA, presenting the medals. 'I remember Lory Meagher going up
to receive the gold medals. He was wearing a white trench coat to keep out the cold;
there were no tracksuits in those days.' The game was preceded by a parade to the
Courthouse grounds and an Irish dancing exhibition at the show grounds.

OPENING OF CUSACK PARK
Kilkenny also came for the opening of the new Cusack Park at Howard's Field in
1936. Former garda sergeant and Clooney player John Scanlon recalls that their
presence resulted from a last-minute hitch in preparations for the opening. 'Mick
Hennessy was a great friend of mine; I could tell so many stories about him. I remember the Saturday evening away back in 1936, the day before the official opening of Cusack Park. Limerick were to play Clare in the hurling game the following
day. Around tea-time word arrived that Limerick were not available to play. It
could have upset the whole colourful programme planned for the morrow.

'I was there when the message came in and Mick asked me to drive with him
to Kilkenny. We sat into his Baby Ford – I still remember the number, IE 2891 – and
hit the road. We were talking to Kilkenny secretary Paddy Grace by 9.45p.m. It
seemed an impossible task but Paddy was equal to it and promised to have a team
in Ennis in time to play. He went around to all the county players at that hour and
Kilkenny arrived in Ennis at 2.00p.m. on the following day. That was Mick, a great
organiser and man of action.'

Mick Hennessy's office was at No. 21 Steele's Terrace. Fellow Clooney man
Brendan Vaughan is one of his many admirers: 'He played for Clare and Munster

and excelled, scoring something like five goals in a championship replay against Cork in 1936. He managed the Clare team that won the league in 1946 and was secretary of the Clare county board for nineteen years. He also started the Clare camogie board. A man for all seasons, he was very broad-minded, liberal and charismatic, a very honourable man.'

Between 6,000 and 7,000 patrons turned out on Sunday 25 May 1936 for the opening of Cusack Park by Mr Bob O'Keefe, President of the GAA. 'A great gathering of priests and laity witnessed a brilliant ceremony carried out with splendid order', reported *The Clare Champion* which went on to describe the atmosphere of the occasion: 'The hurling fixture was preceded by entertainment put on by bands from the Boys National School, Ennis CBS, St Flannan's College and Coláiste Muire. Streamers and bunting were displayed on the houses in the nearby Francis Street and the stewarding was top class, with Inspector Kelly regulating the traffic.

The Kilkenny fifteen, who included Lory Meagher, Johnny Dunne, Paddy Larkin and Paddy Byrne, overcame Clare by 2–5 to 2–2. The Clare side on this historic occasion included Seán Harrington, Raphie Burns and Flan Purcell, who made his inter-county debut that day. Flan recalls the opening well. 'We were togged out for ages; it was a fright and we were frozen. Seán Harrington played also; he had recently joined the Feakle club after winning a senior championship medal with Ennis Dalcassians in 1934.'

Feakle, at the Gaelic Grounds [1936]
Back row l/r: Michael Tully, Martin Hayes, Paddy McGrath, M. P. Loughnane, Jim Malley, Flan Purcell, Jimmy Pepper, Seán Harrington, John Jones [Scariff], Bill Loughnane; Front row l/r: John Naughton, Paddy Durack, Paddy Loughnane [captain], Brud McGrath, Tom Moloney, John 'Hassett' Moloney

Munster champions Limerick went on tour to the United States in 1936 aboard the *SS Manhattan*. As it took a few weeks to get there, play a couple of games, and a few weeks to come back at their leisure, it was proposed that Limerick qualify for the Munster final without playing any qualifying game and the motion was carried by the Munster council.

Clare opened the 1936 Munster championship campaign with a six-point win over Waterford at Fermoy 5–7 to 4–4, but were held to a draw by Cork at Thurles, Clare 4–4 to Cork 3–7. The replay was the following Sunday 12 July in Limerick. Conditions both on and off the pitch were appalling due to heavy rain the night before and during that morning. *The Clare Champion* gave a vivid description of the occasion:

> The sideline seats were packed to their utmost capacity, while hundreds remained in their cars outside on the roadway to await the result. The special train from Ennis brought a very small crowd as rain was falling heavily at the time but, as the day wore on, buses and motors were chartered with the result that there was an exceptionally large crowd from Ennis. Those who braved the elements were rewarded, even though they suffered a severe drenching, because the hurling contest was one of the most exciting witnessed on any field for years. It was an hour of thrills and excitement, and when the Clare team emerged victorious on the huge score of 9–1 to 2–3, the scenes that followed can be more easily imagined than described.

Clare led by a point at half-time, 3–0 to 2–2, but began to dominate the game as the rain eased off. The renowned Cork attack had met their match in a Clare defence comprised of Pappy Callaghan in goal and a stalwart full-back line, which included Mick Griffin, Flan Purcell and Paddy McGrath who 'repulsed raid after raid' according to *The Clare Champion*. The report continued:

> The Clare forwards of Mick Hennessy, Jim Mullane and Jim Houlihan could do nothing wrong and piled in goal after goal to the bewilderment of the Cork supporters. A goal by the Clare captain Paddy Loughnane seemed to change the game and, with a couple of goals by Mick Hennessy in as many minutes, Cork seemed to collapse. Considering that Clare and Cork had played a draw the previous week in Thurles, the result proves that glorious uncertainty must always remain the predominating feature in hurling.

Indeed! This was Cork's first defeat in a Munster championship replay since 1898. Clare's opponents in the semi-final were Tipperary, who had earlier defeated Kerry by a big margin. It was Clare's third championship match in three weeks and a huge Tipperary crowd converged at the Athletic Grounds, not only confident of beating Clare, which they did by 5–7 to 3–2, but of winning the Munster championship. However, the championship eluded them, as Limerick returned from the United States to capture their fourth Munster title in a row. It would have taken five games for Clare to achieve the same result that year!

CBS BANNED

St Mary's CBS, Ennis had first entered the Gaelic games arena in 1927 by fielding three teams for the Western league, a competition organised by the Christian brothers for their schools in the western area. Initially there was a senior and junior football team and a senior hurling team; the junior footballers and senior hurlers were successful.

Br Irwin arrived as superior from Mount Sion in Waterford in September 1937, and held this position until 1942. He saw the school not only as a centre of learning but also a bastion of hurling and football. Then the Dean Ryan Cup [Under 16½] for Munster colleges hurling was introduced in 1936. Brother Irwin realised that he did not have enough hurling talent in the school to win the competition, but he had his mind set on capturing the cup.

For the 1941 campaign the first player introduced was Willie McAllister who looked after the school gardens. As the competition progressed it became more difficult to win each game, so other players such as James 'Dutcher' Moloney were introduced, but not all at the same time. With the aid of these and legitimate students like Gerry McNamara, Joe O'Halloran, Jackie and Joe Cullinan, Austin Hannon, Reggie Connellan, Mick Leahy, Seán Ó Liodáin, Tom Slattery and Seán McCormack in goal, the Dean Ryan Cup was won and Brother Irwin seemed to have achieved success. However, celebrations were short-lived because of an objection to allegedly illegal players and the cup had to be returned. Ennis CBS were banned from entering the competition for many years afterwards, but the record books still show them as champions for 1941.

Mick Leahy was one of the disappointed players on that team and says that the case against Br Irwin and the CBS regarding illegal players was not all that straightforward. 'It was a grey area. Some of the lads worked part-time and maybe went to school a bit as well; it wasn't as it seemed. Brother Irwin had a tremendous love for hurling and he made lads hurl as it should be played. He believed in ground hurling, moving the ball. He lived for hurling and, if he got carried away a bit, it was due to the fact that he loved the game.'

DEATH OF TOMMY DALY

Sports followers were shocked at the tragic death of Dr Tommy Daly in a road accident on 21 September 1936, when his car careered off the road between Tuamgraney and Scariff. Dr Daly's hurling career spanned twenty years from 1914 to 1934, playing both with his native Tulla and Collegians of Dublin. He won an All-Ireland junior medal with Clare in 1914 but, having taken up residence in Dublin, he could only play for that county under the rules of the time. Tommy won four All-Ireland senior medals with Dublin between 1917 and 1927 before returning to the Clare colours. He also won a Clare senior championship medal with Tulla in 1933. Tommy Daly is regarded as one of the greatest goal-keepers of all time. A comment at the time in the *Irish Independent* reflects the national esteem in which he was held: 'While it is widely claimed that he had no equals, it can be safely said that he had no superiors.'

The pitch at Tulla was opened in his memory in 1941 and his sad loss is commemorated in the well-known ballad *The Windswept Hill of Tulla* by Bryan McMahon of Listowel. In my opinion, no other song captures the spirit of Clare hurling to the same degree. I heard Jimmy Smyth give a rousing version of it in Marrinan's public house, Milltown Malbay during the Willie Clancy Summer School, which took place a couple of days prior to the 1995 Munster final. The following are a few of the verses:

On the wind-swept hill of Tulla,
Where the Claremen place their dead,
Four solemn yews stand sentinel,
Above a hurler's head,
And from the broken north lands,
From Burren bleak and bare,

The dirge of Tommy Daly,
Goes surging on through Clare.

No more shall lime-white goal posts,
Soar tapering and tall,
Above the greatest goalman,
That ever clutched a ball,
Nor yet he'll rouse the echoes,
Of ash in native air,
Nor heed the throbbing thousands,
Tense with pride of Clare.

But wherever Clare does battle,
And whoever guards the goal,
Whenever the citadel is saved,
The proud, the noble soul,
Of sterling Thomas Daly,
They shall recall and say,
'God rest you Thomas Daly,
On your wind-swept hill today'.

To think that never once again,
He'll don with lightsome air,
The claret-gold of Tulla,
Nor the blue and gold of Clare,
Perhaps they'll pray when feasts are high,
And healed the wounds of fight,
'God rest you Thomas Daly,
On your wind-swept hill tonight'.

Mourners at the funeral of Tommy Daly

THE COONEY AFFAIR

The Tipperary–Clare Munster championship clash of 26 June 1938 gave rise to one of the most bizarre GAA controversies – the Cooney case. If the outstanding Tipperary hurler Jim Cooney wasn't known throughout the country for his hurling prowess, he certainly became well known because of Rule 27. This rule stated as follows:

> Any member who plays, attends or helps to promote rugby, soccer, hockey or cricket thereby incurs automatic suspension from membership of the Association.

Jim Cooney, a native of Carrick-on-Suir, Co. Tipperary was a student at UCD and played his club hurling with the college. He was also a member of the Tipperary senior hurling team and, as first choice for Tipperary in this position since 1934, was regarded as one of the best mid-fielders playing the game. On 12 February 1938 he attended a rugby international in Dublin, thereby offending against the foreign games rule. On his own admission of the offence, he was automatically suspended for three months and duly served that term. His application for re-instatement was then granted by the Leinster council.

Subsequently, Tipperary, including Cooney, played Limerick in the Monaghan cup in London. It was at this point that matters started to get complicated. According to Tipperary, Cooney had declared to play for them in the 1938 championship. Tipperary claimed that he had signed his form of declaration on 2 February, i.e., before the rugby offence had taken place. Nevertheless, the chairman of the central council ruled that the date of receipt of the application form determined its legality and, because it was received when he was on automatic suspension (i.e., after 12 February), he had played illegally in London and therefore suspended himself for yet another six months!

Then Clare entered the picture, and I spoke with some prominent Clare hurlers of that era while researching this story. However, the most comprehensive account which I came across was given by the well-known Tipperary hurler Tommy Doyle of Thurles Sarsfield's, who told his version of the saga to Raymond Smith in 1955. Tommy won five All-Ireland medals with Tipperary from 1937 to 1951. He first recalled the run-up to the match when another of the Tipperary players, Ned Wade, warned the Tipperary officials against playing Cooney, 'for if you do Clare will take the match from us'. He went on to say that the Tipperary officials were under severe pressure from county champions, Moycarkey, to play Cooney and, in the end, it was decided that he should play:

> So Jim Cooney took the field with the rest of us and a buzz of excitement passed through the crowd when it was noticed that he was playing. To give Clare their due, they gave our officials ample warning of their intentions when we arrived at the Imperial Hotel that morning. Again, as we lined out for the throw-in, Larry Blake said: 'If you play Cooney, you do so at the risk of losing the game on an objection. You are warned on time'. But the die was cast.
>
> Right from the throw-in, when Ned Wade dashed through on a fine solo run to score a point, we hurled in the manner of champions. The game abounded in thrills and open spectacular hurling was the order. I was pitted against the renowned Larry Blake and must say that I came out second-best in my duel with the Ennis man. Only once did I slip him to notch a point. A brilliant stylist, he often dominated and always held his own. He was one of the hardest and fastest pullers I have met in a long career, a terrier to the tackle, quick and tenacious on every ball. Though past his best in 1938, Larry Blake was still considered good enough to keep men like Johnny Ryan and John Maher off the Munster Railway cup team.

However, in spite of the efforts of Larry Blake and the rest of the team, Tipperary had a convincing victory on a score line of 3–10 to 2–3. Clare then proceeded with their objection and this was upheld by the Munster council. Tipperary counter-objected on the grounds that Clare player Michael Griffin also attended the same rugby match as Jim Cooney, but their appeals failed all the way to central council level. Cooney's six-month suspension led to considerable controversy, with copious correspondence to the newspapers and Tipperary even threatening to break with central council at one stage. In the end things calmed down but there was a lingering bitterness over the incident for quite some time, due both to internal Tipperary dissent towards their own county board and a feeling that they had been cheated out of a possible Munster championship and All-Ireland. These feelings are echoed by Tommy Doyle: 'It is not for me to say who was right or wrong. All I know is that I lost an All-Ireland medal for, believe me, the 1938 Tipperary team was every bit as good as that which won the title the previous year.'

Flan Purcell feels that Tipperary lost the possibility of an All-Ireland themselves by insisting on playing Cooney and flaunting the rules. *The Clare Champion* was of a similar opinion, stating that Tipperary showed 'an apparent disregard for the discipline of the GAA and couldn't be ignored'. To be fair to the Clare county board, their statement in the *Champion* of 9 July acknowledged that Tipperary had some cause for grievance: 'On the run of play, Tipperary were superior and Clare will place no obstacle if they are legalised'. However, this was not to be and, at a special meeting of the Munster council in Limerick, Tipperary were eliminated from the Munster championship.

1938 MUNSTER FINAL

On the other side of the 1938 Munster championship, four-in-a-row champions Limerick lost to Cork by eight points in the opening round. Cork were in turn heavily beaten by Waterford, so it was a Waterford *v* Clare showdown at the Cork Athletic Grounds on 31 July 1938. The following excerpts are from *The Clare Champion*'s report of the game:

> It was in the judgement of experienced followers of the native game worthy to rank with the best exhibition ever witnessed in the championship. Clare were short four regulars, but their replacements were worthy of their places. However, to place them to the best advantage needed considerable reshuffling.
>
> The hurling was keen and fast and featured beautiful deliveries on both sides. It was played at a cracking pace, and up to the final whistle was anyone's, so close was the hurling. Clare opened well in the second half but shot four consecutive wides. It was a crisis in which the smallest turn in play would decide the result – Waterford got the turn.
>
> In the final moments, the whole Clare team threw themselves upon the Waterford defence and a terrific battle raged around the goal posts. However, the Waterford defence stood up to the barrage and it must have been a relief to their supporters when James O'Regan finally blew the whistle and left them victors by 3–5 to 2–5. The spectators thoroughly enjoyed the contest, a notable feature being that not a single individual left the grounds before the final whistle.

Larry Blake was described as 'the hero of the hour', Martin Murphy was 'top class' and Jim Mullane and Clement Flanagan were 'outstanding'. Newcomer Martin Hayes of Feakle 'justified his presence'. Joe McNamara was at the Athletic Grounds that day and remembers it well. 'The game was held up for twenty minutes as Clare were late coming out on the field. I believe a share of them didn't want to play that day on account of the Jim Cooney controversy. We were behind the Clare goal in the second half. It was one of the best matches I ever saw but was thrown away. The Clare full-back line of Martin Hayes, Tom Loughnane and Paddy McGrath excelled – all big men. Larry Blake, a cultured hurler and the best centre-back I ever saw, was switched from the half-back line to centre-forward on the great John Keane. Mick Halloran came on for the injured Clement Flanagan in the final quarter. Mick was classed in *The Cork Examiner* the following morning as the longest striker in the country. He relieved the half-back line, lobbing ball after ball into the square. Martin Murphy on the wing and P. J. Quaine scored two of the loveliest points, both struck close to the corner flag – delicate hurling. But I fell in love with Waterford hurling that day; it was very cultured. Charlie and Jim Ware influenced the outcome of the game by 3–5 to 2–5.' Waterford had led by four points to two points at half time, but went further ahead with an early second-half goal. Clare fought back and Seán Harrington placed a well-timed pass to Loughnane to score a goal. Seán Guinnane later put Clare into the lead by a goal, but Waterford finished strongly to win.

FEAKLE V SCARIFF

Feakle probably had their greatest spell in Clare hurling from 1937 to 1944, winning four senior championships, including a three-in-a-row – 1938, 1939, 1940. The most prominent players were John Naughton, M. P. Loughnane, Paddy Loughnane, Jimmy Pepper, William 'The Dublin' Moloney, Flan Purcell, regarded as a pillar of strength at centre-back and Dr Bill Loughnane who won an All-Ireland senior medal with Dublin in 1938. Added to these, the return of Dr Tom Loughnane and the transfer of Seán Harrington (a native of Templederry, Co. Tipperary) from Ennis Dalcassian's forged Feakle into a formidable side.

Flan Purcell had a long spell with Feakle and remembers the great atmosphere at the 1938 Clare Champion Cup final between Feakle and Tulla at Newmarket-on-Fergus, when the Newmarket Brass and Reed Band and the Tulla Pipe Band led the teams out on to the field. 'Some of the Tulla old-timers brought along the Carrahan Flag, won in 1889, to frighten us.' Feakle won that 1938 final, scoring an impressive 6–2 to Tulla's 3–2. However, in his book *Feakle*, Kieran Sheedy describes that club's subsequent decline at the hands of near neighbours Scariff:

> The supremacy of Feakle ended with the arrival of Scariff on the scene as a major force in 1946. In the first round of the 1946 championship, Scariff were held to a draw by Ennis Dalcassian's, but Ennis failed to field a team for the replay. Scariff continued on their winning way, even though they lost the services of the Whitegate players (who assisted them in 1945) because of the introduction of the parish rule, and qualified for the final against Feakle. The Scariff team, which included many inter-county hurlers (Dan McInerney, Joe Whelan, Des Carroll, Alfie O'Brien, J. J. Bugler and Jimmy Fennessy) were on average much younger. The county final was played in good weather conditions and attracted a crowd of 7,000 spectators paying a record gate of £260, an increase of £65 on the previous record. A late goal by Joe Whelan after a spectacular solo run gave Scariff the championship title by 3–4 to 2–5. The match report stated that 'though Scariff had several of the county team, the Feakle team were more balanced and displayed more combination'.

It was Scariff's first senior county championship victory since 1917. Des Carroll won three championship medals with Scariff and remembers a different style of hurling then: 'It wasn't like it is today. It's more professional now, but there's too much picking and running, not enough ground hurling'.

Johnny Moloney remembers Scariff making their first breakthrough when they beat Ennis Rovers in the 1938 intermediate final. 'The Rovers were fine hurlers. We then carried on for senior purposes with a combination of Scariff, Whitegate and Mountshannon. We were beaten in the 1942 senior final by Clooney and in 1943 by Clarecastle. We had a great team but we didn't have the parish spirit. I'm all for amalgamations if it improves hurling.'

CLOONEY

In *The Golden Days of Clooney Hurling*, Jimmy Smyth, who describes himself as a great Clooney supporter, wrote about his experiences playing both for and against Clooney!

> I played juvenile illegally with Clooney. At one stage I was asked to play with them in a senior outing when I was stopped by Joe McDonnell, a Ruan hurler and a great friend of mine, who had made his name on the Clare team. In fact, I had the jersey on, a jersey which was unceremoniously pulled off by McDonnell.
>
> I later played on Austin Hannon, a hard, good and unrelenting player. He had the art of shadowing, that is marking off the ball, forever nudging and laying in – all very annoying. In all my experience of players, he was one nut I couldn't really crack. He was a top-class hurler and played for Clare for many years. I remember Paddy and Joe McNamara, Paddy and Jimmy Kelly, the five O'Halloran brothers, Joe and Brendan Kilmartin, Jamesie and Brendan Clune, Fr John Gaffney, Jimmy Markham, Jim Lynch, Michael Power, Fr Michael McInerney, Cormac McNamara, Cornie Flanagan, Pat 'Duckle' O'Loughlin and Garda Mick Flynn.
>
> There was the bones of a team that could match and did match any team in Clare. They reached four county finals from 1940 to 1944. The 1941 final was a memorable one. Tull Considine, the Ennis trainer and a great man at his trade, used every trick in the book – players lying down when the opposition was going well and substituting at least ten times during the game. There was no limits to substitutes used at this time and play had to stop when a player lay down; it didn't matter whether the player was injured or not. Clooney had a great leader in Mick Hennessy.

Well-known Ennis barber, Paddy White, also recounted for me the goodwill and good relations that existed between Ennis Dalcassian's and the great Clooney team of those years: 'My father Mickey White played on a man called Mick Flynn in the county final of 1941. My father got his kidney shifted, probably from a dig of a hurley, which was part and parcel of the game in those days. When he woke up the following morning, his whole body had inflated and, consequently, he spent about six weeks in hospital. But during those weeks, Mick Flynn, through the goodness of the players in Quin and Clooney, used to arrive to us every Saturday with £3. Amby Power, who played in 1914, used to contribute £1. It was a great gesture as they did not have to do it. £3 then was a lot of money. I never forgot it.

'But, though the Ennis Dalcassian's beat Clooney in the county final of 1941, the sad thing is that we failed to field a team during some years in the 1940s. The Faughs won the intermediate in 1945 and played senior in 1946. Plus the Ennis Commercials were formed, comprised of shop boys. It was a big thing then to work behind the counter of a drapery. Tom Neylon was one of the founders. Flan Hynes was a Faughs man in the 1940s. The hurlers were there; the Faughs had Johnny Fleming, Reggie Connellan, Tony Strand and Paddy Duggan. Plus Ennis Rovers always had good hurlers.'

CLARE'S 'EMERGENCY' YEARS

Flan Purcell declined to play with the county team after a falling-out with some

Ennis Dalcassians, county champions, 1941
Back row l/r: John Hynes, Tom Nealon, Paddence O'Loughlin, Christy Glynn, Johnny Fleming, Jim Quinlivan, Brud McCarthy, Seán Moloney, Tull Considine, Raphie Burns; Front row l/r: Tony Glynn, Arthur Power, Bruddy Mann, Miko Ball, Seán Guinnane, Tommy 'Tonnie' Considine, Joe 'Jeweller' Madigan, Aoner Sheridan, 'Bucky' Flynn
[Mickie White is missing from photograph]

members of the county board around 1938. Nonetheless, in spite of general hard times, he recalls that county teams were always well looked after with dinner at Hanratty's in Limerick or Hayes' in Thurles after matches. He names some of the best that he saw during the 1930s and 1940s, Mickey Grady of Bodyke who, Flan claims, should have been on the 1932 team, John and Haulie Daly, Mick Halloran of Clooney, Lal Rice and of course Larry Blake of Ennis.

He said 'Raphie Burns was a great corner-back; he was dropped for the championship game with Tipperary in 1936, even though he had a great game against Cork in the previous round.' Joe McNamara has some similar, colourful opinions about the lack of development of a county team during this period. 'Dalcassianism cursed us for life. We're a small little tribe in Clare and we're the least Anglicised and Normanised county in Ireland. Everyone was pulling for their own parish and no one could see the overall picture. Thankfully Ger Loughnane broke all this in 1995. In the late 1930s, collective training was dispensed with. There was no proper training; a player might be looked at for fifteen minutes and never again seen.'

There is a general school of thought to the effect that Clare teams suffered in the late 1930s and early 1940s because of a lack of collective training. Jack Hogan of Newmarket-on-Fergus first played with the Blues in the late 1930s and recollects that collective training was banned by the GAA. 'The GAA did not like anything professional or semi-professional. We in Clare abided by the rules while other counties didn't; it was a GAA directive.'

Mick Leahy contrasts the prevailing attitude to match preparations in Clare with that of his adoptive county, Cork. 'Going back to the 1930s, it was said that if Clare won the first round, they'd train for the second round. But they forgot that they were playing in the first round against the great Limerick teams, plus the Cork, Tipperary or maybe Waterford sides of that era. Cork club hurling was at an inter-county standard in those years; the Barr's, Rockies and Glen produced the bulk of the Cork teams. Dunlops and Fords gave huge employment and they were also havens of hurling.'

THE HAMILTON ERA

Michael Hamilton was born in Clonlara in 1894. Having attended the local nation-al school and St Flannan's College, Ennis he went on to study for the priesthood in Maynooth, displaying a brilliant academic aptitude along the way. Following his ordination in 1919, he was appointed to the teaching staff of St Flannan's, then be-came an army chaplain for a few years, before returning to St Flannan's in 1924. In addition to his teaching duties, he was appointed diocesan secretary in 1926, a post which he held until he became parish priest of Newmarket-on-Fergus in 1942.

In parallel to his status as a cleric, Fr Hamilton was a major force in the Clare GAA organisation. He was appointed chairman of the county board on 28 February, 1928 and held this position for twenty-five years. The two big names in the Clare GAA organisation during the 1930s and 1940s were Fr Hamilton and Mick Hen-nessy of Clooney who was secretary. Tom Malone of Clonbony club points out that they could not be considered as natural allies. 'They were opposites politically speaking, but politics didn't come into it. Mick Hennessy's brother Patrick was exe-cuted by the Free State during the Civil War and Fr Hamilton was staunch Fine Gael but they were able to work together in the GAA.'

Johnny Moloney confirms this view of Fr Hamilton. 'He commanded respect regardless of politics; he was an outstanding man, had great personality and dom-inated county board meetings. He was also a national figure in GAA affairs and I had great respect for him.' John Donoghue of Kilnamona was a county board dele-gate from 1940 to 1954 and attended many meetings during the Hamilton era. 'In Fr Hamilton's time, the county board did all the work that's being done now by umpteen committees. At that time there was a lot more business done because of objections; clubs played illegal and overage players. The dates, venues and referees were also fixed at board meetings. He was a very fair man and he used to say that no amount of rules were as good as common sense. He was the complete boss; what he said was law.'

This latter characteristic of Fr (later Canon and Monsignor) Hamilton was one that did not always endear him to the entire body of GAA followers in Clare dur-ing his long reign. It would seem that he was seldom too far away from controver-sy and his memory is not universally cherished by those who came up against his wrath. According to Aoner Sheridan, 'The only man who had decent arguments with him was Paddy McNamara of Labour. The meetings were often adjourned.'

However, many people have also echoed Tom Malone's view that he was instrumental in unifying the Clare GAA after the Civil War split in the early 1920s, which in itself must be considered a significant contribution. He also had tremen-dous organisational skills and was tireless in his efforts to improve standards of dis-cipline and presentation of games. The following statement, issued by him before the 1923 senior county championship semi-final between Feakle and Newmarket is testimony to his crusading nature:

54

I will insist on punctuality and I do not care who suffers. It will not do to be on the field and placing your men etc. at 3.00p.m. They must be on the field lined up at the scheduled time, otherwise there will be no match. I hope that no member of a team will come out in pants to play in a semi-final of the county championship.

A *Clare Champion* report from April 1928 gives high praise to his achievements:

An enthusiastic revival of hurling has taken place all over Clare. Next Sunday will be a day of unique activity in Gaelic circles. There will be no fewer than 28 teams in action involving some 500 players. It will be the first time that the GAA can boast of such numerical strength in a single day in the county or in any other county and it is striking evidence of the popularity of the chairman of the county board, Fr Michael Hamilton, who over the past few years has done Trojan work in support of our national pastimes.

Fr Hamilton was a renowned orator and, when in full flow, could command any audience's attention. John Donoghue can still remember and recite by heart some of Fr Hamilton's speeches, both from county board meetings and other public occasions, so he was a man who obviously left a strong impression. The following piece is from an article which he wrote later in life entitled *The Passing Years*, which casts an eye back over social and sporting developments down through the years and gives an insight into his own vision of the GAA's significance. It also illustrates his passionate style of expression:

Yet, underlying all those passing phases there is the underlying sameness, the same thrill of victory, the same ambition to bring credit to 'the little village' and above all the same passionate desire to hand on to another generation, in spite of change and fashion, the imperishable consciousness of the Ireland of the Gael. Other influences may distract, the passing years will bring further change, but the GAA will be the backbone of Irish national life, the nerve centre of Gaelic feeling, just as truly and forcibly as it was of yore when it withstood the onslaughts of those who deemed it vulgar, and the physical efforts of those who aimed at its destruction.

The passing years will continue the process of evolution; the time will come when our methods and customs will be obsolete, but Ireland's claim to nationhood, Gaelic in thought and action, will endure forever.

On his transfer to Nenagh in 1956, the trophy for the senior hurling championship was presented to the county board by Monsignor Hamilton. His parting comments addressed the question of internal conflict in his own inimitable way: 'There will be and there must be, at all times, differences of opinion and clash of interests and I had my share of them, but the overall outlook and policy of our organisation has sufficient appeal to the national instincts of our people to surmount the temporary divergences, and the genuine Gael forgot animosities as quickly as he begot them.'

THE WAR YEARS

The Clare teams of 1939 to 1942 were easily disposed of in the Munster championship. In 1942, it appears that many of the most prominent players in the county were selected for the junior team, including Pake Haran, Pake Lyons and Bernie Power, who later spent many years playing senior for Galway. The juniors easily disposed of Limerick by 5–6 to 3–2, but the seniors were thrashed by Tipperary 5–13 to 1–3. Pake Lyons, the distinguished Mountshannon–Whitegate hurler of the 1940s, recalls playing about thirteen games for Clare before winning any during this era:

Some of the players used league matches for a day out. The selectors weren't much better either. For each game, the team was chopped and changed and the first time that the same fifteen were concentrated on was 1949. I remember going to a training session in Tulla on a Saturday evening. The person in charge of the team was out canvassing for a council election that day. We had no ball to train with and, after waiting around till near dark, we were getting ready to go home when man and ball arrived. Travelling arrangements for matches that time were also very bad. The other counties were better organised.

CLARECASTLE

Clarecastle finally made the breakthrough in 1943, winning the senior championship and *Clare Champion* cup double. The *Clare Champion* cup was won at the expense of the Twenty-third Battalion, a very strong army side stationed in Dromoland, which included many inter-county players including Brian Moore and Phil Byrnes. They were all-army champions and they had the pick of the county. Also they had the benefit of the best training, with extra rations as well, a significant advantage at that time.

The late Willie McAllister, who made his senior club debut with Clarecastle at the age of fourteen, has said that his happiest memory was winning the double in 1943. The final against the Twenty-third Battalion was a thriller and one of the greatest Clare club matches of all time. The army team had a great reputation and they seemed unbeatable, but the Magpies played like men inspired and won a classic match. In the county championship semi-final later that year, Clooney the holders led Clarecastle by thirteen points three-quarters of the way through the game, when the Magpies staged an extraordinary come-back to snatch victory and a place in the county final by 4–5 to 4–4.

John McInerney was growing up in Clarecastle in the mid-1940s to early 1950s. 'I remember nothing in Clarecastle but success, between county championships, Clare cups and Dr Daly tournaments. The players I remember best are Willie McAllister, John, Haulie and Pat Joe Daly, Paddy Markham, Chris Murphy and James "Dutcher" Moloney. Dick Barron, the Sixmilebridge hurler, often said that Chris Murphy was the best centre-back he saw during those years though he seldom played for the county. Dutcher Moloney from Patrick Street, better known as 'The Pound', was a class corner or centre-back; he played for Clare in the late 1940s and early 1950s.'

ST FLANNAN'S FOUR-IN-A-ROW

St Flannan's were outside the official Munster colleges hurling competition, the Harty cup, from 1928 to 1943. This resulted from a dispute that arose over the extension of the GAA's ban on 'foreign' games to college hurling. Twenty Munster schools abided by the ruling but six didn't. Apart from St Flannan's, others who objected were Waterpark College, Waterford; St Colman's, Fermoy; St Finbarr's, Farranferris; Presentation College, Cork and Christian Schools, Limerick. St Flannan's president, Canon O'Kennedy, became chairman of the breakaway body and an unofficial competition, the Munster cup, was put in place. In his acceptance speech, one of the points which Canon O'Kennedy made to justify the stand taken was that these new GAA restrictions on entry to colleges' hurling competitions constituted 'a violation of the principle of liberty in athletics and the rights of the heads of schools'.

St Flannan's re-entered the Harty cup competition for the 1943–44 season. They had not won the unofficial Munster cup competition since 1934. Tull Considine had played for St Flannan's in his student days and was invited back to train the Harty team by college president Fr M. Quinn. Tull's influence was seen immediately as St Flannan's won four Harty cups in a row, 1944 to 1947, thereby equalling the record set by the North Monastery, Cork who achieved the same from 1940 to 1943. Jimmy Smyth played in five Harty cup finals, winning three. He remembers Tull Considine as a great trainer. 'Many of the things he taught us haven't caught on yet. He was the most articulate and knowledgeable man on hurling I heard before or since.'

The first of the four-in-a-row wins was a replay against Midleton in Tipperary Town on 2 April 1944 on a score line of 4–5 to 2–2. *The Clare Champion* reported that St Flannan's deserved their victory 'as they combined better and were loudly applauded for their accuracy, abandon and skill'. Up to this point, the All-Ireland colleges series did not exist but, due in no small part to the endeavours of Fr Michael Hamilton, the Munster council inaugurated these championships in 1944. The first final was suitably fixed for Thurles between St Flannan's and St Kieran's, Kilkenny. St Flannan's won by 5–5 to 3–3, thereby becoming the first college to win the All-Ireland. Flannan's also won the All-Irelands of 1945 and 1946. They struggled to overcome O'Connell's Schools at Croke Park in 1946 until J. J. Bugler was moved to centre-forward where he gave an inspirational display.

Kieran Hennessy of Quin was a student of St Flannan's from September, 1944 to June, 1949 and remembers some of the students who played during those years. 'The big names included J. J. Bugler, Michael O'Shaughnessy, Harry O'Meara and Jimmy Kennedy of Tipperary. Even then, Jimmy Smyth was star material, and John and Willie Hanly. I remember Michael Considine and Tim Tuohy; Jimmy Carney was two or three years my junior. In 1947, St Flannan's completed the four-in-a-row (a feat they haven't achieved since), beating St Colman's Fermoy by 4–5 to 3–6. John Hanly gave a wonderful display in 1947 and out-played their star player Bill Abernethy at mid-field.'

John Hanly himself also recalls this period. 'I played at centre-field in 1947 with Jimmy Smyth. My job was to knock the ball down to him and he would score points from centre-field. Jimmy Smyth had tremendous strength even then'. Smyth played as wing-back in 1945 while still a second-year and was on the team until 1949. An indication of the esteem in which he was held even then is given by a Tull Considine instruction before one particular match: 'Nobody is to rise the ball except Jimmy Smyth'.

In the 1950s St Flannan's won four more Harty cup titles, beating St Finbarr's in 1952 (1–5 to 1–3), Thurles CBS in 1954 (2–11 to 3–5), North Monastery in 1957 (7–7 to 3–3) and Limerick CBS in 1958 (6–2 to 3–7). They also went on to win the All-Ireland in 1958 against St Kieran's, Kilkenny (3–10 to 0–2), thereby avenging defeat by the same school in the previous year's final. However, after 1958, it was to be a long eighteen years before another Harty cup was brought back through the gates of St Flannan's.

POST–WAR RESURGENCE

Clare re-emerged in the mid-1940s as a major force and a young side ran Limerick very close in the 1945 senior championship. Young, talented players like J. J. Bugler (St Flannan's), Chris Murphy (Ballyea) and Phil Byrnes (a Limerick man then playing with the Twenty-third Battalion) ran Limerick to within three points 3–6 to 3–3 and only faded when an experienced Limerick side began to slow things down in the final quarter.

1946 will always remain one of the high points in Clare hurling history with the winning of three major competitions – the national hurling league, Árus na nGaedheal and the Thomond Feis. The Thomond Feis was a highly prestigious tournament at the time, much sought after by the counties involved. It took place in Limerick every spring between Cork, Clare, Tipperary and Limerick, providing many fine games, and was always a good indicator of how things might go in the Munster championship.

Michael 'Tolly' Guinnane from Clarecastle made his debut for Clare in the Árus na nGaedheal competition. 'I played corner-forward, a position I never played in my life. I didn't expect to be on the team, as I was only called up the night before. We beat Tipperary 4–5 to 2–6 in the final of the Thomond Feis. It was our first win in this competition since 1929. The selectors changed the team for the championship; it was unbelievable.'

Clare's league run had started on a bad note with a two-point defeat by Galway, but they picked themselves up to beat Westmeath and Offaly. They then had a vital win over Limerick to keep their interest in the competition alive. A draw in this game would have been useless to Clare but they rose to great heights when Pake Lyons crashed home a dream goal having broken through a barrage of men and hurleys. Dan McInerney held Mick Mackey scoreless and the mid-field pairing of Des Carroll and Austin Hannon dominated their positions on the way to a Clare victory by 6–2 to 4–3.

After the defeat of Limerick, Clare qualified for a divisional play-off with Galway. With Bob Frost, Dermot Solon, Haulie Daly and Alfie O'Brien outstanding, Clare took command and finished strongly to win by 6–3 to 2–7 at Nenagh. In the league final at the Dublin Gaelic Grounds, the home side led Clare by four points at half-time and, towards the end of the match, a spectacular shot by Pake Lyons was saved by goal-keeper Banks, but Matt Nugent and Alfie O'Brien bundled him over the line before he could clear. The result was a draw 1–6 to 1–6.

1946 LEAGUE FINAL

Clare improved greatly for the replay, with Pappy Callaghan at full-back putting in a Herculean effort and enabling Dan McInerney, Phil Byrnes, Des Carroll and Brian McMahon to deal effectively with the advances of Wade, Herbert, Prior and Ó Ceallacháin. In his autobiography, Seán Óg Ó Ceallacháin recalls the league final of 1946:

> We met Clare in the League Final at Limerick. I got a right roasting from the Clare right half-back, Dermot Solon. Dermot inspired them to a second-half recovery to earn a share of the honours. They beat us by five points in the replay and the hero was Jackie Solon at mid-field. I asked the selectors to move me to mid-field to curb Jackie Solon, but the damage was already done. Clare deservedly won the game. Jackie Solon was their prime marksman and gave a masterful display, totting up 1–5 out of 2–10.

Ned Doyle nominates Jackie Solon as his man-of-the-match that day. 'He won the national league for Clare in 1946. He was outstanding, himself and Austin Hannon (both at centre-field). Jackie cleaned up on Harry Gray the same day'. After the final whistle, four or five thousand wildly excited and rejoicing Claremen surged onto Croke park to greet the players. The cup was presented to the captain Michael 'Haulie' Daly and the team then went to Barry's Hotel where they were given a formal reception at which over two hundred turned up, including veterans of 1914 and 1932.

Johnny Moloney was a selector in the 1940s. 'Mick Hennessy was the manager and possibly complete selector in 1946. He had an advisory committee, which consisted of Larry Blake, John Joe Doyle and myself. I think the 1946 team was our best team'. Matt Nugent also considers this team to be the best that he played on. 'Clare had the ability to challenge strongly for the Munster and All-Ireland titles of 1946. We met Cork in the Munster championship on an awful wet day. It was so bad that lines were washed off the field'. That Clare team in 1946 played eighteen games, comprising thirteen wins, two draws and three defeats.

Clare National League Champions, 1946
Back row l/r: J. J. Bugler, George Frost, Pappy Callaghan, P. Quaine, Fr Jackie Solon, Matt Nugent, John Daly, Brian McMahon, Paddy Markham, Mick Hennessy; Middle row: Haulie Daly, Dan McInerney, Des Carroll, Tolly Guinnane, Joe Whelan, Bob Frost; Front row: Dermot Solon, Phil Byrnes, Austin Hannon

WHERE'S YOUR GREAT CLARE TEAM NOW? (1947–1955)

Growing up in the 1950s, we had two heroes, the Lone Ranger and Jimmy Smyth.

P. J. CURTIS

All we had was a couple of barrels of water.

TOLLY GUINNANE

After the national hurling league victory of 1946, the fortunes of our senior hurlers slumped at the hands of Cork in the first-round championship defeats of 1946 and 1947. However, a narrow two-point defeat by Waterford in 1948 signalled something of a revival. In a game of changing fortunes, Clare, powered by Matt Nugent, Haulie Daly, Austin Hannon and Mick Murphy (who had recently returned to the Clare colours after a spell with Tipperary) almost defeated the future All-Ireland champions of 1948. They also captured the Four-County tournament and Cusack Shield. Both competitions were played on a knockout championship basis and were highly prestigious at that time. On the club front there were a few passionate encounters during this period, some of which led to considerable controversy.

THE LONG FINAL OF 1948
One of the most talked-about county finals was the famous 'Long Final' of 1948 between Ruan and Clarecastle which ended in a controversial draw. It was an encounter that had been eagerly awaited as the following eyewitness account suggests:

> The Ruan convoy left in every mode of transport – horse and trap, bicycles and open turf lorries. Upon entering Ennis, the team togged out in Linnane's yard and marched up Parnell Street and through the square with every man, woman and child from Ruan behind. The rest is history.

Ruan, with victories over Ennis Rovers and Scariff, had earned their place in the final and Clarecastle had accounted for Newmarket in the other semi-final. The game was a fairly hot-blooded affair and, at the final whistle, many of those present in the crowd of 8,000 thought that Ruan had won by three points, 7-4 to 5-7. John Hanly wrote about the game in a Ruan club history and remembered the second half lasting sixty-one minutes (other reports say it lasted forty-six minutes):

> In the hurly-burly of that tempestuous game and in the sporadic intrusions on to the pitch, it is quite understandable that the time factor was misread as much as the final goal for Ruan was not recorded. Truly, Ruan won by a goal and I remember congratulating several of their players on a great victory.

One possible explanation for the confusion is to be found in the following *Clare*

Champion report of 9 October, 1948:

> Asked if he had disallowed any score, the referee (Mick Quain) said he had not. If he
> had missed a score, it was due to an encroachment of spectators around the goal post.
> When our representative said that the green flag had been raised for the last goal by
> Ruan long after the teams were even, the referee replied 'Not only one but forty flags!

The referee's problems may have been added to by the fact that Ruan had borrowed
the jerseys of the Clooney club for the day, apparently because Ruan were tem-
porarily without a complete set. (A good relationship existed between the two
clubs, which originated in a senior championship amalgamation in 1934.) In any
case, this may have impaired the referee's ability to see green flags as the Clooney
jerseys were red and green!

The bards were busy after this county decider and *The Clare County Final of
1948*, written by Jimmy Ward, is an epic ballad which provides a unique match
report, albeit with a slight leaning in the Ruan direction. Here are some of the verses:

> Have you heard of the county final that was played in Cusack Park,
> Ruan boys and Clarecastle they played till it was dark,
> The referee's watch refused to go, at least that's what we're told,
> Though some are apt to differ, they say the game was sold,
>
> The band struck up 'Attention' and the teams lined up behind,
> Spectators still kept pouring in but had no seat to find,
> A lady in from Spancilhill looked round her in despair,
> If we hadn't got such stewarding, she'd fill the bishop's chair,
>
> Six thousand fans with ringing cheers were shouting 'Up Ruan',
> But, undismayed, Clarecastle played like heroes every man,
> McAllister he takes a pass, his shot goes straight and true,
> Though Courtney pulled and pulled again, his pulling didn't do,
>
> But Smyth is there to stem the tide, he rouses up his team,
> The 'Red and Green' are fighting hard, a draw may yet be seen,
> But what is that I see right now, a crowd invades the square,
> We look around for umpires, though we know they are not there,
>
> A Yankee seated near me was quite upset I fear,
> He said, 'why don't they stop that row, it's drawing very near?'
> But I replied, 'don't worry sir, it's only just a lark,
> It's the regular occurrence sir here in Cusack Park.'
>
> The sun was sinking in the west 'ere order was restored,
> And once again the match began, the Ruan spirits soared,
> As Donoghue sends to the net, there stands a mighty roar,
> The long awaited whistle and the marathon is o'er,
>
> Ruan, thought they were winners, the ref did not agree,
> When asked for his decision, 'it is a draw,' says he,
> But the county board thought different at a meeting later on,
> So why the hell bother to bring the ref along!

The awarding of the match to Ruan by the county board, the appeal to the Munster council, the referee's report and the re-fixing of the county final were issues which were hotly debated and generated huge interest both inside and outside the county. As a result 9,000 people attended the replay in April 1949 which Ruan deservedly won.

Ruan were fortunate to have two keen hurling mentors, Fr Gunning and Fr Leamy, in their midst during that period and these priests took a great interest in the game, attending training sessions and generally motivating the players. It is interesting to note that Ruan had been playing in intermediate ranks in 1948. Miko Lyons, who was secretary of the club at the time, takes up the story. 'There was and uneven number of clubs in the senior championship that year, so we decided to apply for senior status to Monsignor Hamilton, the chairman of the county board, and our application was successful'. According to Jimmy Smyth, they had a very strong team in Ruan at this time. 'Possibly, if the Munster club championship had existed, we'd have given the best clubs a game. We had players of a very high standard in Seán Leahy, Joe McDonnell, "Jazzer" Meaney, Christy Courtney, Joe Hassett, etc., but we lost to Clarecastle in 1949 and to Whitegate in 1950.'

DEAD MAGPIES
The depth of rivalry between the Newmarket 'Blues' and the Clarecastle 'Magpies' was as intense as usual in 1948 according to John Hanly. 'The best match played in the club championship of 1948 was the semi-final between ourselves and the Blues. Newmarket left two dead magpies in the village on their way to Cusack Park.' Tolly Guinnane has a slightly different version of events. 'I remember it well; it was hard and Newmarket expected to beat us. They had some dead magpies which they intended depositing in Clarecastle on the way home, but we found out about it. They got a shock that day. Chris Murphy, Haulie Daly and Willie McAllister – the best forward to come out of Clarecastle in my opinion – were the stars.'

John Hanly continues: 'We were playing badly and Jimmy McMahon made a great switch. He came over to me and said, "John, go to centre-forward, Haulie (Daly) is playing badly". But he had gone to Haulie before that and said: "Go to centre-field, John is playing very badly". What a beautiful balance. Jimmy McMahon (a blacksmith from Clarecastle) was one of the great characters; he gave his life to hurling.'

In a series of winning sallies, Clarecastle swept through the Newmarket defence and caused numerous flags to be raised in a pulsating last quarter. Clarecastle won 7–9 to 7–1 having trailed for 45 minutes. Huge crowds, including overseas visitors and contingents from Galway, Limerick and Tipperary witnessed the game. 'It is heartening to see the standard of club hurling so high as we saw from Clarecastle v Newmarket and Ruan v Scariff', was *The Clare Champion*'s verdict on the games.

PAKE'S RETURN
Pake Lyons returned to the Whitegate team for the county final of 1950. He was a great centre-half back, probably one of the best Clare ever had. Whitegate also had great players in Dermot and Percy Solon and Ned Doyle.

The following interview with Pake Lyons is taken from Patrick Madden's *History of Gaelic Games in Whitegate and Mountshannon*. Pake had first retired from hurling in 1947:

> The appetite for the game was gone. I also got married that year and began worrying about injuries. There were no insurance schemes that time and no compensation for

injuries. I started to lose interest in the game as well.

I'll never forget it. I hadn't hurled for three years and never even thought about playing again. Whitegate had reached the county final and, one day I arrived home from work, there was a message for me that Fr Crowe wanted to see me. I had my mind made up going down to see him that I wouldn't return.

When I went down he said to me that there was training in the hall that night and would I go up to it. I eventually agreed to go. There was only two weeks to the final. We did the usual physical training that night and, afterwards, ran to Willie Halloran's cross and back. I wasn't able to stir the next day I was so sore. The following Sunday, we did a bit of hurling at Whitegate. That was the sum total of my training in three years for a senior county final. In the final itself, I was playing centre-back and couldn't run any distance without getting bloated. The two wing-backs that day were Ned Doyle and Tom Thornberry. I used them a lot to clear the ball. I did find it difficult but it was worth it in the end.

The Clare Champion reporter also enjoyed the game:

> By a clear-cut victory of six points over Ruan in the county final, Whitegate left no doubt about their being deserving champions of Clare for 1950. Despite the bad weather and water-soaked ground, the game produced really good passages of play; never once was there a dull moment all during the hour. Striking was lengthy and clean and the determination with which every ball was fought kept spectators keyed up from whistle to whistle.

GENERAL CLUB SCENE

John McInerney of Clarecastle remembers going to Cusack Park in the early 1950s when the Clare hurlers were training. 'It was a huge novelty to watch the greats like Matt Nugent, Jimmy Smyth, Mick Leahy and Willie McAllister training. Because of unemployment in the region, the vast majority of our county players were working in Dublin or elsewhere and this meant that we only had the home-based players training. On the week prior to a championship game I often saw as little as six training, having an unorganised puck-around. Then in the mid 1950s, the county secretary Seán Guinnane, a very affable man, organised the Residents *v* Non-Residents; this was played in Newmarket in the springtime as preparation for the championship. The non-residents had among others Des Dillon, Michael Lynch, Philip Waldron and Johnny Hogan, a real stylist, in their line-out.'

Flan Hynes of St Joseph's considers that the general standard of club hurling in Clare was very high during the 1950s, with practically all of the strong clubs capable of winning senior championship honours in any given year. 'Clarecastle had outstanding men in Willie McAllister and Haulie Daly. There was Des Carroll, Vinny Henchy, Jimmy Fennessy and Harry O'Meara of Scariff, Pat and Jackie Greene of Newmarket. Whitegate had great ball players; they had a

Matt Nugent

style of their own – Paddy Jordan, the Cleary brothers, Jack Kenneally, Pake Haran and all the rest were very difficult opponents.' With regard to players from his own club, St Joseph's, Flan says: 'Matt Nugent was one of the all-time greats; he was revered in all counties. Donal O'Grady was the sweetest of centre-backs. Donal played with the Faughs of Dublin in 1954 as did Tom Fahy (Newmarket). Yes, St

Joseph's were a leading side; you needed to be at your best to beat St Joseph's.'

Ennis seems to have been an exception to this trend in the early 1950s, when hurling had reached a low ebb in the town. The last senior success had been Ennis Dalcassian's in 1941, although the Faugh's won the intermediate championship in 1945 and Turnpike were runners-up to Sixmilebridge in 1951. The Rovers also had a useful junior side but, in general, disinterest had set in amongst the town's hurling followers. The main sporting interest at the time lay in Gaelic football, which was not surprising when one considers that Ennis Faughs won senior football championships in 1947, 1948, 1952 and 1954 and were finalists in 1953 and 1955.

In February 1952 a new Ennis club called Éire Óg was formed in Paddy Duggan's house at No. 5 Steele's Terrace, when a historic meeting was called by a group of young hurling enthusiasts, many of them still at school. A set of jerseys – white with a green shamrock – were made available thanks to the generosity of the residents of the Boreen (now Marian Avenue) and Steele's Terrace. The driving forces behind the new club were Simon O'Donnell, Seán Guinnane, Tim Smythe (trainer), Larry Blake Jnr, Michael Blake, Val McCann and Paddy Duggan.

Bernie Dilger was approached by Paddy Duggan to join the club. 'We played hurling in the fields which are now St Michael's Villas – the Enskos, Cronins, Cosgroves, Loftuses, etc. The hurling didn't necessarily have to come from your parents. We could pick a team from the Connolly Villas area. We spent all our time outdoors; this was the era before television. The effect that television has on people in general is bad; young people spend so much time watching television that they don't acquire the natural everyday skills earlier generations had.'

TOWN LEAGUES

The Ennis town leagues were a major attraction in the 1930s and 1940s. Vincent Sheridan, a brother of Aoner, told me about these great leagues: 'Huge crowds turned out in the fair green. The 1930s was the high point; I think the hurling was better then. The crowds came from far and near to the finals; I remember a great final between The Turnpike and Old Mill Street – Tull Considine, Larry Blake, Christy "Click" Houlihan and "Pharoah" Mahony – the pick of them played for the Dals and the Rovers.'

Frank Malone also credits the Leagues with building up hurling in Ennis. 'We'd have had no hurling without them. Frank worked as a lorry driver during the development of Cusack Park in 1936 but had to give it up. 'My father Pako got sick and I went into the farrier business to help him. It was the hardest work one could get but I got great encouragement. If I was a flute player, I'd have been God!'

The town league final of 1948 attracted 2,000 spectators to Cusack Park. The esteem in which these leagues were held is evident from the fact that the county board saw fit not to fix any other games at the park on the weekend of the final, which was contested between the Turnpike and the Market. These sides had disposed of the Boreen, Old Mill Street, Clare Road and Corrovorrin on their way to the decider. The Ennis Brass Band led the teams on to Cusack Park and the Knights of Malta rendered first aid when necessary according to *The Clare Champion!*

Unfortunately, the final was marred by crowd encroachments. The Market, who had trained hard under former Clare hurler Mickey White, proved too strong in the second half. Mickey's son Paddy spoke to me about this period. 'The ironic thing is that, when hurling was at its very best in Ennis, we had a bad record; there was also some class distinction. Many of the Old Mill Street lads were left off, even though they were great hurlers. In the late 1940s, Ennis fielded the Dalcassian's, the

Faughs (who went senior in 1946) and Ennis Commercials. However, Éire Óg did a great job when they formed in the early 1950s.' Aoner Sheridan, also commenting on the town leagues, says: 'With five or six teams competing in the leagues, we had close to one hundred good hurlers in Ennis. What have we got today?'

Bernie Dilger corroborates Paddy White's views on the effects of class division, even on the hurling pitch, though they seem to lay different emphasis on the influence of Éire Óg. 'There were many players who shone in the town leagues and with the Rovers who didn't get a game with Éire Óg. The Rovers played Junior and they were very sticky. Then we had class distinction, a sort of inferiority complex. Elitism meant that lads who came to Ennis to take up positions were often played before locals, though there were exceptions. Some fellows were picked on merit, like Mick Morrissey and Donal Leahy from Wexford – they had great strength and presence – and Tony Keaty from Tipperary, though of Ennis stock. A real Ennisman, he was fearless.'

1949 MINOR MUNSTER FINAL
In the minor championship of 1948 Clare were well beaten by Waterford; Jimmy Smyth and Seán Dinan were the only ones to impress. However, the 1949 minor team is considered to have been one of the best ever to represent the county. Clare suffered a heart-breaking one-point defeat in the Munster final. Secretary of the county board, Mick Hennessy, had put everything into the minor team for months, sifting and grading to get the proper blend for the final. That minor team of 1949 was regarded as one of the best ever to represent Clare with Paddy Russell, Gerry Ryan, Seán Meehan, Patsy Meaney and Jackie Greene in the line-up. *The Clare Champion* report of the game read:

> Clare had two goals before Tipperary settled down, but Tipperary fought back to lead at the interval, 2–3 to 2–2. With Jimmy Smyth dominant at centre-field, Clare raced into a 4–4 to 2–3 lead. Tipperary fought back to lead 5–6 to 5–5 on the thirtieth minute. Smyth's solo run will long be remembered by the large crowd when he made that gallant effort, racing from centre-field through the Tipperary backs with the ball glued to his hurley, and it was heart-breaking that his bullet-like shot just greased the post from the difficult angle from which he had to shoot.

ALL-IRELAND JUNIOR 'HOME' CHAMPIONS OF 1949
In 1949, the All-Ireland Junior championship was played in two phases. The first involved the 'home' teams, with the winners usually playing London or whatever other team from abroad might qualify. The Clare junior team of 1949 captured the Munster championship with wins over Waterford and Cork in the final. Johnny Moloney was in Armagh for the semi-final against that county. 'We got a warm reception; the Keady Pipe Band played the Clare team through the streets on their way from the field to the hotel.'

Kilkenny as usual provided tough opposition in the 'home' final at Nenagh. Late in the game, Jimmy Smyth gathered a pass from a sixty-five yard free and shot low to the net to give Clare victory by 3–5 to 3–3. The Clare team were chaired from the pitch and the Tulla Pipe Band played a victory march for the huge Clare following. Nenagh remained a Clare stronghold long into the night.

In the final against London, Clare were cruising to a rare All-Ireland victory on a sweltering October's evening in Ennis, when Joe Duggan and Con Burke of

Clare All-Ireland Junior Home Champions, 1949
Front row l/r: Donal O'Grady, Bill Hogan, Mattie Moloney, Jimmy Smyth, Raymond McNamara,
Ned Doyle, Joe 'Jazzer' Meaney; Back row l/r: Tommy Considine, Ned Hickey, Peter Fitzgerald,
Michael 'Starry' O'Keeffe, Marty Marrinan, Pat Greene, ? , Paddy McNamara, Dermot Keane,
Raphie Burns, Pat Halpin, ? , Gerry Browne, Kevin Keogh, Willie Shanahan, Larry Blake, Michael
Garry, Miko Lyons

London conjured 2–1 between them in the dying moments to snatch victory from the Claremen in a sensational finish. The London exiles received great applause when the cup was presented to their captain in the presence of the Taoiseach and various ministers. According to Des Carroll, 'It was thrown away; a friend and I left before the final whistle and went to Carmody's hotel. We couldn't believe it when we heard that London Irish had won it by a point.' Ned Doyle of Whitegate, now living in Bodyke, was wing back on the 1949 team. 'We mostly trained on our own. Smyth was the difference; imagine if we had someone like him now?' For Jimmy Smyth, 'The Junior Final of 1949 was the biggest disappointment of my career. I remember Mick Hennessy crying. It's a game I'll never forget.'

That same year the Clare senior team suffered defeat in the Munster championship at the hands of the Tipperary three-in-a-row team of 1949–1951, which included a young John Doyle, Pat Stakelum and the legendary Tommy Doyle, then at the veteran stage of his hurling career. Many shrewd hurling people have since told me that both Smyth and O'Grady were left off the senior side for the 1949 championship to help win the junior title.

TRIP TO 'THE SPA'
Tolly Guinnane was a member of the senior championship team from 1949 to 1952, which also included Haulie Daly, Paddy Jordan and Willie McAllister. 'I've always said that if we had Jimmy Smyth with Haulie Daly and Willie McAllister we'd have beaten Tipperary in 1949. Clare were good in those years, but we seemed to be that bit lacking; maybe it was mí ádh. I remember training in Tulla and all we had was a couple of barrels of water and we'd be hosed down afterwards, but we enjoyed it. Larry Blake was a great man to talk. He could say more in five minutes than another would say in a day. Fr Jackie Solon also trained us in Lisdoonvarna and Tim Smythe was a great masseur. Fr Solon tried to get permission from the bishop of Galway to play for Clare, but to no avail. He was a huge loss. (The Church at that

Recent picture of Michael 'Tolly' Guinnane'

time excluded priests from playing hurling and this led to the loss of Fr Solon from the team after he entered the priesthood.) We trained collectively for ten days but people were under the impression that it was up for the booze we went!'

The Clare goal-keeper at this time was Eugene Small of Ardnacrusha who also remembers collective training at Lisdoonvarna. 'It was very strict and we were watched closely after evening meals, but the mentors were right. We were close enough to the great Tipperary team but they beat us by three points in the 1950 championship'. Eugene regards the 1946 league team and the 1954 Oireachtas team as the best Clare teams of this era and has great memories of the outstanding full-back Pappy Callaghan as well as Tolly Guinnane, Mick Murphy, Flor O'Brien and Jimmy Smyth. 'There was no one to touch Jimmy Smyth'. His last championship match with Clare in 1954 resulted from the unavailability of Mick Hayes. 'I was walking into the first round of the Munster championship against Tipperary in 1954 when a car pulled up and Fr Corry and Mick Hennessy got out. They asked me to play as they didn't have a sub goal-keeper. I said: "You can't expect me to play as I have no real hurling done all year." I was reluctant to play but I couldn't let them down.'

Jimmy Smyth regards the 1953 senior team as the best side he played on during his long career. 'Mick Hayes made his debut that year and the team also included Jackie Greene at full-forward, Des Carroll and Matt Nugent, but the man that I remember most from this side was Michael Considine of Ennis. He was a big, strong, able man, tough as they come, a great centre-field player. He never got the full credit for his greatness. We beat Limerick 10–8 to 1–1 in Cusack Park, but Cork beat us by three points and went on to win the championship.' Smyth scored 6–4 against Limerick in 1953 which, forty-three years later, is still a record in Munster Championship hurling and a feat hardly ever likely to be equalled.

RAILWAY CUP
Jimmy Smyth played on every Munster railway cup team from 1953 to 1964 and probably played longer in the company of Christy Ring than most Corkmen. Jimmy himself recalls: 'It was very hard to get on the railway cup team, especially as a Clareman in those years. It was a special kind of game and, coming from a weaker county, one was expected to pass the ball. I only got two passes in my time playing for Munster. Everyone went for their own scores. I got on very well with Christy Ring and we often socialised together; he was the greatest in my time; I've seen nothing like him. He was devastating, had great charisma and thousands came to see him; he often put 10,000 extra into a stadium. Mick Mackey was a selector. He was a reticent kind of man, an idol.'

Speaking recently about Jimmy Smyth, Michael Arthur of Newmarket-on-Fergus had this to say. 'Smyth is held in the highest regard throughout the country wherever GAA is talked about. Whatever our contribution was for Clare or our club, we have never reached the same pinnacle as he has without having won a Munster championship or All-Ireland.'

Other Claremen to play with Munster in those years include Dermot Solon (1948), Haulie Daly (1948–49), Willie McAllister (1950), Dan McInerney (1951), Matt Nugent (1951 to 1954), Donal O'Grady (1953 and 1955), Des Dillon (1955), Jackie Greene (1955), Jimmy Carney (1956), Mick Hayes (1957). Both Matt Nugent and Donal O'Grady of Tubber were on the 1953 team, a tremendous achievement for a small parish.

1953 COUNTY FINAL

The 1953 county final between holders Scariff and Newmarket-on-Fergus is considered by many to be one of the most memorable ever. Scariff were a strong, established side and had beaten Sixmilebridge in the 1952 final. A record crowd witnessed one of the toughest and most entertaining county finals for many years. *The Clare Champion* described 'some great duels between players such as Des Carroll and Jimmy Halpin, John Walsh and Jack Hogan, though the rugged and the robust nature of the exchanges didn't leave much room for the classical.'

Scariff lead by just a point at half time but dominated the game in the third quarter to build up a lead of eight points at one stage. Newmarket fought back at the end to narrow the gap to four points, but Scariff held on to win by 5–2 to 2–7 with J. J. Bugler and Mick Guilfoyle scoring two goals each for Scariff. For Jack Hogan, the Newmarket centre-back on the day, recollections of a trojan struggle are still intact. 'I remember Mick Guilfoyle coming back at full forward where he was devastating. Newmarket were hot favourites with many fine ball players, but Scariff were physically stronger; they had the McInerneys – Dan at centre back, Frank at full back and Vincent. They were whole-hearted and got stuck in.'

Michael Arthur recalls that Newmarket went through a lean spell from 1936 to 1955 even though they had great players like Gerry Houlihan from Cork and Chris Keane. 'It's not unusual to get barren spells, it's the pattern. We just couldn't win the championship in those years. Scariff were a bogey team for Newmarket.'

OIREACHTAS VICTORY 1954

One of the most attractive competitions which took place during these years was the Oireachtas. Many hurling followers consider the Oireachtas to be a relatively modern competition but this is not so. The GAA and the Gaelic League first allied in 1910 and, within a few years, teams lent valuable assistance to League activities by participating in the Munster Feis competition and the Thomond Feis. When the first Oireachtas was held, the events included a hurling match and this continued to be the case until this Gaelic festival was abandoned during the mid 1920s.

The Oireachtas was revived in 1939 when the GAA gave permission for a game of either hurling or football to be played in Croke Park between selected teams. In 1939, only a handful of people turned up to see the Limerick hurlers defeat Kilkenny and the promoters switched to football for a few years until 1944. From there it went from strength to strength and became one of the most prestigious hurling competitions in the GAA calendar of the early 1950s. The largest crowd ever was in 1956 when Wexford defeated Kilkenny – 37,227 paid to see it.

Clare reached the final in 1953, having beaten All-Ireland finalists Galway by 2–7 to 1–2, but fell disorganised and nervous to Wexford. Mick Leahy was based in

CLARE'S GALLANT FIGHT WAS UNREWARDED

Clare team in the Gaelic Grounds, 20 June 1954 [v Tipperary]
Front row l/r: Matt Nugent, Eugene Small, Jackie Greene, Donal O'Grady, Dan McInerney, Johnny Hogan, Tom Fahy; Back row l/r: Pat Halpin, Gerry Ryan, Pat Greene, Paddy Jordan, Gerry Browne, Jimmy Smyth, Haulie Donnellan, Johnny Purcell

Kilkenny at the time and could easily have been playing for Wexford that day. 'I was asked to a trial for the Wexford team. I played club hurling in Wexford, but I was supposed to play under the name Jack Jackman. If Jackman didn't make it, the excuse they gave was that this Jackman was a bit eccentric; he could be wonderful; he might not get a puck of the ball; or he might not turn up at all. I played on Paddy Keogh in the Oireachtas final of 1953. He obviously knew about the Wexford trial, but I asked him not to say anything about it to the Clare players.'

Prior to the 1954 Oireachtas, Clare were invited to London and entertained by the London county board. They defeated London 2–6 to 2–5 on 19 September. Smyth had a brilliant spell and, midway through the second half, he sent a long sixty-yard pass to Tom Fahy, who rattled the net to level matters. Des Carroll shot the winning point from an acute angle.

Clare and Tipperary clashed in the semi-final of the 1954 Oireachtas at Nenagh. The Clare backs played tremendous hurling, with Mick Leahy outstanding, and the home county trailed by five points at the interval, but pulled back the lead to level the match 1–6 all. The national league game between the same counties had to be deferred to accommodate the replay in Limerick and it was an outstanding game, rated as good as a Munster final by many. Clare won by 3–5 to 2–5 and so qualified again for a re-match with Wexford in the 1954 final.

The teams were level on six occasions, including the final whistle, on a score line of 2–8 all. The Clare half-backs, Noel Deasy, Donal O'Grady and Tom Fahy held the two Kehoes and Tim Flood in admirable fashion and Paddy Russell did well on Jim English. The replay, in front of an attendance of 29,289, co-incided with the annual observance in Croke Park of Bloody Sunday and saw Clare triumph over the 1954 All-Ireland finalists by three points 3–6 to 0–12. Corn Thomáis Aghas was raised by the Clare captain Matt Nugent and many people felt that, if this game had been an All-Ireland, it would have been rated the best for years.

The Wexford attack, with Nicky Rackard on the edge of the square, had failed to raise a green flag that day. Mick Hayes in goal added to his reputation and was fronted by Dan McInerney who held Nicky Rackard scoreless. This made all the difference according to Jimmy Smyth, whose opinion is also supported by Johnny Moloney, describing McInerney's performance as 'rock solid'. The newspapers of the day were also highly complimentary. Donal O'Grady was described as 'regal' at centre back. Dermot Sheedy, described as the 'hardest worker on the team', had a great game at midfield, while Jimmy Smyth had the upper hand on Ned Wheeler. Matt Nugent was 'the sweetest ball player of all' and Jackie Greene scored two great goals.

Dr Des Dillon, a native of Lisdoonvarna, made his Clare debut during the 1954 Oireachtas. Des first came to prominence with UCD in his student days and led the Combined Universities *v* Ireland in one of the early games of that series. He had previously played for Dublin and Leinster before declaring for his native county in 1954. Des led the Clare attack on Oireachtas final day, curbing Bobby Rackard. For Wexford, goal-keeper Art Foley brought off some incredible saves, Nick O'Donnell and Billy Rackard were very solid, Tim Flood was outstanding in the forwards and Jim English also played well. A final word to *The Clare Champion*: 'Clare kept the ball moving. The dilly-dallying trait of play attached to Clare teams for too long, but now it has been discarded and a more determined style employed by players of ability.'

HISTORIC WINS OVER CORK AND TIPPERARY IN 1955

Michael Arthur reckons that the greatest Clare team that he saw was the 1955 team. 'They were a multi-talented side and a strong, physically big team like Wexford – Dan McInerney, Des Dillon, Jim Carney and Dermot Sheedy – all big men. Donal O'Grady was probably the best centre-back playing in those years, Jackie and Pat Greene were clever forwards and Jimmy Smyth had tremendous qualities – intelligence, physique, great skill and ability – there was no stopping Smyth'. So hopes were high.

Clare and Tipperary clashed again in 1955, this time in the league at Cusack Park, and again Clare triumphed 3–4 to 2–3. 'Tipperary seemed to have found an answer to their attacking problems,' reported *The Clare Champion*, 'for the two lines they fielded were beyond compare, but it was not too much for the peerless trio of Mick Leahy, Dan McInerney and Haulie Donnellan.' Clare went on to defeat Limerick but lost to Tipperary in a play-off (now the semi-final stage) before a crowd of 22,000.

For this game, a young twenty year-old Jimmy Carney made his first appearance as a sub on the senior team. Carney, originally from Bealaha in West Clare, was retained for the first round championship game against Cork in Thurles. Jimmy Smyth remembers him as an unknown quantity. 'Suddenly, he was playing in Dublin and discovered by a great Clareman, Paddy Canny from Tulla. Paddy scouted for hurling talent in Dublin and generally looked after the Clare lads. He produced Carney and he played in a couple of practice matches; he had this unorthodox style. He came out against Cork in the championship and played great, smoothing the road to victory with some fine scores.'

Prior to the start of the Clare *v* Cork game, a miniature 12 inch hurley, signed by the Rackard brothers of Wexford, was presented to the Clare team. A first-minute goal from Jackie Greene followed by another from Jimmy Smyth put Clare in a strong position by the end of the first half. However, Cork stormed back and had drawn level by the eighteenth minute of the second half. Thanks to a great team

The Clare team that stopped Cork achieving Four-in-a-Row, 5 June 1955 in Thurles
Back row l/r: Mick Hayes, Willie Stritch, Jimmy Smyth, Dermot Sheedy, Des Dillon, Johnny
Purcell, Noel Deasy, ?; Front row l/r: Jimmy Carney, Matt Nugent, Gerry Ryan, Mick Leahy,
Donal O'Grady, Jackie Greene, Dan McInerney, Haulie Donnellan

effort however, the All-Ireland champions of 1952, 1953 and 1954 fell to Clare with
Smyth scoring the winning point. A new determination swept through Clare's players and officials alike, urged on by a subsequent good win over Kilkenny in a gold
watch tournament in Birr.

In the meantime, Clare's march to the Munster championship of 1955 wasn't an
easy one, with league champions Tipperary to be overcome. This Tipperary side
had many of those from the great era of 1949–1954, including John Doyle, Tony
Reddin, and Liam Devanney, Theo English and Jimmy Finn, all famous names in
their day. It was played on 19 June and was a tense low-scoring affair. The only goal
of the game came from a Clare move involving Matt Nugent and Jackie Greene.
Greene's shot was saved by Tony Reddin but Jimmy Carney, tearing in, first-timed
the rebound to the net under Reddin's body. Donal O'Grady (centre-back) and Dan
McInerney (full-back) were the Clare stars in this game, with McInerney giving one
of his greatest displays ever in a Clare jersey.

Once again, Clare had won by the narrowest of margins and just about held off
a final Tipperary onslaught. Controversy raged afterwards when Tipperary
deemed Carney to be illegal (echoes of the Cooney case of seventeen years earlier).
However, Carney was legal, the result stood and Clare were through to their first
Munster final since 1938. Limerick had earlier defeated Waterford; it was their first
championship win since 1949.

1955 MUNSTER FINAL

I doubt if any match involving Clare has ever produced such controversy and
rumours as the Munster final of 10 July 1955 between Clare and Limerick.
Obviously Clare were red-hot favourites going into the game, but things went
badly wrong. Well-known hurling writer Raymond Smith was there and described
the atmosphere in his book *The Clash of the Ash:* 'Clare's dream of winning their first
All-Ireland since 1914 was to die before the scorching speed of "Mick Mackey's

Greyhounds" on the sun-baked pitch that day and I reckon that it was one of the most sensational results in the history of Munster hurling'.

Many theories have been conjured up and 'explanations' put forward for Clare's collapse. These generally take the form of alleged sightings of team members indulging in 'pre-match celebrations' in a multitude of hostelries around the county, which have increased with the years. Raymond Smith refers to them as 'a golden crop of rumours' suggested by 'Banner County men who find it hard to accept that so many of their men could have been so bad on the one day.' He goes on to say that, given the lack of evidence to substantiate these rumours, 'it would be grossly unfair to malign a side which I believe was caught napping on the day.'

Team member Mick Leahy feels that, as a team, they didn't get much opportunity to train together. 'The Clare team of the early to mid 1950s was scattered; many of the players were Dublin-based – Des Dillon, Donal O'Grady, Tom Fahy, Johnny Hogan, Jackie Greene and Jimmy Carney were all in Dublin. I was in Kilkenny and had to train on my own, or occasionally train with the Kilkenny players. It wasn't the ideal build-up to a Munster final.'

Jimmy Corry had seen Clare beat Cork and Tipperary. 'Against Cork, Noel Deasy had held Christy Ring. For the Munster final we thought we had only to go down. It was a magnificent summer's day. I can still see it; the ball was thrown in and Jimmy Smyth picked it up, raced through and put it over the bar, but things began to go wrong'. In Tolly Guinnane's opinion, 'The selectors dropped Paddy Russell, which was a big mistake. He had played very well on Jim English the Wexford right wing-back during the Oireachtas. They brought Matt Nugent, a natural forward, to wing-back for the game against Limerick; no one could believe it.'

However, Tommy Small, a Clare selector from 1952–1955 disagrees with this analysis. 'The selectors are blamed for every game lost. Garrett Howard (another of the selectors and a former Limerick hurler) got a lot of slagging after the game

Five great players of the 1950s, pictured at Cusack Park, county final day, 1995
L/r: Mick Hayes, Dan McInerney, Haulie Donnellan, Donal O'Grady, Jimmy Smyth

"picking for Clare and playing for Limerick", but it was the team that let us down.' This latter view is supported to some degree by Flan Hynes, who reckons that Clare were close enough from 1948 to 1955, but that the 1955 team was the best he had seen. 'They showed great character against Cork and Tipperary and losing to Limerick was an awful disappointment. Limerick were "speed merchants". Vivian Cobbe, Dermot Kelly and Ralph Prendergast (a champion sprinter) ran Clare ragged.' Another St Joseph's man, Matt Nugent, also described Limerick as the fastest team that he had played against.

The game certainly threw up its share of scapegoats. The celebrated centre back, Donal O'Grady, who was then playing his club hurling with Dublin Faughs, seems to be the one most hurt by what Mick Leahy refers to as 'public house talk'. According to Jimmy Smyth: 'Donal O'Grady was probably the finest centre half-back ever to don the saffron and blue. He was singled out after this Munster final for unfair and hurtful criticism. Great men such as O'Grady often find that a day comes when luck, the run of the ball, and a skilled opponent with a rub of the green hitting scintillating form, come between him and his best form. Dermot Kelly (Limerick) hit a purple patch as I had in 1953, and unfortunately, when county pride is at stake a scapegoat has to be found.

'O'Grady's talents should have been employed elsewhere and we didn't utilise his greatness to best effect. The true position is of course that having overcome Wexford in the 1954 Oireachtas, and having beaten Cork and Tipperary in the previous rounds, we were lulled into a false sense of security. It must also be remembered that Limerick were well on top in most positions all through the game: that at least two-thirds of the team were not playing with their customary dash whilst Limerick seemed to thrive in the sweltering conditions.'

In *The Clash of the Ash* Dermot Kelly himself concedes that it wasn't only the sun that shone for him on the day but Lady Luck as well. 'Donal O'Grady was no more to blame that day than any of his team mates. With Clare beaten in the flanks, more often than not he had to challenge an oncoming Limerick forward, leaving me on my own. He was a fine hurler and a great centre-half back. My team mates passed me the ball unselfishly when I was in a scoring position and, allied to this, I had extraordinary luck and it seemed that nothing could go wrong for me.'

Bernie Dilger was watching from the sideline. 'Clare were caught in the Munster final of 1955; they didn't bother to check Limerick out. Then we didn't have television to analyse Limerick and they were prepared. I sat opposite the half-back line so I could study the Limerick wing forwards. Clare had a great full-back line of Leahy, McInerney and Donnellan, but the Limerick corner-forward Vivian Cobbe was operating out on the wing as an extra wing-forward and this seemed to throw our wing backs into confusion, forcing Donal O'Grady to cover back and forth and leaving Kelly too much freedom.'

These hurlers' recollections of the game are strongly supported by the reporter from *The Clare Champion* of 16 July 1955:

Clare were wiped off the field by a rampant Limerick team which could not be matched for speed, accuracy and dash. Apart from two early points, this Clare team that had rattled into Cork and Tipperary never led. The sun beat down relentlessly throughout the game, making this final one of the greatest endurance tests. Limerick set to their task from the first minute with a zest and vigour reminiscent of the Limerick team of the 1930s and 1940s. They commanded the game throughout and were the dictators of the pace from the start.

Limerick played havoc with the Clare backs by employing criss-cross movements and deft touches. The Clare selectors, who also included Haulie Daly, tried everything, bringing Matt Nugent to corner forward in a direct switch with Johnny Purcell and Jimmy Smyth to centre field, but all to no avail. The final score was 2–16 to 2–6. Only two of the Clare team scored, Smyth getting all six points and Jackie Greene scoring both goals. Clare goal-keeper Mick Hayes made several brilliant saves, which helped stave off an even more crushing defeat by Limerick.

The Clare Champion headline after the final was 'All-Ireland Lost', a bit premature perhaps? Well, Jimmy 'Puddin' Cullinan, then a young schoolboy in Newmarket-on-Fergus, was also thinking along the same lines. 'This was a fine team with a stonewall defence in Leahy, McInerney, Nugent, O'Grady, all powerful lads. I felt they should have won the All-Ireland.' Another Newmarket man, Liam Danagher, also has youthful memories of the game. 'Both my parents came from Limerick, Fedamore and Kilmallock. I remember lying on the bed after coming from the Munster final. My father looked in the door and said "Willie, where's your great Clare team now?" I burst out crying'.

The bitter disappointment of 1955 was a severe setback to Clare hurling and seemed to sow the seeds of lingering doubts about Clare's ability to deliver on the big day. While it would be totally unfair to attribute all of Clare's subsequent woes to that great 1955 team, it appears to be true that 1955 was a watershed era and had a detrimental effect on the confidence of later teams, however unreasonable this might seem. It took a full forty years for Clare to regain their Munster pride and, ironically enough, it was raging favourites Limerick who were taken by surprise on another hot day in July 1995, this time by a fast, fit and determined Clare. Such is the joy and heartbreak of hurling!

IF YOU WANT TO GO TO HEAVEN (1956–1971)

If you want to go to heaven when you die
You needn't wear a collar and a tie
Just wear a baby's bonnet
With blue and yellow on it
And you're sure to go to heaven when you die.

ENNIS CBS CHANT

I always liked Clare's style of hurling; they were good sticksmen and played direct.

LEN GAYNOR

The 1955 Munster final defeat had a devastating effect and set Clare hurling back considerably. Although they defeated Limerick in the national league later that year, Clare lost two subsequent league games, one against Tipperary, 2–5 to 2–3, in a torrid clash at Cusack Park and the other against Galway, 3–7 to 1–7, in Tuam.

The great rivalry of that era between Clare and Wexford was renewed once again in the semi-final of the 1955 Oireachtas with Wexford gaining the upper hand on this occasion. The Clare team was weakened by the fact that St Joseph's withdrew their players from the panel following a dispute. Tony Grimes (Smith O'Brien's) was promoted from the junior team to play in goal that day and Tolly Guinnane, who was recalled to the panel, remembers the game. 'It was a Clareman beat us – Christy Casey from Sixmilebridge. He moved to Wexford and played in goal for Wexford; he played a great game against us that day.'

The Kincora cup, in aid of the Killaloe parochial house fund, was one of many tournaments played in those years and Clare contested the 1956 final against Tipperary in Nenagh, but once again lost 1–13 to 2–2. Newcomers Phil Waldron (Feakle) and Charles Murphy (Tulla) had joined the panel at this stage and preparation for the 1956 championship included a challenge match with Faughs of Dublin. Prior to the championship, Seán Meehan (Sixmilebridge) and Tom McInerney (O'Callaghan's Mills) were introduced.

LIMERICK RE-MATCH

If any doubts persisted over Clare's Munster defeat of 1955, they were well and truly laid to rest at the Gaelic Grounds in the first round of the championship on 17 June 1956. The Clare team was very similar to the 1955 line-up except for Charles Murphy at wing back, Aidan Raleigh at wing forward and Michael Blake at centre back. Limerick triumphed 1–15 to 2–6, a score line very similar to that of 1955 (2–16 to 2–6). 'Limerick, playing fast clever hurling, removed all doubts in Munster contest', reported *The Clare Champion*.

Des Carroll was then coming to the end of his inter-county career. Speaking of the period from 1955 on he says: 'Mick Mackey's team were very fit and athletic;

they ran us into the ground. That's not to say they didn't have hurling skills.' It is interesting to note that this Limerick team came very close to retaining the Munster Championship in 1956, but then Cork's Christy Ring had other ideas and scored three goals in a final onslaught to deny Limerick. His team mate Willie John Daly later commented in *Giants of the Ash:* 'We were very wary of Limerick. I'd seen personally what they did to Clare in 1955 and 1956.' According to Pa Howard, Willie John Daly and fellow Corkman Mattie Fuohy were linesmen at the 1955 Munster Final between Clare and Limerick.

WEMBLEY TOURNAMENT

On 3 November 1957 Clare defeated Waterford to qualify for the first ever Wembley tournament final; this game featured a tremendous display by Johnny Purcell. The Wembley game was played on 25 May 1958 and the other finalists were Kilkenny. Tolly Guinnane remembers it well. 'Jimmy Smyth scored a goal that day as good as ever I saw scored; if he beat one man, he must have beaten six. "Doc" Doherty and I went over, though we didn't play. I went for a weekend and I stayed 21 years. I hurled with Pearse's, Michael Cusack's and Emerald's. Cusack's were comprised mostly of Claremen, Joe O'Grady, Larry Blake Jnr, Paddy Duggan and Jimmy Walker, a Kerryman who had earlier played for Éire Óg, a lovely fellow and a great hurler.'

Kilkenny and Clare gave an exhibition of hurling that day. Clare included many Éire Óg men in their line-up including the highly-rated Dilgers, Bernie and Michael ('Gruggy'), and Pat Kirby who later made a huge name for himself as a handballer. Also on the team were Bobby Burke, Matt Nugent, Jimmy Smyth and Naoise Jordan. The 'Cats' prevailed in a high-scoring game 6–10 to 5–7,* calling upon the likes of Ollie Walsh, Seán Clohessy, Dennis Heaslip and Billy Dwyer. Bernie Dilger played in Wembley: 'The Wembley tournament was first organised in 1957. The GAA in London were very strong and fanatical. Clare had a surprise one-point victory over Waterford, the Munster champions, to qualify for the trip to London. As I ran out on the turf at Wembley, I thought of Stanley Matthews. The only time I'd seen soccer was on the Pathé News during the interval at the Gaiety Cinema. The stadium was probably a bit big for such a tournament game, though over 33,000 paid in. Many of the great players of the 1954–1955 were retired, so we had a fairly new-look team. We gave Kilkenny, the All-Ireland Champions, a great game.'

In the opinion of Pat Danaher, 'Bernie Dilger was a class hurler; he'd have got his place on any team.' Pat reckons that the two best half-back lines in club hurling that he saw were Dilger, Michael Blake and Jimmy Cronin of Éire Óg: and Jim Cullinan, Gus Lohan and Joe Hannon of Newmarket-on-Fergus in the 1960s.

'REBEL' VICTORIES

The senior teams of 1957–1960 continued to be a force in hurling despite not having any real success. Clare were defeated by Cork 4–10 to 2–6 in the 1957 championship. In the 1958 first round Clare led Cork by ten points after a magnificent first-half display. Jimmy Smyth recalls a free given against him during a great spell for Clare from which Christy Ring collected and scored a goal which changed the game. Clare were again badly beaten by Cork in the 1959 championship but were unlucky to lose 2–12 to 1–11 against the Rebels in 1960 with John O'Riordan at centre-forward and Ollie Naughton and Mick Frost at centre-field. They 'tore into'

---

* *Also 5–11 to 5–7 as the last Kilkenny point was recorded as a goal in some accounts.*

Cork that day. 'The inferiority complex was gladly missing' according to *The Clare Champion*, but once again Cork came from behind. It is interesting to note how close Clare came that year to a Cork team which ran Tipperary 4–13 to 4–11 in what is regarded as one of the hardest Munster finals of that era.

ÉIRE ÓG V ST JOSEPH'S

In 1958 St Joseph's and Éire Óg clashed in the Dr Tommy Daly memorial cup at Tulla where the result was a 2–6 to 2–6 draw. Shortly afterwards, the same teams met in the O'Doherty cup and Gold Watch tournament final. According to *The Clare Champion*, 'The crowd of 3,000 was in a tense but good-humoured mood as the starting time approached. It raised the spirits of old and young alike and will be talked about for many a day. Many sported the rival colours and each team had their cheer groups.' Once again the sides finished level at 2–5 each. The replay was yet another draw causing *The Clare Champion* to proclaim: 'St Joseph's and Éire Óg Still at it'.

After a total of three draws and at the third attempt to decide the winner of the O'Doherty cup, Éire Óg were leading by a couple of points when, according to *The Clare Champion*, the referee blew full time after fifty-three minutes on a score of 2–6 to 1–7. St Joseph's had a player sent off early in the game and Pat Kirby was the star for Éire Óg at centre field, with Hugh Ensko capping a fine performance in the dying moments when he dived full length to stop a shot. Others to star in these epic games were Paddy Kerin, Paschal Brooks and Noel Gilligan (Éire Óg), Flan Hynes, Pat Hynes, Paschal Sheridan and Justin Gleeson of St Joseph's.

This tournament was a significant feature of the club calendar at the time and was taken seriously by both players and supporters. Michael Gallagher of Kilkishen feels that it was a great complement to the championship. 'It should never have been dropped from the hurling calendar. Éire Óg always reminded me of Cork with the red jersey and the dapper tap on the heels. They could turn it on and they brought something new to hurling in the 1950s – Michael Blake, Paddy Duggan and Paddy Loftus.'

Len Gaynor was a student of St Flannan's from 1956 to 1961 and remembers the great games between Éire Óg and St Joseph's. 'It was cracking stuff; the standard was great. I recall Matt Nugent and Bernie and Michael Dilger; great excitement; I can remember it vividly.'

ÉIRE ÓG V RUAN

Michael Gallagher remembers cycling to the 1959 county final between Éire Óg and Ruan at Cusack Park. 'The 1959 final captured the imagination of the public with two classy teams – Éire Óg, the champions in 1956 and 1957 and a resurgent Ruan team. The Ruan side of 1959 to 1962 was one of the best club sides I ever saw. Every cog fitted into the wheel; every fellow knew what he was doing. They had the Barrett's (from Lisdoonvarna), the Custy's, Seán and Frank, and they had a natural leader in Jimmy Smyth. They were masterful in defence – Joe "Jazzer" Meaney, Paddy Feighery and the Lyons' brothers – they shackled the Éire Óg attack.'

Pat Danaher remembers Frank Custy giving one of the greatest displays in goal that he has ever seen. Frank himself puts forward some possible reasons for the lull in Ruan hurling after the success of the 1948–1952 team. 'Very little was done with young lads for seven or eight years; they held on to the older players. We won the minor B championship in 1953, beating Smith O'Brien's by 4–8 to 1–3. Cheating was unbelievable. Most of the players who started out in the first or second round weren't there for the final. Ruan won the minor B final with the Clare minor goal-keeper, Paddy Hewitt, from Ennis. I was in goal for the earlier rounds but Hewitt was brought in for the final as I was only fourteen. The paper that week read: "Ruan fielded a team of exceptional height and strength". They objected to Gus Whelan but, as it happened, Gus was under-age; he was tall and strong. Killaloe had some fine players – Tony Grimes in goal and Tony Haran, their captain, at centre-back.'

Jimmy Smyth

Michael 'Gruggy' Dilger was one of the most feared forwards in the game at this time. He got his nickname from his habit of 'getting down on his grug' or bending down to get or retain possession. Contemporaries say that he had a beautiful body-swerve and was deadly accurate on the run. He had great hands but Ruan held him in the 1959 county final. In fact, Éire Óg were held to just four points in total. Bernie Dilger remembers being well beaten by Ruan in 1959. 'It was very tense. Their backs were on top of our forwards and we were forced to shoot from far out. Smyth was like Ring; he could make three or four decisive moves which won games.'

ÉIRE ÓG AND ST JOHN'S

Many young players came through to the senior county team because of the work being done at St Flannan's College, Ennis CBS, the Rovers and St John's minor clubs. Back in 1951–52, the Dalcassian's were the only club catering for under-age hurling in Ennis. Michael Nihill remembers how other aspiring hurlers practised their skills. 'When I lived in the Causeway, we played Clonroad every Saturday on the patch of ground that was outside Cusack Park. We played eleven-a-side but none of us were ever considered for the Dal's juvenile or minor teams of that era.'

St John's was founded in 1953 by a group of enthusiastic hurlers who felt that another club was needed in the town to cater for a growing number of young players. Apparently, it was originally intended to call the team St Francis club in view of the fact that it was formed mainly by people from the Francis Street area, but this was changed simply because a number of founder members were named John! Chief among these were Seán Cleary, Seán O'Gorman, Frank O'Gorman, Joe Daly, Des McCullough, Rev. Fr Carthridge, OFM, Rev. Fr Justin and many others who committed time and money to the club. As Michael Nihill went on to explain, things developed from there: 'We recruited Paddy McInerney and we got in touch with Paschal Brooks and John O'Donoghue, basically people who were GAA followers but had no involvement with Ennis Dalcassian's. Our first set of jerseys were given to us by Ennis CBS, blue with a gold hoop. So we entered teams in minor B and junior championships in 1953 and, ironically, we got to the juvenile final against the Dal's in our first year, which proved that the town warranted a second team. It was a draw but the Dal's won the replay. The following year, we won minor B and then minor A in 1955 and 1956. Finally we won the intermediate championship and were entitled to go senior.' Joe McNamara of Newmarket remembers St John's players as 'Fine lads, tall and well-built. They won every honour in minor and junior and were a very well-run club. Seán O'Gorman and Joe Daly were the financial brains behind the club. It was a travesty that they didn't go senior.'

Éire Óg, the senior club in Ennis, objected to St John's going senior. 'Looking back on it,' says former St John's player John McCarthy, 'it was detrimental that St John's didn't go senior. We played the great St Joseph's team of that era in *The Clare Champion* cup (senior league). We gave them a good game and I remember Mick Hayes saying to me afterwards that he felt we were strong enough for senior championship. Four of the St John's team were taken by Éire Óg for the quarter-final replay with St Joseph's in 1957, Jack Daly, Brendan Doyle, Joe Ensko and myself.

'The mentors of St John's were upset by it, Des McCullough in particular. They felt that Éire Óg were poaching from St John's. St Joseph's and Éire Óg had played a draw before that, a fairly acrimonious affair. With the extra players, they put Ensko into goal and brought out Pat Kirby to centre field which was a great move; Kirby was very powerful.' Commenting on their objection to a second senior club, Éire Óg's Paddy White had this to say: 'In all honesty, at the time I did believe that there wasn't room for two senior clubs. We were convinced of this; we thought we were right and I don't know now if we were wrong or right.'

St John's went into a decline, partly for the above reasons, but partly because Ennis Rovers were beginning to flex their muscles. Rovers were outstanding at minor A and U–21 level, dominating the scene from 1961 to 1966. Michael Brennan, P. J. Summerly and John 'Dugger' Kearney were the chief movers with Paschal O'Brien, Noel and Dick Pyne, Vincent Loftus, Michael Hanrahan, Paddy Flynn and Jim McMahon.

ÉIRE ÓG'S RISE AND FALL

Pat Brennan has long associations with Éire Óg club, both as a player and mentor. He gave me his views on what were for him the highs and lows over the years. 'After coming from seven o'clock Mass, we played hurling on the streets from Tuttle's corner down to the Old Ground Hotel; we didn't break too many windows! The same on the concrete patch in Hermitage: twenty to thirty from veterans to young lads. The same in Summerhill: Terry Hurson, the Loftus's, the Darby Cullinan's, John Nevin, the Ryan's and McCullough's. We played full-scale matches. Sixpence might be thrown in for the winners by Eddie Breen or Don Ryan.

'My main interest in hurling started with Éire Óg around 1955 to 1957; they always built on youth. In the mid-1960s, the minors, U–21 and seniors always trained together; it meant that the senior selectors were viewing every bit of talent. If you were able to hurl a senior player, they realised you were good enough for the senior panel. Now they all train separately. The young lads aren't getting the experience of hammering into the senior players; I played my first senior game at sixteen. The 1965 Éire Óg team was the best I played on. We beat a Mount Sion side powered by Waterford inter-county hurlers Martin Óg Morrissey and Frankie Walshe. We were cock-a-hoop going into the 1965 county final against Newmarket.

'Nobody has ever had the same influence on

John Dunne

me as Brother Jim Hennessy. He gave everyone a chance, a belief. He looked after Ennis Rovers and they went on to win three minor and three U–21 titles, also providing eleven of the side that won the senior championship for Éire Óg in 1966. But for circumstances in the first round against Tubber, that team could quite possibly have been as effective as the Newmarket team of the 1960s and 1970s. We beat Tubber at an awful cost. One of the Tubber lads got injured and it went to a court case; that court case hung over the heads of the whole team for about eighteen months.

'The following year, Dickie Pyne went to the north, Vincent Loftus and Gary Stack went to Dublin. The Éire Óg team broke up as a unit, the team never came back together as a satisfactory unit again and in the 1970s, players were coming and going – Massie Dilger, Paddy Flynn and myself'.

Jimmy Cullinan transferred from Newmarket-on-Fergus to Éire Óg in 1971 and stayed for three years. 'Things weren't going right at the time; it wasn't to my liking. The same commitment wasn't being put in as I was accustomed to in Newmarket. I knew all the lads at Éire Óg such as Paschal O'Brien and Vincent Loftus. Éire Óg were ragged in those years. I remember playing a Clare Cup game against Newmarket and we had to go looking for players on the Sunday morning. Consequently, we had to give a walk-over to Newmarket; it upset me'. It is worth recalling some of the Éire Óg players from the mid 1960s – Des Neylon, Des Loftus, Jim Blake, Seán O'Driscoll and Terry Hurson gave great service.

WEST CLARE

Tom Malone of Milltown Malbay, who has given a lifetime of dedication to hurling, remembers when the Kilkee–Kilbaha area was a haven of hurling in the early 1950s. 'Bealaha produced a great man in Jimmy Carney, who came to prominence in 1955, and Kilrush supplied a man called Young who worked in O'Doherty's. Clonbony produced a few good hurlers over the years. Paddy (Mahony) McMahon, the outstanding footballer of the 1960s, was a very fine hurler. He could have played with a more glamorous club, but he remained loyal to us. I always had a great grá for hurling; I remember cycling to Limerick to see Joe McDonnell and Alfie O'Brien in action in the senior championship in 1946.

'Mickey Shannon of Kilrush starred with the Clare minors in 1957. Other prominent players to come from West Clare include Jimmy O'Neill, Pete McMahon, Cyril Jones and Mickey Wilson. In more recent years we had Marty Morrissey. A West Clare amalgamation ran Scariff very close in the senior championship; Mick McCarthy from Kilkee excelled. Occasionally you'd get a good hurler in from the traditional strongholds; we had Seán Minogue from East Clare and Liam Ryan from Ennis. Cahircanivan in the parish of Kilmihil had a nice team and they reached the junior B final in 1963.'

'THE RISING OF THE MOON'

In 1957 a major controversy erupted in West Clare over a film called 'The Rising of the Moon', which attracted record crowds to cinemas in the west. It was directed by John Ford and consisted of a trilogy of short films on Irish life featuring Abbey actors such as Cyril Cusack, Maureen Connell, Noel Purcell, Frank Lawton and Jimmy O'Dea. Locals were used as extras.

The controversy centred around one scene which was shot in Kilkee and featured about forty locals depicting bloodstained hurlers returning from a match on stretchers and crutches. The GAA was alerted to the situation during filming and the then general secretary Mr P. Ó Caoimh, later stated that he had received assurances from Lord Killanin that there would be nothing offensive to national traditions in the film.

However, when the film was released, the scenes were included and presented the participants in somewhat stage-Irish fashion. According to Tom Malone 'it cast a slur on the GAA.' The film seems to have managed to offend a wide cross-section of Irish society at the time as it was also banned by Belfast Corporation because of a reference to the fight for freedom.

1961 COUNTY MINOR TEAM

Clare had produced a highly-talented minor team in 1961, beating Galway by twenty-five points in the opening round of the championship at Nenagh. Later they ran riot in the second round and led Tipperary by thirteen points. Then Michael 'Babs' Keating was moved to full forward for Tipperary and this changed the game. Liam Danagher was in goal for Clare that day. 'Earlier, Keating hadn't got a ball off Paddy Flynn our centre-back; then he rattled in three goals past me. I came out of goal and scored the equalising point, but Tipperary finished much stronger.'

Liam Danagher

A team mate of Danagher's, Tony Maher, comments: 'We had a great minor team that year with Vincent Loftus, Paddy McNamara, Tony Marsh, Richard Pyne (Lissycasey) and Tony Loughnane, all of whom would become household names in Clare hurling. We should have done better but we didn't last the pace'. *The Clare Champion* castigated the county board saying, 'It seems scandalous that the parent body did not see fit to provide finance for the purpose of training this team.'

ENNIS CBS V ST FLANNAN'S

Ennis CBS re-entered the Harty cup competition in 1955–56 after a long absence. John McCarthy played with the CBS in 1956. 'I don't remember a Harty cup team before that. Br Fagan, a native of Dublin city, was principal. He came to Ennis from the North Monastery and took a very keen interest in hurling as did Br Burke, but Fagan was behind the whole thing. We had a good crop of players in Colm Madigan, Hugh Ensko, Larry Walsh and Pat Henchy, good enough to win the cup.' This talented 1956 side lost the semi-final to the North Monastery CBS by 6–2 to 4–6.

Ennis CBS's first success of this era was in the Dr Rodger's cup final of 1961, beating Sullivan's Quay by 8–4 to 8–3. Ground hurling was the order of the day and the scoring for Ennis was done by Derry Dinan 3–1, Vincent Loftus 2–0, Michael Hanrahan 2–2 and Jim McMahon 1–1. Tony Maher enjoyed his playing days at the CBS 'I played in goal in 1960; we weren't very well organised and Charleville beat us in the first round. With the introduction of Br Hennessy, whom I would regard as one of the best trainers I ever encountered, we became a force in colleges hurling. He was a fantastic motivator and just lifted the team before going out. We beat Coláiste Chríost Rí and St Finbarr's to reach the semi-final.'

Ennis CBS did indeed show their worth at Buttevant in early December 1960 when they led St Finbarr's after sixty minutes, only to lose after four minutes of extra time. However, following an objection by the CBS, the match was replayed and they overcame St Finbarr's by six points 2–5 to 1–2, a margin that scarcely did them justice.

HARTY CUP FINAL

The 1962 Harty cup final was an all-Ennis affair, featuring the CBS and St Flannan's and is regarded as one of the most memorable ever staged. It generated tremendous excitement and hurling fever in the town for weeks beforehand. Noel Pyne, who was a St Flannan's student, recalls the divisions that existed even at home in a piece which he wrote for the 1989 Harty cup final programme:

> My brother Dickie was centre forward on the Flannan's team and I was a sub. One other brother Derry was a second-year in the College while four younger brothers, Liam, Louis, Brendan and Tom were at Primary School in the CBS. They say that blood is thicker than water but I'm afraid that this just did not apply when it came to Harty cup finals. All four of my younger brothers were fully committed, enthusiastic and very vocal supporters of the CBS. Not only that, but they were also the bearers of all kinds of friendly threats and messages from the brothers camp. It was certainly a time of fun and excitement in our house and town but the whole tone was very good-natured and had no effect whatsoever on the good relationships and mutual respect which existed between the two schools.

Marie Barrett, a former student of Coláiste Muire, Ennis, also gave a graphic description of the prevailing atmosphere coming up to the match in an article which she wrote for the *Irish Independent* in 1983 entitled 'The Day Ennis Split in Two'. Here is part of her account:

> Looking back, the match itself pales into insignificance when compared to the pre-match rituals. Then you wore your heart on your sleeve for the final and loyalties, friendships, homes, and in particular the local Coláiste Muire, were split in two, depending on the colours worn.
> The convent was the major battleground, for 'us girls' were the most fervent, loyal and ferocious supporters both colleges had. Nearly all of us had a brother or a cousin in one or other college and blood was thicker than water. The first split was between day-girls and boarders; the boarders were the ones with relations in Flannan's and the day-girls had ties with the brothers.
> So, sporting our colours, we stalked the corridors of education, eyeing each other up with barely concealed venom. We walked on a tightrope of tension and fear and finally turned to the Almighty for comfort, support and, most of all, the gift of prophecy. But even He did not escape the bitter feud. Unbelievably, the convent chapel itself was not even sacred. We nearly burned the church down with the hundreds of candles we lit and the heat was unbearable.
> Final day arrived and, packed into the park, the enormity of the occasion began to dawn on us. Some shouted and roared to camouflage the empty feeling of fear. Others remained silent and tight-lipped, but all watched the hands of time move steadily towards three o'clock with a mixture of impending doom and hysterical elation.

sausage, beans and chips in the Savoy, there was only the funeral procession home through an exultant town, to nothing more attractive than bread and raspberry jam in the college.

LOCAL RIVALS CLASH AGAIN ... AND AGAIN!

Ennis CBS and St Flannan's remained very strong during these years. The CBS qualified for the Harty cup final again in 1963 with wins over Limerick CBS and St Coleman's, Fermoy. The semi-final win of 6–2 to 1–8 over St Colman's was fashioned just before half time when Pat Coffey scored four goals in five minutes at Kilmallock.

In the final at Thurles, Conor Smythe got the CBS off to a great start when he goaled in the opening minute of the first half, but the Cork side took over with centre-back Connie O'Leary in top form, ably supported by Tom McEvoy and Liam McAuliffe. Three goals from Seánie Barry in a ten-minute spell put paid to CBS hopes. The final score was 4–9 to 4–3. Future Clare goal-keeper Paschal O'Brien played in goal in the 1963 final. He recalls that St Finbarr's were a bigger side physically and the wet conditions at Thurles suited them, but he also acknowledges that they were better on the day. St Flannan's contested the final in 1964, losing to the up-and-coming Limerick CBS, a top class side, by 6–12 to 4–9.

From the point of view of trophies won, both Ennis colleges went into a hurling decline in the mid 1960s though they both competed. I remember the CBS playing Mount Sion and Limerick CBS during these years and doing fairly well. My most vivid memory of Ennis CBS is a Harty cup game in the 1968–69 season against the North Monastery. Ennis won 2–11 to 3–4. On our way back home, the bus drivers, prompted by the CBS leaving certificate class (a colourful bunch in 1969!), drove into the hallowed grounds of St Flannan's, flags and banners waving and victory songs in full voice. One that comes to mind is the following, sung to the air of 'The School Around the Corner':

If you want to go to heaven when you die,
You needn't wear a collar and a tie,
Just wear a baby's bonnet,
With blue and yellow on it,
And you're sure to go to heaven when you die.

Needless to say, the presence of 300 raving students from the CBS disrupting study wasn't appreciated by St Flannan's, but wouldn't it be lovely to have such a diversion today for the same reason! Prominent hurlers from the CBS included Flan Hegarty, Ollie O'Regan, Jimmy McNamara, Michael Smythe, Noel Ryan, Seán Lynch, Seán Liddy, Niall McInerney and Martin and Michael Leahy.

During the 1967–1970 era, Ennis CBS contested Rice cup (All-Ireland CBS) U–14 finals in 1967, 1968 and 1970. The stars of these teams were players like Kevin Kennedy, Jimmy Spellissy, brothers Don and Kieran Ryan, Michael O'Driscoll, Barry Smythe, Davy and Eric Connellan, Michael Skelly, Mike McEnery, Seamus and Haulie O'Connell, Tony and Paddy Piggott.

In the quarter-finals of the 1970–71 Harty Cup, St Flannan's had beaten St Colman's Fermoy and Ennis CBS had beaten Limerick CBS, a team which included Seán Stack and Martin McKeogh. The backbone of the Ennis CBS team had come from the talented Rice cup teams of 1967–68. The semi-final between St Flannan's and the CBS was played in Tulla and was eagerly anticipated by a capacity attendance, whose memories of earlier contests between these great rivals had been rekindled. Fleets of buses were laid on to bring the crowds to Dr Tommy Daly Park. John Callinan played with St Flannan's and related his memory of the game to Brendan Fullam in *Giants of the Ash:*

> The first time I felt the presence of the crowd was when I played with St Flannan's in a Harty Cup game versus Ennis CBS in Tulla in 1971 before a crowd of 8,000–10,000 students, teachers, parents – St Flannan's with players from Tipperary, Clare, Limerick and Ennis CBS with all local players. You could feel the tension, the partisanship.

St Flannan's had won the Munster Colleges U15$^1/_2$ in 1969 with a talented side which included John Callinan, Tim Crowe, Ger Loughnane and Brendan Gilligan. David Connellan, a member of the Ennis CBS Harty cup teams of 1970 and 1971 questions the pre-match preparation of that team and decisions made during the game: 'For 1971 against Flannan's we trained on the Saturday morning coming up to the game but we never got going. I felt that we were over-trained and tired.

'We were instructed to go for goals in the opening minutes, especially from frees. It didn't work as their goal-keeper Gerry Ryan stopped everything. We got a dream start when Noel Glynn scored a goal in the opening minute, but an opportunity was missed with the sending off of St Flannan's corner-forward Donal O'Dwyer in the final quarter. Tony O'Donnell was left in the corner-back position on his own. Our forwards Haulie O'Connell and Kieran McNamara, who were both outstanding players, were getting nothing.'

As it turned out, St Flannan's pulled away in the final ten minutes in a disappointing, rugged and over-physical game. St Flannan's led 1–3 to 1–2 at the interval, after which the Ennis CBS forwards were guilty of some dreadful misses. The CBS backs Davy Connellan, John Sheehan, Michael McNamara, David Barry and Tony O'Donnell were outstanding but their highly-acclaimed forwards never got going, especially when John Callinan and Liam Heffernan took control of centrefield in the final quarter. Colm Honan's late goal in the closing minutes gave Michael Skelly no chance and the final score was 2–7 to 1–4.

As I left, a disappointed CBS supporter, a Cork man who was at the game said: 'Sure boy, The Mon would beat the pick of them'. I doubted it, knowing that none of them had done themselves justice because of the tension and the hype. Many of these players filled the ranks of a very talented Clare minor side which beat Tipperary 3–13 to 1–7 on their way to a Munster minor final against Cork in Killarney, where they were unfortunately beaten. That team included Ger Loughnane, John Callinan, Colm Honan, John Treacy and Tim Crowe of St Flannan's, Michael 'Haulie' O'Connell, Kieran McNamara and Michael Skelly of the CBS and Martin McKeogh and Seán Stack of Limerick CBS.

The following season, 1971–72, hurling frenzy again took over the CBS primary and secondary schools leading up to yet another Harty cup semi-final clash with St Flannan's and little else was spoken about in the school yard. Ennis beat Limerick CBS in the previous round. However, a Flannan's team inspired by John Callinan and Seán Stack easily won the day on a score line of 7–9 to 2–3 despite good displays by Michael Griffin, Kevin Kennedy, Paddy Neylon, Paddy Hill, Tony O'Donnell, Michael Nugent, Brian Stenson and Paddy 'Cuss' Kelly who battled to the end.

The CBS did not enter the Harty competition for 1972–73 despite the fact that they reached the semi-final stage in Munster during the previous two years. They re-entered the competition for the 1973–74 season, but a very talented side lost to

Thurles CBS by a solitary point at Emly, 3–10 to 3–9. Ennis were probably over-confident as they had beaten a lot of top-class opposition in challenge matches prior to their game against Thurles. That CBS team included Patsy Hehir, Denis O'Connor, Donal Fitzpatrick, Denis Mulcaire, Michael Clohessy, Gerry Pyne (Kilmaley), Ollie and Gerry O'Loughlin (Ennis), Peter O'Loughlin – an outstandng corner-forward (Ballyea) and the suspended Seán Heaslip, who was a huge loss.

Commenting on this recently Seán still protests his innocence: 'I played for Ennis Dal's minor team and I got a six months suspension from Bord na nÓg for allegedly abusing a referee, which I didn't do. Br Miniter and Br Donnellan brought me to Broadford to appeal it but the committee couldn't lift the suspension. We had a good side but we missed a late twenty-one yard free. Declan Coote was man of the match.' Sadly, the school's fortunes have slumped since then, apart from occasional successes like winning the Corn Phadraig 'B' group in 1979 with the talented Pat Lynch, Michael Dinan and Michael Glynn.

Finally, I would like to mention the amount of time given to hurling in the CBS from 1963 to 1974 by a dedicated few; Bros. Bridges, Clancy, Cavanagh, Power, Miniter, Fitzgerald and McGrath. Also, there were the lay teachers who gave their time in the evenings, Joe 'Jeweller' Madigan, Cyril Brennan, Bobby Burke, Kieran Kennedy and many more. Ennis CBS had a great tradition but very little to show for it.

CBS TOWN LEAGUES

CBS under-age town leagues had existed for years in Ennis. In earlier decades, teams went under names such as Na Piarsaigh, Na Sairséalaigh, Eoin Ruadh's, etc. By the 1960s however, they were called after localities such as Hermitage, the Town, Lifford, the Boreen, the Country, St Michael's/Árd na Gréine, Cloughleigh and the Turnpike. These leagues were a huge success and very popular, producing many notable players.

The finals were played during sunny June evenings, attracting great crowds to the Fair Green and generating a great sense of occasion in the town. Finalists were led out by the school band and there were hundreds of spectators, including women with prams coming out to cheer for their favourites. One final that sticks out in my mind is the U–11 decider in 1965 between favourites the Town and St Michael's. The Town, which included star players Kieran Ryan and Paul McNamara, had beaten all and sundry along the way, but fell to a rampant St Michael's team, which included 'man of the match' Paddy Piggott as well as Martin Corry, Seán Dinan, Gerry O'Connell, Seán Hahessy and Ian Bidulp, a young German whose family had come to live in Ennis and who took to hurling like he had been playing all of his life. The cup was presented to Gerard Hanrahan, captain of St Michael's, who was shouldered from the pitch. I remember as a Boreen player watching enviously from behind the goal posts and wishing I was out there in the middle of the fray! The team paraded through the town with the cup aloft, halting at Jack Heaslip's for refreshments, where the cup was filled with red lemonade.

RUAN V SIXMILEBRIDGE

Jimmy Smyth's senior hurling career lasted over twenty years from his debut in 1948 to his last club games with O'Connell's of Dublin and Ruan in 1970. 'Ruan were going very well. Without the Ruan club team, I wouldn't have survived for that length. The club is important and we had a very good side in Ruan. We always felt we could win and we trained hard. Much of the credit for Ruan's success in these years must go to the Castle Rovers club'. In an article entitled *Down Memory Lane,* Michael Henchy of Ruan writes about the origins of Castle Rovers:

> Hurling had reached a very low ebb (in Ruan) and days of former glory were but a dream. During the fifties, men working on the forestry near Ballygriffey Castle used to amuse themselves with a 'puck about'. Interest grew and it was decided to form a Junior B club. This was done with a mixture of all ages and a team was first put on the field in 1952. The enthusiasm was enormous. The players met and trained and thought of little else but getting the best team possible together. As a separate club, they had not only all the necessary administration to take care of but, in addition, the problem of expenses had to be overcome. Funds were nil and jerseys, hurleys and balls, etc., had to be got somehow and travel organised.
>
> Castle Rovers won the Junior B championship in 1955 and some of the victorious members of the Ruan teams of 1959, 1960, 1962 came through Castle Rovers. A succession of good wins against strong opposition were put together in early 1959, including a first ever win over Newmarket-on-Fergus in a major competition. Éire Óg were the opposition in the final, a team of skill, speed and dedication – the glamour team. A margin of eight points stamped Ruan with quality and brought them two more championships, in 1960 against Scariff and in 1962 against Sixmilebridge. The 1962 final was drawn and it was not until the last ten minutes of the replay that the scores came that clinched the game. Sixmilebridge were the best parish team never to win a county championship (all that would change from 1977 to 1995). They were hard, vigorous, muscular men with no weakness in any position and this made them hardy opponents. The clashes between the 'Bridge and Ruan were always fair and many friendships were formed from their relentless tussles on the field of play.

Sixmilebridge had won the intermediate championship in 1951, beating the Turnpike (Ennis) by one point and remained a strong force in senior hurling throughout the 1950s. Seán Meehan was a long-serving member of the team and feels that they were in hard luck not to win a senior championship. 'We were close every year, but 1962 was the end of the road for us.' His clubmate Pat 'Whack' O'Shea recalls that dissension had set in by 1963: 'But, thankfully, John Joe Nihill, Michael Murphy and Fr Navin were responsible for the far-sighted youth policy which paid off a decade later.'

Ruan had a great spell from 1959 to 1962, an era which yielded them three senior championships. Des Crowe describes Jimmy Smyth as 'A national figure; also, we had great men in Johnny Cullinan, Tony Meaney, Kevin Smyth and Paddy Feighery. Hurling was a way of life in Ruan: the whole parish followed the team, not just the hurling followers.' For Paddy Feighery, 'Work was all part of hurling. You got up the following morning for work; it was a way of life then.' Paddy names Gerry Ryan (Meelick) and Mick O'Shea (Sixmilebridge) as amongst the best he played against.

Frank Custy was the Ruan goal-keeper in those years. He pays tribute to the great work done by Joe McDonnell, Joe Hassett, Miko Lyons and Fr Gunning, who had a great record in every parish where he worked. Frank also credits Jimmy Smyth as the person who made the differ-

Pat Henchy

87

ence to Ruan hurling during this period. 'He was an inspiration and he made fellows who were poor hurlers by comparison look good and brought more out of us. I had great backs in Pat and Frannie Lyons, Gus Whelan and my brother Seán. The 1962 team was our best, even though the win in 1962 was nothing in comparison with the win in 1959. After the success in 1962, Ruan players scattered, Jimmy Smyth to Dublin and Seán to New York. Many retired, including Willie Kitson and Paddy Feighery. Others retired when they got married as that was the tradition at the time. The Bridge were good and no club deserved a championship more than they did; they were great sportsmen. The standard of hurling in the 1962 draw and replay was very high.'

NEWMARKET AND WHITEGATE
In a piece entitled *The Best Years of My Life,* Jimmy Conroy, a Galway inter-county player describes how he arrived at his adopted hurling home in Whitegate:

> I remember it well. It was January 21st, 1961 when I stepped off the Limerick-Portumna bus and got my first glimpse of Mountshannon. It was cold and dark and I looked for the garda station which was my destination. I asked myself did I do the right thing by coming to Mountshannon. I had spent a very restless winter in the non-hurling village of Kilmihil in West Clare. Around Christmas, I got a letter from Michael Cleary asking me would I play with Whitegate. I knew very little about the place but I did know that it was a strong hurling area and that Naoise Jordan played with them.
>
> After a few weeks, I began to settle in. The hurling season began in March; we played Broadford and Crusheen on my second outing. I came off second best in a collision with that great character Tom Mac who was playing full back for Crusheen. Spring turned into Summer and everything was on course for the championship. I cannot recall any close calls until the semi-final against Sixmilebridge and, after a great struggle, Whitegate had reached the final for the first time in four years. The preparation was hectic and I can recall those rounds of Whitegate field with Fr Murray doing the 'driving'. The famed 'Blues' from Newmarket-on-Fergus were our opponents on final day at Cusack Park. Newmarket had arrived on the scene with a young talented team.

Flan Purcell describes the 1961 final between Whitegate and Newmarket as one of the best ever. 'It was hard from the throw-in. Naoise Jordan was a smashing hurler as well as Ned Cahill and the Doyles. Paddy McNamara and Liam Danagher of Newmarket were all good men. In Jimmy Cullinan's view: 'It was Jimmy Conroy beat us that day from centre back. Tom Turner scored two goals. Whitegate were fine hurlers, the Kenneally's, Jordan's and Tom Holland.' According to Ned Doyle, substitute Michael Hayes who came on for the injured Percy Solon played a blinder. Ned Cahill's point clinched it at 5–7 to 3–9. Scenes of jubilation followed and the homecoming to Whitegate was hectic.

Pat Danaher of Tulla has great memories of Naoise Jordan's prowess as a goal-scorer. 'You couldn't keep nets up; he bursted more nets and raised more flags than any man. The only men I saw to hurl him were Eamon Russell (Sixmilebridge) and Pascal Sheridan (St Joseph's) in the 1957 Clare cup final.' An interesting aspect of this Whitegate team related to me by Ned Doyle was that thirteen of the fifteen players were non-drinkers.

Newmarket and Whitegate met again in the decider of 1963 and this time the result was reversed. Liam Danagher attributes a lot of the improvement in the Newmarket team to the fact that they had gained a lot of experience playing tournament games against clubs like Toomevara, with players such as Matt O'Gara, Donal O'Brien and Matt Hassett, who also played for Tipperary. In hindsight, Pat

Cronin of Newmarket feels that the 1961 defeat by Whitegate was the best thing to happen to Newmarket. 'Had we won that day, we may not have become the force we were in the 1960s, winning six senior championships.'

CRUSHEEN

Crusheen became a major force in senior hurling in the mid 1960s when they defeated Éire Óg in the Clare cup final of 1965. Many of their players had tasted success at minor B, junior and intermediate ranks, winning the latter in 1960. Crusheen contested two senior finals, 1970 and 1974. On both occasions they were unlucky to come up against established clubs like Clarecastle in 1970 and Newmarket in 1974. Yet both of these titles could have been won, especially in 1970 when they held Clarecastle to a draw in a tense final. A Dermot Fitzgerald goal for Clarecastle in the replay was a major factor in separating the teams.

Again in 1974, they were most unlucky to lose to Newmarket 1–6 to 2–2. Big-match experience gave Newmarket the edge and they just about held on for victory. In the meantime Crusheen had won the Clare Cup again in 1970 which was some compensation. The players I remember most from Crusheen during these years include Tommy O'Donnell (goal-keeper), the great centre-field man John O'Donnell, the veteran Tom McNamara, Enda Mulkere, Jerry O'Connell, and of course their inter-county representatives Owen O'Donnell, Paddy Vaughan, Michael Moroney and Michael Culligan.

UNDER 21 COMPETITION

The highly-attractive U–21 grade for hurling was inaugurated in 1964. Clare's first ever game was against Limerick and the Shannonsiders featured Eamon Cregan, Bernie Hartigan and Ned Rea in their line-up. Clare triumphed in a high-scoring game 9–7 to 7–4. The Clare backbone consisted of Jim Woods, Pat Brennan, Gary Stack, John Nevin and Michael O'Leary, but it was Paddy McNamara who stole the show with an incredible tally of five goals, all from play. Tipperary again proved too strong for Clare in the semi-final when they pulled away in the second half. Many future stars were on this Tipperary team including Len Gaynor, Mick Roche and Francis Loughnane.

SENIOR TEAM RE-EMERGES

Clare senior hurlers re-emerged from the doldrums in 1964 to defeat Limerick 4–14 to 2–6 at McDonagh Park, Nenagh in front of 8,000 spectators. A rampant forward line of John Nevin, Pat Henchy and Pat Cronin played immaculate ground hurling. Jimmy Smyth, Paddy McNamara and Naoise Jordan combined well to score 4–13 between them. This was Clare's first senior championship win since 1955. *The Clare Champion* described it as 'the best team for years from the Banner county'. It is interesting to note that Clare played in the Newmarket-on-Fergus colours that day. Their usual jerseys were considered too heavy for what was a very hot day. Mick O'Shea of Sixmilebridge, better known as an outfield player, kept goal for the 1964 championship.

In preparation for their semi-final clash with Tipperary, Clare went into strict training. However, a vastly experienced Tipperary swept the Clare challenge aside in the second half of their encounter on 5 July, 1964. This youthful Clare team put up a strong challenge and trailed by only 1–5 to 0–4 at half time, but they were crushed in the end 6–13 to 2–5. The Tipperary side of 1960–1965 is considered by many authorities to be among the greatest. A stonewall defence of John Doyle, Mick Maher and Kieran Carey combined with lightning forwards like Jimmy Doyle, John

Milo Keane

'Mackey' McKenna and Michael 'Babs' Keating. Jimmy Smyth describes Jimmy Doyle as 'having something extra.' While a twenty-point defeat in 1964 and an eleven-point defeat in 1965, both at the hands of Tipperary, might look bad, it is worth noting that the hidings which were also dished out to Cork, Kilkenny and Wexford by Tipperary during this period were just as bad if not worse! For instance, Cork lost the 1964 and 1965 Munster finals by cricket scores.

Pa Howard describes the 1964–67 Tipperary team as the greatest hurling team he has ever seen. Len Gaynor was a member of that team and remembers some lively encounters against Clare. 'I played U–21 for Tipperary in 1964 against a good Clare team, Paddy McNamara and company – Paddy was a fair detail. Consequently I got picked for the Tipperary senior team for the Oireachtas final in 1964. Tipperary then were a tremendous team to read a game; they could see where the danger was coming from and shut it out; they could cope with any situation that arose. The 1967 Clare team that lost the Munster final to Tipperary was good. In the end they ran out of self-belief; they just lacked the killer instinct.'

John McCarthy was another prominent member of the Clare team in the 1960s. 'I played for Clare from the early 1960s but, around 1965, Newmarket, Éire Óg, Whitegate, Clarecastle and the 'Bridge were all producing quality players. A good team began to develop from 1965 to 1967. In 1965, we were ten points in arrears to Galway at half time. Seán Guinnane gave a fiery speech and woke us up, so we qualified to meet Tipperary in the semi-final of the Munster championship. I played on John Doyle; he was tough but fair. He pulled hard but took it as well.'

Clare enjoyed two glorious spells in the second half of that game when Mick O'Shea was moved from corner back to full forward. John McCarthy gave John Doyle a torrid game with his hard first-time hurling. However Jimmy Doyle and Tipperary went on to take the All-Ireland title, their twenty-first.

Noel Pyne

SUSPENSIONS

In 1966, Clare were drawn against Cork in the first round of the championship but, prior to the game, some members of the panel were invited to New York. Jimmy Cullinan recalls the ensuing controversy. 'We were asked to assist the Clare team in New York that year. It was very hard to turn it down at the time as it wasn't often you'd get trips like that. The New York Board were a great group of people and they

The CBS had a big lead by half time; Bobby Burke takes up the story in an article which he wrote in 1977:

> The second half opened in a welter of excitement. The blue-jerseyed St Flannan's swept into the attack and scored a point. Michael Hayes then brought off a sizzling save. The ball was swept up-field to Vincent Loftus, who passed on to corner-forward Dessie Guerin, who centred beautifully to Jim McMahon, who rounded the full back and slammed the ball home.

That goal put CBS into an eleven-point lead but, as it turned out, they needed them all because the game ended 4–2 to 2–7 with CBS holding on by just one point. Jimmy Quinn of Clarecastle was a member of the Ennis CBS Harty cup teams of 1962, 1963 and 1964 and has great memories of the 1962 final. 'St Flannan's had a strong team, and with players of the calibre of Jimmy Lillis, Tony Loughnane, John Nevin and Richard Pyne (Ennis), they were favourites to beat us. It was a huge occasion. I remember Br Lee, the superior, going down on his knees at the end of the game and being knocked over by a stampede charging to greet the CBS team! I had been due to take part in a boxing tournament before the Harty final but Fr Kenny, who was a very keen hurling man, asked my father not to allow me fight before the match, such was the fever generated. I came on as a sub in the 1962 replay against St Peter's in the All-Ireland final at Croke Park, but it was all over at that stage. We were well beaten by a powerful Peter's side with Dan Quigley, Ned Colfer, etc., in their line-up.'

Joe McNamara was a spectator at the 1962 Harty final. 'The CBS defence won it for them. Paddy Flynn was a most promising hurler as was Vincent Hogan. Flannan's took over in the last twenty minutes but the clearing of the CBS backs was unbelievable'. In his very humorous book *Over The Bar*, the late Breandán Ó hEithir wrote that the Harty cup final of 1962 was the most exciting colleges game that he saw during that period and continued: 'I got so involved during the last quarter that I forgot to switch on my machine to record the commentary'. Marie Barrett also witnessed the unusually passionate responses which the atmosphere awoke in some of the other spectators:

> It was the first time in my life I heard priests and brothers swear and that in itself seemed to make the occasion more awesome. I can still remember my shocked innocence and can also see the smashed splinters of the big black umbrella of a local 'respectable' teacher. He had hurled so ferociously off the field, both with directions and damnations, that all that remained of his umbrella was a battered and battle-scarred tangle of cloth and metal – symbolic of our torn nerves. The details of scores and scoring I fail to remember, but the final result I will never forget. We won by a point and the CBS were victors and our heroes for life.

For St Flannan's, however, hometown defeat added to the feelings of dejection. Arthur Ford was a first-year boarder in Flannan's and remembers trudging back to cold comforts:

> Defeat was bad enough; that it should be by our neighbours was worse; but it was that journey home that made it worst of all. Usually a Harty cup match entailed a journey to such exotic places as Thurles, Fermoy or even Emly, and win, lose or draw, there was always the hour's freedom in Limerick city to look forward to. But this time, instead of

were doing a lot for the game, trying to keep it alive out there. We didn't ask permission as we knew we'd be back for the Cork game and we felt we were doing no harm; travelling to and from the States was rampant with all counties.

'The New York Clare board had paid to bring us out and, after travelling so far, we couldn't let them down. Little did we think that Tony Marsh, Paddy Mc-Namara, Jim Woods and I would be suspended by the Clare county board; I felt very sore over the suspension. I had gone in and out of New York on several occasions and the Clare team had brought me out in 1964.'

So Clare went into the first round of the championship against Cork without some of their key players. Though leading by two goals at the interval, Cork barely survived against this depleted Clare team. Clare had hit back with three second-half goals plus great displays by Noel Pyne and Mick O'Shea to lead 3–8 to 2–8 in the dying moments. Then disaster struck when a thirty-yard free struck by Justin McCarthy was deflected past Paschal O'Brien to salvage a draw.

In the replay Clare were well beaten. According to Vincent Loftus, in *The Clash of the Ash*, 'Cork came out a far different team from the first day, and before we had really got to grips with them, they had gone in at half-time with an eight points lead on the board. We could never regain the initiative and they ran up a score of 5–11 to 1–7 against us before it was all over.' 'Clare's Blackest Day Since 1955' screamed *The Clare Champion* headline. Cork and Gerald McCarthy went on eventually to lift the Liam McCarthy Cup, beating firm favourites Kilkenny by 3–9 to 1–10 in the All-Ireland final.

Justin McCarthy, a Cork hurler who went on to play a significant role with Clare in later years, remembers playing against Clare in the 1966 championship. 'Clare should have beaten Cork in the drawn game at Limerick in 1966; we were outplayed. It was a humid misty afternoon and Clare were flying – Noel Pyne, Pat Cronin and Liam Danagher. Clare had us on the run and we were lucky to draw, but we were always good in a replay. We learned from the drawn game and steadied up the team. Clare never played with the same authority in the replay, but we had great belief in ourselves.'

NEW YORK

The New York hurling championship runs in parallel to the home championship, with different county teams and their dedicated band of followers. Inevitably, of course, there is a greater involvement of players and even mentors who are adopted by various counties. A good example is Bernard (Benny) Connaughton from Athleague, Co. Roscommon who emigrated to the United States in 1949 and immediately became involved with the Clare hurling team. He played in many positions, but mostly in goal, and his brothers Terry and Rory also joined the Clare club. In the early 1950s, Clare teams in New York found it necessary to recruit non-natives such as Brian Molloy (Galway), Dan and Steve Murphy (Limerick) as well as the Connaughton brothers. However, by the mid 1960s, Clare were mostly comprised of native-born men such as Jimmy Carney, Seán Custy, Gus Whelan, Noel Firth, Pat Kirby and Hubbie McCabe.

In spite of this talent, Clare had little success and had not won a championship since 1921 when they defeated Offaly by 7–6 to 4–2. Things changed when Terry Sheridan of Cavan was brought in to assist in the training at Van Cortlandt Park – he had won an All-Ireland football medal with Cavan in the Polo Grounds in 1947. Under his guidance Clare went on to win the New York Championships of 1967, 1968, 1969, 1972, 1975 and 1978. The first of these contests for the Patrick J. Grimes

Clare Champions, New York 1967
Back row l/r: Paddy Markham, Tom O'Meara, Seán Custy, P. J. Noone, John Joe Naughton,
Pat Marsh, Michael Gleeson, Noel Firth, Michael Fitzgerald, Michael Clune, Jimmy Carney, Pat
O'Neill, Hubbie McCabe, John Lynch, Benny Connaughton; Front row l/r: Pat Baker, Pat Culligan,
Joe Malone, Larry Kelly, Eddie Brandon, Pat Fagan, Pat Kirby, Rory Connaughton, Tony Egan,
Henry Condron, Terry Sheridan; Sitting: Joe Firth, Mick Reynolds, Paddy Rynne, ?

Trophy was against Galway in Gaelic Stadium in 1967. Clare were one point behind at half time, 1–4 to 0–6, but had improved considerably in the second quarter of the game. John Byrne of the *Irish Echo* takes up the story:

> Pat Kirby won control of almost every ball after a quiet first quarter and rained long dri-ves into Galway territory. For a while the Galway backs held off these dangerous thrusts, but Kirby's amazing anticipation, his deft catches in the air and his masterful and lengthy strokes eventually penetrated the champion's defence and Clare were on the road to victory.
>
> Another star was Seán Custy at right full-back. This was the Custy of a few year's ago, blotting out his opposite number completely and generally dominating the whole full-back line. There were other Clare stand-outs. Michael Clune's flashing goal from John Joe Naughton in the fiftieth minute when the issue was still in doubt was the turn-ing point of the game. From there on Clare never looked back. Clune's first-time pull from outside the square was beautifully executed and gave Ken Croke no chance.
>
> Clare goal-keeper Henry Condron was beaten only once, full back and captain Eddie Brandon, Pat O'Neill, Mick Reynolds – all had a big share in fending off the Tribesmen's search for scores. Hubbie McCabe started at left-half back but switched with Joe Firth at mid-field. This change benefited both McCabe and Firth. Others to play well were P. J. Noone, Pat Fagan and Tony Egan, but the man of the match was Jimmy Carney of Bealaha. The West Clare man contributed nine of Clare's fourteen points.

Players from the Clare team were also members of the New York team of course. Seán Custy was on the team which went on a world tour in 1968. 'We stopped off in San Francisco, Auckland, Hong Kong, etc., before coming to Ireland to play

Clare players with the Patrick J. Grimes trophy, New York 1967
L/r: Christy Moynihan, Rory Connaughton, Jimmy Carney, Seán Custy, Tony Egan

Wexford the All-Ireland champions and Tipperary the other finalists.' Seán went on to comment on the perception that there was a significant amount of financial gain to be had from involvement in New York hurling. 'The biggest fallacy of all time is the amount of money changing hands. I get sick when I hear this. The players got a bit of expenses; that's all ... New York had a great team in the 1960s which included Mickey Reynolds of Roscommon, Brendan Hennessy of Kerry and Jimmy Carney. The success behind the Clare team over the years is down to a couple of great men, Paddy McMahon of Killanena, who was president of New York GAA for many years, and Paddy Markham of Clarecastle – two great Clare men. They put their heart and soul into it. Paddy Markham came to New York in 1954, having played minor, junior and senior for Clare. The Clare team in New York had a manager, Benny Connaughton, before any team in Ireland. He was the financial genius behind the team and managed most of the Clare teams that won the New York championships.'

Cork hurler John Horgan has great memories of playing in New York and also attests to the high standard of hurling which was being played there. 'I think that the league is a great competition; you can express yourself more easily in the National League. The 1970 second leg game in New York was the toughest hurling that I ever played in. Gaelic Park at 90°– it was torrid! We were over there with a swagger after winning the championship and league double. We were there to be got at and the dust was flying. They were flaking games.'

1967 Munster Final

Undaunted by their defeat in 1966, this Clare team rediscovered their best form again in 1967, reaching the league semi-final and trouncing Limerick and Galway in the Munster championship with a cultured brand of hurling. I recall vividly being a young programme seller at the semi-final meeting of Clare and Galway and seeing the Fair Green packed with cars. The recall of Jimmy Smyth to the team after a two-year absence gave added interest to the game. Jimmy Cullinan was also back and had governed centre-field in the previous game against Limerick.

There was a tremendous atmosphere and Clare were willed on with tremendous vocal support from the home crowd. Liam Danagher and Tom Ryan dominated mid field with great confidence and fed in a plentiful supply of ball to the forwards. Clare were in control after the first quarter when Pat Cronin cracked home a goal from a twenty-one yard free. Shortly afterwards, Milo Keane made a brilliant connection with a cross from Naoise Jordan to leave Clare 2–7 to 0–6 by half time. Two more goals from Jimmy Smyth and Naoise Jordan in the second half put the game beyond Galway's reach to give a final score of 4–12 to 1–11.

The 1967 team was considered by many to be the best side since the mid 1950s. The Rovers club from Old Mill Street in Ennis, a great nursery, produced one-third of this team. Newmarket were also coming to the fore in Munster club hurling. The strength in depth of the team can be gauged from studying the list of substitutes, which included seasoned campaigners like Pat Henchy, Jim Woods and John Dunne plus future stars Jackie O'Gorman and Michael Considine. Former Tipperary All-Ireland medal winner Tom Ryan had recently joined the Éire Óg club and declared for Clare. With other players like Vincent Loftus, Eamon Russell, Naoise Jordan and Noel Pyne, Clare had a good chance of upsetting Tipperary in the Munster final.

The Munster final of 1967 (in effect the All-Ireland semi-final) was played at the Gaelic Grounds and once again expectations were high. Clare full back Martin Bradley, commenting before the game, exhorted the Clare supporters to get behind the team: 'This team has been moulded together for the past few years and a wonderful team spirit has grown amongst the players. I appeal to our supporters to put petty parochial differences aside and lend the team whole-hearted support.' However, as it turned out, harmonious supporters were not enough to eliminate Clare's difficulties, both on the pitch and on the sideline.

After thirty-eight minutes the sides were level 2–6 to 2–6 when Clare abandoned their fast, first-touch hurling and began to over-elaborate. A couple of Michael 'Babs' Keating goals changed the game. Towards the end, Jimmy Cullinan and Larry Kiely of Tipperary were sent to the line. Cullinan, though playing in select company, had his best hour to date in the Clare jersey until he was sent off. Vincent Loftus felt that Tipperary's physical superiority had much to do with their success against Clare. 'You cannot win championships without strength down the middle – Wexford have been able to knock the Tipperary machine out of gear because they have the physique to upset them. I believe that physically our team has not been strong enough in certain vital positions'.

A few weeks later, the same sides clashed in the Oireachtas in Cusack Park on a wet and miserable 1 October. Clare held Tipperary almost scoreless at half time, 3–7 to 0–1, and eventually won by 4–8 to 3–5; it was Clare's first win over Tipperary since 1955. Writing in the *Irish Independent* the following day, John D. Hickey was impressed with the standard of hurling and gave particular mention to the honorary Clareman on the team:

It bordered on the fantastic how Clare, winners by 4–8 to 3–5, and Tipperary contrived to serve up wondrous hurling at Cusack Park in conditions that looked totally impossible to the non-combatant. After a few minutes, the hurling had become an enchanted spectacle. Clare, inspired by the magnificent Tom Ryan, who mastered Mick Roche at centre field, led Tipperary at half time by 3–7 to 0–1. It was Clare's first senior victory over Tipperary in twelve years.

1967 OIREACHTAS FINAL

Clare met Kilkenny in the 1967 Oireachtas final at Croke Park. Kilkenny won by 4–4 to 1–8 but Clare had stayed with them right to the end, trailing by just a point until Kilkenny scored a goal and a point in the final moments. In his book *The Kilkenny G.A.A. Story,* Tom Ryall describes it as 'a game that maintained the tradition of Oireachtas finals, with players freed of championship tension and producing their best form. With the will to win evident on both sides, the match spilled over into an excess of fervour and led to some regrettable incidents on both sides. Apart from this, it was a very entertaining encounter.' Mick Dunne writing in *The Irish Press,* described the closing stages of the game:

> Kilkenny played with power and authority in the final quarter befitting their status as All-Ireland Champions, when they retained the Corn Thomáis Aghas in the thrilling Oireachtas final before a crowd of 15,879 at Croke Park, and they needed it all to repel an eminently persistent challenge from Clare.

CLARE V KILKENNY MARATHON

In 1968, Clare qualified for their third successive league semi-final appearance. Clare goal-keeper Paschal O'Brien considers this team the best he played on, when Clare and Kilkenny had to meet three times to decide the issue. 'They were the best games I remember from that era. I particularly remember the great motivating influence of Fr Tim Tuohy on the team.' Jimmy Cullinan feels that Clare should have beaten Kilkenny the first day. With the sides level at 2–10 to 2–10, Pat Cronin won a close-in free. 'I think he played for the free and got it,' says Liam Danagher. 'It was taken by Pat Henchy, normally a good free-taker. The arrangement was that, if Cronin got injured, Pat Henchy was to take the frees, but he only drove it about fifteen yards. Our wing backs in those years were Eamon Russell, one of the best ever, and Jackie O'Gorman, fantastic hurlers.'

The replay was excellent; Clare played marvellous ground hurling and led 3–8 to 1–8 with a few minutes remaining, but Kilkenny hit back with two late goals to equalise again. It was one of our best performances against Kilkenny. According to *The Clare Champion*, 'Clare hurled with splendour'. Kilkenny, the reigning All-Ireland champions, won at the third attempt 1–11 to 1–7. Clare defeated Kilkenny shortly afterwards in the Ground's tournament semi-final, 4–2 to 1–6, but lost the final to Wexford in Croke Park, 4–6 to 2–8, with Jack Berry of Wexford scoring three goals, the first after only twenty seconds.

MUNSTER CLUB CHAMPIONS

For Jimmy Cullinan, growing up in Newmarket-on-Fergus in the early 1960s, 'Hurling was a religion; we were at it day and night. Every chance we got we were flicking with a ball.' Liam Danagher recalls matches in Newmarket between Glencragga, the Street and Dunkirk. 'Tim Cronin used to referee; he brought us up from juvenile. Tim Cronin and Ned O'Connor originally came to Newmarket from

Action from the Clare–Kilkenny league semi-final, first replay 1968
Included are Ollie Walsh [K], Michael Arthur [C], Jim Treacy [K], Pa Dillon [K], Liam Griffin [C],
Pat Henchy [C] and Pat Henderson [K]

Kerry when Shannon Airport was being built. He started this combination hurling which later paid off for us. We always knew instinctively where each other was on the field of play. We won the juvenile in 1957 and later had two minor teams in the parish, Newmarket and Moohaun.'

Mick Arthur was one of Newmarket's greats and is credited with much of their success. For Jimmy Cullinan, 'Mick Arthur was a great leader. He had played for the county as far back as 1958, but he began playing rugby and soccer, although he returned to the Newmarket colours in 1966. He was a great athlete and an all-round sportsman. We loved training; you have to get enjoyment out of training and we were hurling morning, noon and night, even in the handball alley.'

Mick Arthur himself recalls the circumstances of his temporary absence from hurling. 'I played a soccer tournament with the Shannon Duty Free team around 1958 and was subsequently suspended; it was ridiculous. Consequently, I went on to play a lot of soccer and rugby; I played League of Ireland for Limerick and I won an inter-provincial rugby 'cap' with Munster. I returned to the Newmarket team in 1966 because Jim Cullinan, Paddy McNamara, Jim Woods and Tony Marsh (Broadford) were suspended for assisting the Clare team in New York. I trained diligently in the ball alley to get my eye for hurling back. I loved the game and, following some displays with the Blues, I was called into the county team about 1967.'

Liam Danagher compares Newmarket's training regime with that of the present Clare team. 'They're talking about the present Clare team training at seven in the morning. "Arthurs" used to take us up around Dromoland in the middle of the night and Mary, his wife, would have a bowl of soup for us. We always trained with the hurley; there's so much physical fitness training now. If you can position yourself and anticipate the flight of the ball, that's more important. Our trainer Fr Tim Tuohy believed in wrist work, left and right. He came from Feakle and was curate here in Newmarket.' Paddy McNamara also credits another Newmarket mentor, Jimmy Halpin, with the development of training methods. 'He brought in a new type of training; more physical training. Jimmy Halpin was a big influence on me.'

Newmarket, having been lords of Clare hurling for many years, reached the pinnacle of their hurling success in the late 1960s. Who could forget the great county finals of 1965, 1971 and 1973, all won by Newmarket, and the 1968 and 1969 Munster club championship, with wins by their fabulous team over top-class opposition such as Glen Rovers, Ballygunner and Carrick Davins. They became the first Clare side to capture the coveted Munster club title, inaugurated in 1964, when they defeated the holders Carrick Davins of Tipperary by 3–9 to 2–7. In doing so, they also became the first Clare side to win a Munster championship since 1932. This achievement was acknowledged in *The Clare Champion*'s report of the game:

> Newmarket have unlocked the golden gate which has proved impenetrable to Clare teams over the years. The foundation of this historic win was led by their solid half-back line of Jim Cullinan, Gus Lohan and Joe Hannon. Cullinan played the game of his life giving a display that is unlikely to be witnessed in any hurling field.

Glen Rovers were one of the teams beaten by Newmarket on their way to that 1968 title. Liam Danagher had a high regard for the Glen. 'Patsy Harte, Denis O'Riordan and Flynn at full forward was a big man. They were a tough outfit. They were great days.' Mick Arthur remembers well the day Glen Rovers came to Newmarket:

'We played Glen Rovers in 1968; they arrived early one Sunday morning in a fleet of Austin Princess cars and walked around Newmarket re-splendent in blazers, shirts and ties. The old-time hurlers like Mick Rourke, Bob Doherty, 'Bocky' Connery, Jim Clancy, Jim Guerin and Miko Fox said we wouldn't hold a candle to them. We did and we beat them by one point 3–8 to 4–4 in a cracking game with no quarter given.'

The Blues retained the Munster crown in 1969, beating Ballygunner 5–8 to 4–3. They started the defence of their title that year at Pearse Stadium, Galway, where they hammered Liam Mellow's by 11–21 to 1–5. The Liam Mellow's challenge had evaporated by half time when they trailed by 6–9 to 0–2. This game marked the return of the free-scoring Pat Cronin who contributed 2–6. Newmarket remained a strong force in Munster club hurling until 1981 when they lost the Munster semi-final to South Liberties, Limerick by 2–9 to 1–5.

An intense and at times over-robust rivalry has always burned between Newmarket and neighbouring Clarecastle, but some of it was laced with good humour. Jimmy Cullinan felt that Newmarket had even more incentive than usual to win the county final in 1968. 'The fact that Eileen Slattery (1968 Rose of Tralee) was to present the cup in 1968 was a great motivation. No way was she going to present it to her brother Tom (captain of Clarecastle) as far as we were concerned'. And indeed she did not!

According to John Hanly, 'Clarecastle should have beaten the "Blues" in a couple of county finals, the 1969 drawn game and definitely in 1973 – but I have to say this – Newmarket were very unlucky that the All-Ireland club championship did not exist in the late 1960s, because no team in Ireland would have beaten them; they were a fantastic club side.'

Clarecastle were indeed very unlucky to lose the 1969 county final. The game was played on a cold, wet 17 August and was a hugely enjoyable, sporting contest. Clarecastle got off to a flying start, with Michael Slattery and Frankie McNamara on top at centre field, and a fine opportunist goal from Christy 'Wax' Guinnane, followed by a Tom Slattery point. The sides were level on four occasions during the game, including half time (2–2 each), but Clarecastle had slightly the best of the exchanges, with Gerry Commane, George Horan and substitute Martin Kelly doing well. With time ticking away and the sides level, 'Wax' Guinnane forced a 70 and the task of scoring the winning point fell to Tom Slattery.

Michael Arthur takes up the story. 'In the excitement that followed the ball was incorrectly placed, maybe ninety yards from goal. Tom Slattery struck it magnificently and we were perspiring; after all we were about to lose our Munster club title as well. But he just barely missed – inches wide – veered to the left. Clarecastle left it behind them that day'. Jimmy Cullinan also looked on as the free was taken. 'They should have beaten us the first day in 1969. Clarecastle would have beaten any other club in those finals, but they had no answer to us in the 1969 replay.' I can still see the disappointment etched on Tom Slattery's face when the whistle blew as he walked away with the Clarecastle supporters. Sean King, writing in *The Clare Champion*, credited one player in particular with Newmarket's win:

> Liam Danagher, hurling artist supreme, made a sensational comeback to the Newmarket colours when, at Cusack Park, Clarecastle's stonewall resistance of the drawn game completely disintegrated before the sorcery of this hurling wizard in the county-final replay.

The referee Frank Murphy of Cork also described Newmarket's display that day as one of the finest he had ever seen. The final score was Newmarket 9–13, Clarecastle 3–6. Again in the 1971 county final Clarecastle led Newmarket by 2–11 to 1–9 in the dying moments when Jim Woods scored two late goals to put Newmarket ahead. A point by the ever reliable Christy 'Wax' Guinnane saved the day for Clarecastle. However, three weeks later Newmarket regained the championship by 2–7 to 1–7.

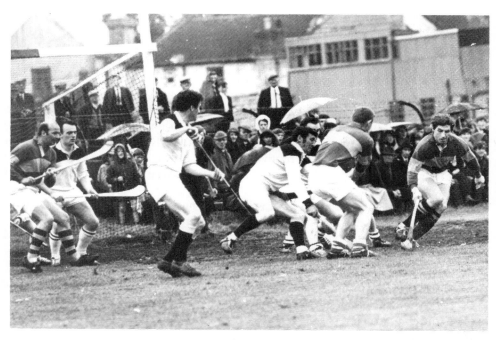

Action from the 1969 drawn county final
Photograph includes Michael Arthur [N], Paddy McNamara [N], Tom Slattery [C], Chris Hanrahan [C], Michael Donnelly [C] and Hubbie McCabe [N]

1973 County Final

The 1973 county final between Clarecastle and Newmarket was probably the finest played in those years. A late goal gave Newmarket their seventeenth title against a gallant Clarecastle side on a score line of 7–10 to 4–16. *The Clare Champion* report describes a hurling game with everything:

> It was a game right out of the top drawer. Played at a very fast pace, it was a thriller right from the word go, particularly the second half where the fortunes of this heart-warming struggle swayed to and fro with bewildering rapidity. This was hurling at its best and the sportsmanship was exemplary. Judging from the standard of hurling served up by both teams, hurling is in a very healthy state and certainly our players have the skills to emulate the heroes of Limerick and put Clare on the All-Ireland map.

Centre-forward Paddy McNamara proved to be Newmarket's hero in that game with a personal tally of 4–1; Timmy Ryan notched 1–7. For Clarecastle, Dermot Fitzgerald proved himself to be an outstanding forward scoring 3–1, with Paschal Russell scoring 0–7 in this memorable county final. The Blue's went on to contest the Munster club finals of 1973 and 1974, losing to Cork teams Blackrock and St Finbarr's respectively. Blackrock player John Horgan recalls playing against Newmarket. 'We won five Cork senior championships and three club All-Irelands from 1971 to 1979. I captained at least two of the national title teams. The club matches were fabulous; I remember a great Munster final against Newmarket-on-Fergus in 1973. We won it by two points, 1–13 to 0–14.'

Speaking about Newmarket in 1969, Jimmy Smyth had this to say: 'The present Newmarket team are as good a club side as ever I saw. They won the Munster club championship, a feat which Ruan would have found very hard to accomplish even in their greatest days.' The Newmarket team of the 1960s and 1970s included a host of regular inter-county players, but other top players I remember from this era include Val Arthur, Tom Melody, Vincent Hogan, Louis Halpin, John O'Leary and Eugene Moore (of Laois).

1968–1969 Munster Championships

Clare defeated Waterford in the first round of the 1968 Munster championship by the narrowest of margins and qualified to meet Tipperary. Gus Lohan, formerly of Galway, made his debut with Clare. Also on the team was Liam Griffin of Wexford, then playing his club hurling with Newmarket, and Tom Ryan of Tipperary in his second year with Clare.

Tom Ryan and Mick Arthur were the Clare heroes that day and 'led Tipperary a merry dance' according to *The Clare Champion*. When Tipperary used the ash however, Clare had no comeback. Mick Arthur and his immediate opponent Noel O'Gorman were sent off. The dismissal of Arthur was a big loss to Clare as he had found the net on a couple of occasions. Paschal O'Brien, Vincent Loftus, Gus Lohan, Tom Ryan and substitute Paddy McNamara all excelled but, despite this, Tipperary prevailed by 5–11 to 5–6.

Cork were the first-round opponents in the 1969 championship at Thurles. Naoise Jordan scored one of the finest opportunist goals I've ever seen at a hurling match. Tearing in behind the Cork defence, he glided the ball to the net. A Charlie McCarthy goal was disallowed when the advantage wasn't applied, and a point was secured from the resulting free to draw the game, Cork 2–11 to Clare 4–5. Some of the Cork supporters were incensed and jammed the entrance to the pitch

The Clare team that drew with Cork in the championship, 11 May 1969
Back row l/r: Johnny Cullinan, Jackie O'Gorman, Eamon Russell, Vincent Loftus, Noel Pyne, Gus Lohan, Mick Considine, Michael Arthur, Paschal O'Brien; Front row l/r: Noel Casey, Naoise Jordan, Liam Danagher, Jim Cullinan, Paddy McNamara, Tom Ryan

demanding the ref. In any event, Cork won the replay five weeks later on a cold and wet Sunday, and went on to win the Munster final against Tipperary. John Hanly, however, was not impressed with one of the umpire's decisions in the drawn game. 'Charlie McCarthy, who was clearly in the square before a ball arrived, palmed the ball to the net. One umpire signalled a square ball and the other put up the green flag. Then they both signalled a goal. I went in and said to them "don't ye think it's hard enough for Clare to beat Cork on the field of play fairly and squarely?" The Munster council gave me a term of twelve months suspension.'

TEAM IN TRANSITION
1970 marked the beginning of a decline for this Clare team. There were sparse attendances at training with the non-appearance of some of the established players and this culminated in a disastrous league campaign. New blood was introduced for the championship. The Clarecastle trio of Dermot Fitzgerald, Pat Moloney and Christy 'Wax' Guinnane, together with Michael Moroney of Crusheen, rejuvenated the team, but the retirements of Eamon Russell, Noel Pyne (due to studies) and Tom Ryan (transferred to Galway) coupled with the injured Gus Lohan severely depleted the squad.

Clare met Limerick in the first round of the 1970 championship. Though Clare led by ten points at half time, it took an injury-time point from Pat Cronin to salvage a draw in Thurles. The replay, which took place at the Gaelic Grounds, was a bad-tempered affair with Limerick winning in the end by a good margin and two players from each side being ordered to the line. Shortly afterwards, Paschal

O'Brien, Liam Danagher, Noel Pyne and Pat Cronin announced their retirement from hurling. Incidentally, O'Brien's last competitive hurling game was for Munster in the railway cup final of 1971. He was only 25 when he retired.

Clare introduced much-needed new blood in 1971, reaching the league quarter-final at Thurles on 9 May, and hammered Wexford by 4–10 to 1–7, their light young forwards tearing the Wexford defence to shreds. Clare fielded many young players such as Timmy Ryan, Paschal Russell and Michael Kilmartin plus seasoned campaigners like Tom Slattery, Oliver Plunkett and Jim Rochford, who were long overdue a senior county call-up. Unfortunately, they went on to lose narrowly (1–11 to 2–6) to an up-and-coming Limerick team with talent.

In the 1971 championship, Clare almost pulled back a fourteen-point Tipperary lead when Michael Moroney and Michael Pewter got on top at centre field in the second half. Though defeated 1–15 to 3–4 by the future All-Ireland champions, many young talented players like Michael Moroney, Michael Kilmartin, Johnny McMahon, Jimmy McNamara and Paschal Russell had arrived.

VETERAN'S EXHIBITION

On 30 May 1971, GAA president Dr Donal Keenan opened the Ruan hurling pitch. For the occasion, a novel match was played between a national selection captained by Christy Ring and a Clare selection of the 1950s–1960s captained by Jimmy Smyth. The game was refereed by former Clare captain Des Carroll and the Tulla Pipe Band led the teams on to the pitch. I had gone to the game with my parents and Des McCullough to see these former greats, players I'd only read about in *The Hurling Immortals* and other books. The Ring selection boasted 42 All-Ireland medals between them.

The Clare selection included Michael Lynch and Paddy Russell of Clarecastle along with Matt Nugent and Dermot Sheedy. Christy Ring, then 51 years old, astounded me. He played like he was in a Munster championship. According to Jimmy Smyth, 'He played every game like it was a Munster championship. When he came to Ruan, he wanted to play well; he wanted to give a display, but he was disappointed because Mick Hayes was stopping everything.' Other players to line out that day were Jimmy Brohan and Willie John Daly (Cork), Jimmy Duggan (Galway) and Pat Stakelum (Tipperary). John Doyle, Mick Mackey and Tony Reddin were other famous hurlers amongst the attendance at this nostalgic occasion.

COUNTY TEAM DEVELOPMENT

So, what were the major influences over the development of Clare hurling during this period? During the early 1960s we had the excitement and rivalry of colleges hurling, which generated huge interest and produced some great players. Clare were very close to Tipperary and Cork in Munster and also on a par with Wexford and Kilkenny during the years 1966 to 1970. The League saga with Kilkenny in 1968 is a highlight – maybe it was an inferiority complex which prevented success. In the words of Paschal O'Brien, 'We beat everyone in 1967 and 1968 but won nothing'.

Jackie O'Gorman

Three Hurling immortals pictured at the opening of the Ruan grounds, 30 May 1971
L/r: John Doyle (Tipperary), Christy Ring (Cork), Jimmy Smyth (Clare)

Rather than look back with regret, Paschal recalls the joy of playing the game, especially to have played in the company of Jimmy Cullinan, Jimmy Doyle (Tipperary) and Eddie Keher (Kilkenny). It is also worth noting that Clare produced talented players who were honoured on the Munster inter-provincial (Railway Cup) teams of this era. The names of Pat Cronin, Jimmy Cullinan, Liam Danagher, Michael Considine, Vincent Loftus, Paschal O'Brien, Jackie O'Gorman, Noel Pyne and Paddy McNamara all spring to mind. Then, there was the dominance of a small number of clubs like Ruan, Éire Óg, Clarecastle and particularly Newmarket, whose inspirational leader Mick Arthur gave me his views on the highs and lows of involvement with the county team at that time. 'We had a fine side from 1966 to 1969 with the likes of Paschal O'Brien, Eamonn Russell, Tom Ryan, Liam Danagher, Milo Keane, Pat Henchy, Noel Pyne and John Nevin – a fabulous team. Colm Flynn is a great trainer and he came in to the set-up about 1966; he's given great service to the county.

'Paddy Cronin was the top scorer at that time with 11–71 in one season. Cronin regularly got goals from twenty-one yard frees regardless of how many lined the goal. Jimmy Cullinan was a ball of fire; he could play anywhere. Paddy McNamara was a tremendous man and had fire, courage, skill; he was the kind of player that was focused on Croke Park. The players on that Clare team had vision; we were desperate to win a Munster or All-Ireland title.

'Fr Tim Tuohy was a brilliant coach to the Clare team. It was very hard to talk to the Newmarket players because you'd imagine we knew a lot about it considering our success, but Fr Tuohy had great control over us as had Fr Rodgers; they complimented each other. Fr Tuohy was a quiet deep-thinking man and he believed in ground hurling. The essence of his plan was that we moved the ball quickly from corner back to wing back, from wing back to wing forward and from wing forward to corner forward. He insisted on playing ground hurling. In the two drawn games against Kilkenny, particularly the replay, Kilkenny didn't know what was going on – we were moving the ball so fast. I believe in fast distribution; if you release the ball quickly, you can get involved again. That Clare team was good enough to win All-Irelands.

'I called a players' meeting at the West County Inn around 1969. The backbone of the New York team at that time were Claremen – Seán Custy, Hubbie McCabe and Pat Kirby. It was proposed to bring a few of our players in New York home to strengthen the team. Most of the players were for it and we called a meeting with the county board, but they just wouldn't entertain it. But we got on exceptionally well with the county board, John Hanly (Chairman) and Michael McTigue (Secretary), a great honest man. Dr McGrath from Kildysart (the team doctor) was another great man; he took it as an honour to look after the players. They looked after us like we were winning an All-Ireland.'

Jimmy Cullinan made his debut with the county team in 1960–1961. I put it to him that the team went into something of a decline from 1961–1963 but he disagreed. 'The players were there – Michael Blake, Eamon Long, Jimmy Smyth and Naoise Jordan – but not enough was put into it. I don't remember much collective training; maybe the funds weren't there. We had great players in Mick Hayes and Jimmy Smyth. Matt Nugent was still there in 1963 (recalled in 1963), but not enough work was put into the team.'

Seán Custy, who played for Clare during the early 1960s, also says that there was very little preparation put into the county team. 'Training was almost non-existent and we got together only four or five times – we hadn't a hope! Waterford hammered us in 1962. Munster hurling then was at an all-time high.' Bernie Dilger also laments the lack of training. 'Very little was put into it though we had great players. I remember probables versus possibles plus a few training sessions – that was all. Many excellent players from less successful clubs, like John "Tar" McCarthy of Smith O'Brien's, who often carried a team on his own, didn't get a fair chance. Cork and Tipperary by comparison were very organised.'

John McInerney of Clarecastle feels that there was too much familiarity between Newmarket, Éire Óg and Clarecastle. 'There were good hurlers in East Clare. Is it possible that from Clooney to Whitegate (with the exception of the two Whitegate players Naoise Jordan and Seán Cleary) and down to Killaloe, taking in Broadford and O'Callaghan's Mills, we hadn't one player worth his place in the 1967 team?'

According to Newmarket's John McMahon, 'Dermot Fitzgerald was lost to Clare hurling in the 1970s. A big, strong man with plenty of hurling, he had a lot to contribute. Michael Kilmartin was lost as well; he had great ability. Timmy Ryan and D. J Meehan also plenty to offer. Timmy had great ability and could destroy you; he could have made a fabulous contribution.'

It is certainly a shame that the Clare team of the 1965–1970 era, which included many talented players, failed to win anything significant. In Joe Power's book on Clarecastle, Kevin Marren blames the intense club rivalry at that time for a lack of success. 'Neighbouring parishes invariably generate rivalry and tension on the playing field, and there is little doubt that the rivalry in question here generated a little too much tension. The Clare teams that lost to Tipperary in 1967 and 1968 had probably more potential in the group of players than there was in the group that won two National League titles ten years later. It is now water under the bridge but stands as a warning to future generations of players that parish success should not be the ultimate goal for any player or official.'

Newmarket players Liam Danagher and Jimmy Cullinan disagree on the level of division which existed within the Clare team. Liam remembers players in different groups in the dressing-room. 'Players were separated and this was a League semi-final in 1970–71. I'll never forget it; it saddened me; there was no communication.' Jimmy, however, doesn't remember things as having been that bad. 'I don't think it rubbed off from club to county level; we went out as a team.'

Clarecastle's John Hanly became chairman of the county board in 1965 and tried to introduce a different approach to coaching, etc. This was not met with universal approval initially, partially due to an inherent resistance to change and partially due to the fact that players from other clubs may have felt that they knew how to hurl already and were not in need of coaching! While this can be a problem within many counties and has perhaps led to the trend in appointing outside managers and coaches, it has to be re-iterated that inter-club tensions seem to have been particularly acute in Clare around this time. This was a major impediment to making the most of the talent and resources available. I'll leave the last word to John Hanly himself, whose views bear an uncanny resemblance to those of Joe McNamara of Newmarket speaking about the 1930s. Not a lot had changed it seems. 'I introduced coaching and Brendan Vaughan formed the Schools Board for the primary schools leagues. Even with great players like Ger Loughnane, Seán Hehir and Joe McKenna (Limerick), St Flannan's were unsuccessful from 1958 to 1976. There was a period when coaching was looked down on and people were of the opinion that hurlers were born not made. Some clubs had more pride in the parish jersey than the county jersey and the last vestiges of the feudal system weren't thrown off in Clare. It was a slow build-up and it has taken thirty years. Remember, Ger Loughnane was only a boy of eleven then.'

ON THE WINDSWEPT HILL OF TULLA (1972–1979)

We in Clare had a passion for hurling equal to that of Tipperary, Cork and Kilkenny, no matter how many All-Irelands they won.

FR HARRY BOHAN

We were virtually unbeatable in Tulla.

JOHN CALLINAN

1972 CHAMPIONSHIP

Clare threatened to withdraw from the Munster championship in 1972 because first-round opponents Limerick were very reluctant about coming to Cusack Park. A home and away arrangement between these neighbouring counties existed since 1970, when Clare gave home advantage to Limerick for a replay in that year's championship. John Hanly recalls that Limerick did everything in their power not to come to Cusack Park. 'They criticised the pitch and, in a nutshell, they were afraid to come to Ennis'. Prior to the game, Aidan Tuttle invited a special meeting to discuss the care-taking of the pitch. Des McCullough of Ennis Dalcassian's suggested at the meeting that all clubs should send a representative to help renovate the park and have it in good playing condition for the game. This was done and the game went ahead as planned on 2 July 1972.

Limerick came to Cusack Park in an extremely confident mood. This was an accomplished side, which had been most unlucky to lose the 1971 Munster final to Tipperary by 4–16 to 3–18. The Shannonsiders included such household names as Pat Hartigan, Eamon Grimes and Eamon Cregan in their line-up, but it was Clare's hurlers that erupted, giving one of their most memorable displays of the 1970s.

Limerick trailed by twelve points with only seven minutes remaining after a breath-taking opening quarter from the home county. Noel Casey and Jimmy McNamara rattled the Limerick net in the opening minutes and a third goal from the flamboyant Michael Keane of Kilnamona put the game beyond Limerick's reach. The Clare defence of Gus Lohan, Vincent Loftus, Paddy Moloney and Jackie O'Gorman were tremendous, with newcomers D. J. Meehan and Jim Power coming through their debut championship game with flying colours. A brace of Limerick goals in the closing minutes only served to put a more respectable look on the scoreboard.

To say that the outcome was a shock would be an understatement, as is indicated by a comment from *The Clare Champion*'s pre-match analysis: 'Only a supreme optimist could venture a forecast on a Clare triumph'. The 1971 Limerick captain Tony O'Brien had also been interviewed by Cormac Liddy in the *Our Games Annual* and had made the following prediction:

The Clare team that shocked the favourites Limerick on 2 July 1972
Back row l/r: Paddy McNamara, Vincent Loftus, Michael Keane, Seamus Durack, Jackie O'Gorman,
Noel Casey, Jim Power, Michael Moroney; Front row l/r: Jimmy McNamara, Timmy Ryan, Gus
Lohan, Jimmy Cullinan, Pat O'Leary, Paddy Moloney, D. J. Meehan

> I am confident that 1972 will see us land that elusive All-Ireland. Men like Jim Hogan and I cannot go on forever, but I think we are playing with some of the best hurlers the county has ever seen. I look forward keenly to 1972.

Sadly for Clare, the subsequent Munster final against Cork was an anti-climax with Cork winning 6–18 to 2–8. 'We were out-classed; Cork destroyed us,' says John Hanly. Brendan Vaughan also reckons that we just weren't good enough. 'We were totally out-classed. Two vital players, Seamus Durack and Michael Moroney were injured going into the game. The 1972 team were the relics of a good side going back to 1965.' A Cork team powered by Gerald and Charlie McCarthy, Mick Malone and Ray Cummins romped home. It was over at half time and Raymond Smith had the following to say about that game:

> I remember a golden goal scored by Ray Cummins against Clare when he pulled back and picked his spot before sending in an unstoppable shot. I recall from that Munster Final in Thurles, the wonderful backing title-starved Clare supporters gave their team and, as Cork crushed them down to crushing, depressing defeat, there was the hurling of Jimmy Cullinan like a beacon in the gathering gloom that descended on the Banner County. He went nearly the length of the field in one run. If there was a 'Fairest and Best' award to be given to the losers, I would have awarded it to him gladly.

In spite of this defeat, John Callinan has great memories of the period. 'We were young – fanatical I suppose. We were playing under-age and senior. It was one roller-coaster after another and I went from playing juvenile to senior in 1972. I remember playing Dean Ryan (U–16½) one afternoon and turning out that evening

106

for the county U–21 team. I found playing minor tougher because more was expected of me. The 1972 Munster final was my first senior championship game. The seniors and U–21s were training together and the late Haulie Daly was a selector. I think Haulie wanted to see me play minor, U–21 and senior in 1972, as he thought it was my final year at minor level and he wanted me to equal Jimmy Smyth's 1949 record of playing minor, junior and senior; but I played minor again in 1973. I only barely remember the Munster Final of 1972. Cork were very experienced and we qualified out of the blue. Though our preparation was good, we were hammered.'

Justin McCarthy was on the Cork team that day. 'Clare were reared on defeats; it's very hard to get over a defeatist attitude. Deep down they weren't sure of themselves, but they didn't realise how much respect we had for them. Basically, they were beaten on the day by hurling mistakes. They didn't realise it; they thought it was Cork's craft. Cork played a quicker brand of hurling and made less mistakes.'

1973 CHAMPIONSHIP

After the debacle of the 1972 final, Fr Harry Bohan, with the assistance of Seán Guinnane, Michael Slattery, John Daly, Matt Nugent and Pa Howard, formed an Action Committee to put Clare hurling back on the map. Clare's recovery was further aided by the appointment of Matt Nugent as manager/selector of the senior team. He did a fine job and introduced many young players including Enda O'Connor, Billy Meehan, Noel Ryan, Michael McNamara and Niall McInerney (later to star with Galway).

Speaking about the Action Committee Fr Bohan says: 'We wanted to give moral support to the players. I thought that it was of crucial importance to go to every club and look for players. One of the reasons that we set up the committee was to identify players in the less successful clubs and to have them recommended to the selectors. I didn't worry how raw a player was initially if he had the right character and commitment.'

Clare's final league game that year was against Kilkenny at Tulla where Noel Casey overwhelmed the Noresider's defence. In the 1973 senior championship, Clare were pitted again against Limerick and just failed to cause another shock on this occasion, losing to the subsequent All-Ireland champions of that year by 3–11 to 3–9 in a torrid game at Thurles. Clare's Michael Moroney had been suspended and was a huge loss. A great goal by Timmy Ryan was disallowed and a free awarded to Clare instead which only yielded a point.

'Lucky, Lucky Limerick', lamented *The Clare Champion* headline, which went on to describe Noel Ryan as 'Clare's most polished forward that day'. The only consolation to be derived from this defeat was that it signalled the emergence of new talent, with young players Timmy Ryan, John Callinan, Niall McInerney, Martin McKeogh and Seán Hehir coming to the fore.

UNDER 21

Clare teams in the U–21 grade have always done well, but the teams from 1972 to 1976 were exceptional, though ultimately unsuccessful at gaining even provincial honours. The 1972 side that contested their first Munster final included Paddy Hickey, Haulie Russell, Enda and Michael O'Connor and Timmy and Noel Ryan. They outplayed Tipperary for most of the hour, but faded in the dying moments to lose by 4–10 to 3–10. Timmy Ryan at wing-forward and Seamus Durack at corner-forward were particularly effective.

The U–21 defeat to Waterford in 1974 was possibly the most galling of all. This talented Clare side had easily disposed of Tipperary, 3–12 to 1–8, and ran Cork into the ground by 3–16 to 3–4 at Limerick, but lost to a gallant Waterford team by 2–5 to 1–3 on a wet and miserable Sunday on 14 July in Thurles. John Galvin gave a tremendous display for Waterford at centre-back and the free-flowing Clare hurling that we had witnessed against Tipperary and Cork never materialised.

The side included about nine future seniors plus top players like James Keogh, Michael Gough and Johnny Boyce. Their strength can also be gauged by the subs bench which included the likes of Mickie Murphy, Peter Golden, Tony O'Donnell and Mickie Burke. The team included no fewer than nine senior players and read like a Who's Who, with extraordinary talent in Con McGuinness, James Keogh, Ger Ward, John Treacy, Colm Honan, Ger Loughnane and many others. The loss of Martin McKeogh through injury before the game was a major blow.

McKeogh remembers the game from the sideline. 'In 1974, you were effectively looking at the minors of 1971 in addition to Pat O'Connor and Christy Ryan. Unfortunately, it was a combination of over-confidence and meeting a most incredibly bad evening , a deluge of rain, but it was the same for Waterford. We didn't play at all on the night. I was a selector and it added to the disappointment.'

Ger Loughnane played centre-back on that side. 'No doubt about it, that was a great team. Many of the senior side of the late 1970s came from that team. We beat Tipperary and Cork comprehensively but lost to Waterford on a dreadful evening at Thurles. They had Tom Casey and John Galvin, later to become All-Stars, but I feel that we should have done better.'

In 1976, Clare defeated Tipperary for the third time in succession 2–13 to 3–5 to qualify for yet another U–21 decider. Again a gallant Clare team went down to a late Cork goal 2–11 to 3–6, with Brendan Gilligan giving an outstanding display, ably assisted by Peter Golden, Tommy Keane, Gerry O'Connor (Kilmaley) and Pat O'Connor.

NEW MANAGER

Fr Harry Bohan was appointed manager of the Clare team in September 1973. His period in office ushered in a new approach at both organisational and team level, thereby helping to inspire a surge of Clare hurling fever throughout the 1970s. There were of course the inevitable voices of dissent, especially towards the end of his reign, but I asked some of the players from that time what Fr Bohan had meant to them.

For Martin McKeogh of Smith O'Brien's, 'he brought a more professional approach and put a lot of effort and commitment into it. He was good with people and players. He brought the best out of them and got a lot of commitment from the panel of players he put together. He brought in youth but, ultimately, success was linked to a mixture of youth and experience.' John McMahon from Newmarket remembers him as 'Very single-minded, a great organiser. He liaised well with the county board and put more into the players.' Jimmy Walsh of Bodyke praises him for involving players from the smaller clubs. 'Myself and a lot of others would never have got a trial with the Clare team except that Fr Bohan came in.'

Pat O'Connor of Tubber was a student at Our Lady's secondary school in Gort when he was called into the senior team. He got valuable experience over a couple of seasons before making his championship debut and says: 'Fr Bohan was a revolutionary figure and brought innovation. He worked tirelessly behind the scenes looking after the minutest details so that players could concentrate on the game. The county team at that time were very close. We toured the United States in 1976;

it was a great experience. We also had tremendous support from West Clare – Lahinch, Liscannor, Kilkee, etc.'

1974 MUNSTER FINAL

Limerick returned to Cusack Park in October 1973 as All-Ireland champions for an action-packed league tie. Clare had two players sent off, Enda O'Connor and Vincent Loftus, together with Limerick's Willie Moore. Having been sent off, Vincent Loftus returned to the fray, stopping a certain Limerick goal from where he was standing near one of the Clare goal posts, and cleared it out the field. He received a six-month suspension for this unorthodox intervention. With a few minutes remaining, Clare led the All-Ireland Champions 0–14 to 1–8 when Limerick got through for two goals to win the match.

Writing about this game in the *Irish Independent*, John D. Hickey was of the opinion that Clare's lack of discipline had cost them dearly:

> I feel sure that shrewd Clare hurling men will not disagree with the viewpoint that they would surely have brought about the downfall of the All-Ireland Champions had they been as disciplined as they were power-packed and fervent.

After a fairly dismal league campaign, Clare caused a major shock with a 1–8 to 1–7 victory over Tipperary in the 1974 championship. Tipperary trailing by six points, fought back to force a hectic finish. Con Woods and Michael Moroney were in command at centre-field and it was only when Woods retired due to injury that Tipperary came into the picture in this sector late in the game. Colm Honan was Clare's most effective forward, scoring six points while Tipperary's Roger Ryan and Michael Keating were held by the Clare defence. In the subsequent Munster final, however, Limerick took command at an early stage, scoring three quick goals in the opening ten minutes. Clare's spirited and second half rally was not enough to stop Limerick retaining the Munster Championship. On a brighter note Ger Loughnane became Clare's first All-Star award winner. The Feakle man was picked from six nominations 'for his alertness in defence and his all-round contribution to Clare's revival in 1974'.

CLUB AMALGAMATIONS

Amalgamations for the senior county championship were very popular in the mid to late 1970s. Colm Wiley of Bodyke remembers this period. 'I played with the successful Brian Boru's amalgamation. The amalgamations of that era such as Inis Cealtra, St Flannan's, St Brendan's, Sarsfield's, etc., produced great players but the County Board dropped the idea a few years later. I think that in the future Clare hurling will go back to amalgamations for senior purposes. Brian Boru's (comprising players from Tulla, Bodyke and Killanena) beat Newmarket in the 1975 championship. We were very lucky to beat Sixmilebridge – Noel Casey was sent off – and we beat Éire Óg in the county final. We were the first East Clare side to win the senior championship since Whitegate in 1961. With the tradition of East Clare hurling, it's hard to beat when it's going well.'

In 1972 St Senan's from Cratloe–Clonlara contested the county final but faded in the second half to Newmarket-on-Fergus. This south-east Clare combination included Jackie O'Gorman, Colm Honan, Martin McKeogh, Johnny Boyce and Michael O'Connor. Another amalgamation side St Flannan's were drawn from Kilnamona, Inagh and Ennistymon and featured well-known inter-county players

Milo and Michael Keane, plus Flan Hegarty and Tom Harvey, Jnr. In the 1975 semi-final, a tremendous display by Éire Óg's Tony Kelly was the difference between the sides to leave Éire Óg winners by 1–10 to 3–3.

Brian Boru's proved too strong for Éire Óg in the 1975 county final at Cusack Park. The East Clare side, which included seasoned players like Pat Danaher, Colm Wiley, Jim Power, Jim Rochford and goalkeeper Pat Kirby, raced into an early lead which they never lost. Kevin Kennedy at centre-field and Seán O'Halloran at wing-back caught the eye, with Pat Danaher subsequently being awarded Clare Hurler of the Year. The Ennis side proved disappointing, but Noel Ryan, Declan Coote, Tony Kelly and Massie Dilger played well.

In September 1988, Fr Bohan was interviewed by Josie Kerin on West Coast Radio and cast his mind back to the 1970s. Fr Harry Bohan points out that a large number of the Clare team from the 1975–1979 era came from junior and intermediate clubs. 'When you are picking a county team, you have to handle them a certain way but, in addition to that, you don't need to take club hurling as your gauge. You take individuals and try and blend them into a team that can rise to it. Kerry are acknowledged as the most successful county in Gaelic football and the bulk of their players come from amalgamations. I think we should look at this; we could have a very good intermediate competition and amalgamations for senior. With the exception of the city clubs like Glen Rovers, Blackrock, St Finbarr's and Na Piarsaigh, Cork have very few senior clubs. My own club Feakle, there is enormous credit due to them for a small parish of 800 people. Going back one hundred years, Feakle–Killanena were one parish when there were thousands of people living in the area. Obviously, amalgamations should be looked at in this context.'

CLARE IN TULLA

Around 1970, Clare gradually started to use Dr Daly Park, Tulla for their home league games. Cork hurler John Horgan reckons that his best memories of hurling are National League games. 'I remember Nowlan Park and Tulla, travelling up the night before. Enda O'Connor and I had some great tussles, manfully tough. I also liked Jim Cullinan and Jackie O'Gorman – they had great cutting. Seán Hehir and Seán Stack were great stylists.'

For John Callinan, 'the games in Tulla were great. This aura built up around Tulla and we were attracting great crowds. There's great hurling support in East Clare and it was easier for people from Scariff and Killaloe to go to Tulla. We were virtually unbeatable in Tulla.' Clare's record at Tulla was remarkable in this decade. Out of twenty home games played, Clare won seventeen, drew one and lost only two. After twelve straight victories and one draw, Wexford broke the spell in the 1977–78 campaign when traffic choked the roads to Dr Daly Park, with a two point victory of 2–12 to 1–13.

1975–76 LEAGUE FINAL

Clare reached the knockout stages of the 1975–1976 league, defeating Waterford 0–18 to 0–7 at Thurles, with Con Woods and Seán Stack on top of mid-field and Mickey Burke and Seamus Durack in great form, before returning to Thurles to meet Wexford. In a game of swaying fortunes, Michael Moroney blasted a late free to the net past a wall of Wexford men to force a draw. The replay was fixed again for Thurles with the Cork *v* Kilkenny game making it a double-header. Over 30,000 witnessed one of the greatest games of the decade with Clare and Wexford serving up excellent fare. Peader O'Brien reported on the game in the *Irish Press*:

The huge crowd basking in the sunshine enjoyed every minute, such was the pace, flow and uncertainty. Both teams got a standing ovation at the finish and they deserved it. Just as they did in the drawn game, Clare came back and, in almost deathly silence, with the last puck of the game, Colm Honan pointed that equalising free to leave the score at 2–14 to 2–14.

The game went to extra time and I remember Jimmy McNamara giving an exhibition of hurling when he pointed several times from play in a glorious first period of extra time, during which Clare raced into a six-point lead, 2–20 to 2–14. I also recall the good-humoured comments of the large Cork crowd sitting near me and being almost in tears from their wit as they urged on Clare. True to form, this Wexford team of Willie Murphy, Mick Butler and Martin and John Quigley fought back in fine fashion, but Clare held on to win 3–24 to 4–16 in a game that I will always remember. In the other game that day, Kilkenny disposed of Cork by 2–17 to 3–10, though it was the beginning of a new era for both Cork and Clare.

In the league final, Kilkenny led by 0–15 to 0–10 with eight minutes to go when Noel Casey and Tom Crowe scored a goal each to take the lead. However, with almost the last puck of the match, Matt Ruth levelled matters 0–16 to 2–10. Shortly afterwards, we were back in Thurles again when Clare beat Waterford 3–15 to 3–12 in the first round of the Munster championship. Noel Casey scored two goals in the first half of that game but was sent off, which meant that his availability for the replay against Kilkenny was not clear for some time after the Waterford game; this seemed to have an unsettling effect on the rest of the team.

He eventually received a two-week suspension and was back just in time for Clare's meeting with Kilkenny on 20 June 1976. Kilkenny, leading 3–8 to 1–8 at the half–time stage, gave one of their greatest displays in what was a great era for them – 1971 to 1976. A rampant forward line of Paddy Delaney, Mick Brennan, Billy Fitzpatrick and Eddie Keher tore the Clare defence to shreds to clock up a final score line of 6–14 to 1–14. Interestingly, the same Kilkenny team was crushed a couple of weeks later by Wexford in the championship.

TRIP TO THE UNITED STATES
'Clare's Bubble finally Bursts', was *The Clare Champion*'s comment on semi-final failure to Limerick in the 1976 Munster championship. The teams were level on seven occasions, but two late Limerick goals from Eamon Cregan and Joe McKenna put a gloss on the Limerick score, giving a final tally of 4–12 to 1–13. It was our seventh trip to Thurles in as many weeks and the team then headed for New York and a much-deserved break.

'The trip to the United States was the making of the team because the players got really close – we became like a club team and came back to win two league titles'. So says team member Michael Murphy. Mick Morrissey, president of New York GAA was very impressed with the team and commented: 'They are one of the finest groups of players to visit New York'. Another great Clare Gael Michael 'Brud' White had a more poetic interpretation of Clare's visit; 'it was like sunshine in winter'! Clare returned from New York a rejuvenated team and collected full points in their league campaign before disposing of Offaly 2–15 to 0–7 in the semi-final at Thurles and qualifying for another showdown with Kilkenny.

NEW HURLING COACH
Former Cork hurler Justin McCarthy was appointed team coach in October 1976.

Michael Murphy points out that he brought great confidence to the team. 'He taught us to play every ball to its merits rather than playing to a set pattern all the time. He could analyse every opposition player and was a big influence.' In the view of John McMahon, he made a difference to Clare's hurling. 'He speeded up our striking and our picking. He brought us on that extra bit and told us where we could improve. He brought a new dimension and looked after the little things.'

John Callinan is also loud in his praise for McCarthy: 'Justin was terrific – he elevated us to a pitch beyond anything I'd seen before. As inter-county hurlers, he expected us to behave in a certain way and demanded that we respect ourselves. His training sessions were very enjoyable. John Hanly and Justin McCarthy were ahead of their time and gave it the status it deserved. They were deep thinkers about the game and they challenged you to think about it yourself. Justin came up to Tulla from Passage, an extraordinary man.'

There was also a significant addition to the sideline team in McCarthy's home county during 1976. Jimmy Barry-Murphy takes up the story. 'In 1976 a new regime came in to the Cork scene. Christy Ring became part of the selection committee with Frank Murphy and others. It became much more organised and more intense as regards training and preparation for games; it was very demanding.

'The fact that Justin McCarthy trained Clare from 1976 to 1979 was a big factor in Cork. We all knew him and we had tremendous respect for him. When a fellow county man is training another county it's bound to galvanise the team. It added a cutting edge to the whole thing.'

Clare hurling maestro Fr Harry Bohan and Clare coach Justin McCarthy in the late 1970s

1976–77 LEAGUE TITLE

The early stages of the 1976–77 league final were won by Clare. A long free from Jackie O'Gorman was won by Pat O'Connor, who flicked it into the square to Jimmy McNamara, who drove it home for the opening goal. Clare goaled shortly afterwards when Noel Casey drove in a long ball which was saved by Noel Skehan, but with Skehan harassed by Tom Crowe, he lost control and Crowe scored an amazing goal while on his knees. The Clonlara man followed this with a point while under extreme pressure to put Clare 2–1 to 0–2 ahead after thirteen minutes. This was a lead that Clare were never to lose.

In the closing minutes, Noel Casey scored a great point from a move involving brothers Pat and Enda O'Connor. Kilkenny had the final point to leave the score at 2–8 to 0–9, with the celebrated Kilkenny forward line of Delaney, Mick Crotty and Mick Brennan well held by Clare's stalwart defence. Jimmy McNamara lifted the League Trophy amid jubilant supporters. It was Clare's first major trophy since the Oireachtas in 1954.

Team physio Colm Flynn recalls one particular difficulty in selecting that team. 'I remember the selection of the team for the League final; it went on for two and a half hours. One of the corner-forward positions was in doubt. The selectors argued for two hours on that one position. Fr Harry was vindicated as Tom Crowe got the decisive goal. He was a good manager and had a good hurling brain, but the ultimate team make-up and switches were down to the selectors. It was a team effort; it was never a one-man thing.'

Tom Crowe played only about a dozen games for Clare during the years 1972–1978 but was very effective. He scored and set up a litany of great goals and he worked very well with Noel Casey. Crowe was plagued with injury which curtailed his service to the county team.

1977 MUNSTER FINAL

On 5 June 1977, the new league champions took on Tipperary at the Gaelic Grounds in Limerick in the first round of the championship. A crowd of twenty thousand turned up to see Tipperary race into an 0–11 to 0–2 lead just before half-time, when Tom Crowe passed to Noel Casey, who drove a powerful shot past Pat McLoughney for a decisive goal, bringing Clare back into the game.

Clare won the replay 0–13 to 1–7 to qualify for a semi-final meeting with Limerick. The Shannonsiders, who had led by a point at the interval, went further ahead in the ninth minute of the second half when Eamon Cregan drove a powerfully-hit penalty to the net. The Clare mentors then made a great move by bringing Pat O'Connor to centre-field; he proceeded to give one of his greatest displays in the county jersey and turned the game around. Clare survived by 0–14 to 1–9 to qualify for a Munster final with Cork.

Jim Power was certainly held in high esteem as a hurler at this time, both within Clare and amongst hurling followers in general. This piece from Paddy Downey's match report in the following day's *Irish Times* is evidence of this:

> Jack Lynch arrived at the stadium to watch the second half. One jubilant Clare supporter, by name Aidan Tuttle, said that if the Taoiseach-elect could go outside his parliamentary party when choosing the members of his cabinet, he might be tempted to select Jim Power as his Minister for Defence. That is a generous compliment to the hurling skill of the Clare full-back.

As always, the Cork crowd brought their own sense of colour to the Munster final, sporting Confederate and Japanese flags and a Soviet one proclaiming that 'Even Stalin was a Red'! Con Houlihan described the scene in the *Evening Press* the following day:

As the teams paraded, the stadium was awash with war cries. For once Clare's hordes did not outnumber the rival tribe; so numerous were two-poled red-and-white flags that Cork's followers seemed out to prove that theirs too was a banner county. And the first-half play was never less than gripping and often delightful. Cork's game was the more even in texture; Clare tended to come in fervent spurts.

Pádraig Puirseál reported on the game in *The Irish Times:*

> Cork got off to a great start when Tim Crowley goaled from a penalty, but Clare hit back with great goals from Noel Casey and Enda O'Connor and, playing some beautiful, cultured hurling, Clare raced into a 2–4 to 1–1 lead. This proved to be the high-water mark of Clare's endeavour. Cork came back and, from a Jimmy Barry-Murphy centre, Ray Cummins fielded and palmed the ball to the net. Cork brought John Crowley to centre-back and began to get on top. Just before half-time, Jim Power was sent off following an incident with Ray Cummins. It was a sad blow to Power, a man who always played the ball, to be sent off.

The second half produced some great goals from Clare's Colm Honan and Cork's famous goal-scoring specialist of that era, Jimmy Barry-Murphy but, in the end, Cork prevailed by 4–15 to 4–10. Con Houlihan singled out one particular Cork player for special mention:

> The most important element in their play was the great anticipation and decisive striking of John Horgan. Nominally at left full-back he was in fact sweeper. All his teammates had their great moments, but beyond question John was man of the match.
> Clare's failure to attempt to tie him down by a change in tactics was surprising; so too was the freedom allowed Jim Barry-Murphy who seemed to have a private road through the middle of Clare's defence.

As far as Fr Bohan is concerned the loss of Jim Power was crucial to the outcome of the game. 'We were most unfortunate that Jim Power was sent off; we were flying and we had Cork on the rack. I have no doubt that if Power had remained, we would have beaten Cork and would probably have gone on to win the All-Ireland. We were only beaten by five points, even though we played almost forty minutes with only fourteen men, playing against forwards of the calibre of Jimmy Barry-Murphy, Seánie O'Leary and Charlie McCarthy. They were household names and will go down as greats.'

Naturally enough, I suppose, Clare's hard-luck story did not hold much currency in Cork. Speaking to the *Irish Press* after the game, the Cork captain Martin O'Doherty said: 'We would have won in any case as we had got on top before the end of the first half'. His view was supported by Cork county board secretary, Frank Murphy. 'I believe we had the game won before the Clareman was sent off'. But Justin McCarthy disagrees with his fellow Leesiders: 'The game wasn't over before Jim Power was sent off; we were well in the game at that stage. We could have won that Munster Championship had Power not been sent off. He didn't do a whole lot to be sent off.'

1977–78 LEAGUE TITLE

Clare bounced back from this major disappointment to retain the league title in 1978. The turning point for Clare in this series was another great display in the preliminary rounds against Kilkenny at Nowlan Park, when Clare triumphed 2–8 to 2–5. Martin McKeogh excelled at full-forward with a personal tally of 1–5; so Clare and Kilkenny reached the League final for the third consecutive time. Kilkenny led seven points to three at half time, but a terrific second-half display saw Noel Casey score one and Martin McKeogh two goals. Clare's winning total of 3–10 all came from play. Speaking to Seán Óg Ó Ceallacháin in *The Irish Times*, Fr Bohan declared: 'We made history today; this is the first Clare team ever to win two National League titles in a row'.

The *Times* reporter continued: 'This Clare side is now a real team, hurling almost as a unit and with cool authority and a confidence in their ability that will not easily be overcome'. Kilkenny secretary, Paddy Grace, was also gracious in defeat and wished Clare well in the Munster championship. 'I hope it's a Kilkenny *v* Clare All-Ireland final', he said. Johnny Moloney believed that this was the best Clare team for many years and attributed much of their success to their manager Fr Bohan. Clare selector Gerry Browne judged Clare's second-half display to be one of the best ever. 'Casey's goal was fabulous, but McKeogh's first goal was one of the finest I've ever seen.' Trainer Colm Flynn considered them 'the fittest team I ever trained and I never had any doubts about the outcome.'

At the presentation of the League cup to Seán Stack, the Clare captain made only a casual reference to the trophy just won and the main thrust of his speech dealt with the forthcoming championship, which he said 'is our real objective'. Thousands of supporters turned out at the square in Ennis on the following Monday night. The team was paraded in an open lorry from the West County Inn to O'Connell Square via the Turnpike, Carmody Street and Parnell Street. All along the route, supporters cheered and applauded as Seán Stack proudly displayed the trophy. In the magazine *Gaelic Sport* 'Moondharrig' wrote:

> Now the championship lies ahead for Clare, with only two matches between the league and a return to Croke Park on the first Sunday in September. Clare now are a cooler, more competent and more resourceful team than they were a year ago. They are now a team, not just a collection of talented individuals. On form, they must start favourites to bring the All-Ireland home for the first time in sixty-four years.

This reflects the general tone of optimism about Clare's prospects as they headed into the 1978 championship.

1978 MUNSTER FINAL

In preparation for the 1978 championship, Clare were invited to the Ballyragget Festival in Kilkenny and to Bansha in Tipperary for the opening of the Canon Hayes Memorial Park on 21 May. 'Congratulations on retaining your league title. We wish you luck in your quest for the championship, but not at the expense of the blue and gold' were the sentiments expressed by one Tipperary speaker at the opening.

Clare opened their championship campaign against Limerick at Semple Stadium, Thurles, where they ran up an early lead with the half-back line of Loughnane, Hehir and Stack completely on top. Clare led 3–12 to 0–8 coming into the final quarter when Limerick sprung to life and rattled in three quick goals to bring the crowd to their feet. Following this, Eamon Grimes set up another Limerick attack, but his move was well read by Seán Hehir, who sent a low pin-point pass to Colm Honan, who passed to Brendan Gilligan, who goaled. This put the game out of Limerick's reach 4–12 to 3–8 and Clare had qualified for another showdown with Cork.

Prior to the Munster final, Clare entertained Galway in the Oireachtas at Roslevan. The selectors introduced new blood for this game in Tommy Keane, Leo Quinlan, Barry Smythe and Tom Glynn in goal. Galway qualified for the Oireachtas final on a score of 2–13 to 1–10.

The Munster final at Thurles in July 1978 attracted an official attendance of 54,000, probably the biggest crowd since the epic 1960 final between Cork and Tipperary. The gates were shut about half an hour before the game, leaving three to four thousand supporters locked out. Cork's John Horgan remembers the chaos. 'I was stuck in traffic and things were looking bad; the clock was against me. I told a guard who I was and explained that I wasn't using my position as a player, but I had to get to Semple Stadium. He gave me a garda escort and got me out of the jam; otherwise I wouldn't have made it. The tension was fierce – we were highly strung, taut – we were wired and the tension was flowing. There's no enjoyment playing championship hurling; it's just pressure; you're holding on for dear life. Obviously, one can relish it afterwards.' John Callinan also recollects the enormity of the occasion. 'I could feel the tension coming out. It was different and the crowd was massive. Ger Loughnane, Seán Hehir, Seán Stack and I were twenty-three or so and we felt it was time to deliver.'

In the opening moments both teams were guilty of poor finishing before John Horgan broke the deadlock after ten minutes with a magnificent free from one hundred yards after a foul on Tom Cashman. Michael Moroney replied with a super point from a sideline ball. The first half saw very little open play with both defences dominating. It is interesting to note that Cork's six forwards failed to score in the first thirty-five minutes' hurling. Clare's remaining points came from a Colm Honan free after a foul on Pat O'Connor and a blistering point from Noel Casey which seemed destined for the roof of the net but skimmed over the crossbar.

Having studied the complete RTE video of that 1978 game recently, it revealed a lot to me. Early in the second half Enda O'Connor scored a great point from a Seamus Durack puck-out which should have signalled the beginning of Clare's assault. However, most of Clare's forwards played badly by their own high standards and never moved with their usual flowing style. Like the Cork forwards, they seemed to be stuck to the ground and were never allowed to open it up. With fourteen minutes to go, Brendan Gilligan was introduced for full-forward Martin Mc-Keogh. He made a great burst, cutting past Crowley and Horgan, but was bottled up. His pass to Callinan went astray but Honan pointed when Pat O'Connor was fouled, leaving the score at twelve points to ten.

The Clare defence excelled throughout. Loughnane was inspirational and Seán Hehir dominated Jimmy Barry-Murphy. Seamus Durack was in magnificent form behind them, his flamboyant defence and counter-attacking style in full flow. He made a series of brilliant saves from Cork substitute Eamon O'Donoghue and, time and again, emerged from the goal area clearing long deliveries up field. A magnificent clearance from Ger Loughnane was the final throw of the dice for Clare, but the wind just carried the ball a little and it went over for a point leaving the final score 0–13 to 0–11. It was the first Munster final that failed to produce a goal since Waterford beat Tipperary 0–11 to 0–8 in 1963.

John Horgan remembers his feelings at half-time. 'We were only two points up after playing with a stiff wind. I don't remember any talk of defeat at half time. I don't remember any speech from Christy Ring; I found Christy Ring a quiet man. No player needs to be motivated when playing Munster championship.' However, his team-mate Jimmy Barry-Murphy had a different recollection of the half time

At a St Flannan's function
Back row l/r: Fr Seamus Gardiner, Ger Loughnane, Colm Honan, Jim Power, Seán Hehir, Brendan Gilligan, Barry Smythe, Fr Willie Walsh; Front row l/r: Leo Quinlan, Fr Harry Bohan, Fr Seamus Mullins, John Callinan, Seán Stack, Michael Murphy

atmosphere. 'The Clare supporters were roaring on their team at half-time; it looked like Clare would win. It was the one time in my involvement with Cork that one man galvanised the dressing-room and that was Christy Ring. No doubt about it, he was firing, he lifted the whole team.'

John Callinan recalls the atmosphere in the Clare dressing-room at half-time. 'We knew at half-time we were there or thereabout. It's a pity the game didn't produce a goal; it might have opened it up, because every ball became too important when it's point for point. I was supposed to mark Tom Cashman in 1978. We did not take into account that Cork didn't want this to happen and didn't allow it to happen.' Justin McCarthy also remembers how their strategy didn't go according to plan. 'Tom Cashman and Tim Crowley switched on John Callinan and Michael Moroney. We switched back but they switched again.'

Jimmy Barry-Murphy recalls: 'We took the game to Clare in the second half. Tom Cashman had a magnificent game and Charlie McCarthy got some magnificent points from frees. John Horgan, a great character, was inspirational and Denis Burns played well in the other corner. Clare had some great players – four or five of them would get on any team of any era – but it's very hard to make the breakthrough.'

I put it to one of the Clare subs, Michael Murphy, that the Clare bench seemed reluctant to make changes. 'The game was so tight, it was hard to blame the mentors, as they were expecting that we would get this goal which would change the game. It was very close, dour, dogged hurling. If either team had got a goal, it would have opened it up.' John McMahon agrees and reckons that even a goal for Cork might have improved Clare's lot! 'I felt that if Cork got a goal, we might have got two. It was a non-event, a dour struggle and a strange game. Cork could have been beaten on the day.'

I can still see the broad smile on John Horgan's face as he was surrounded by jubilant Cork supporters. He gave me his opinion on the game. 'My immediate opponent Pat O'Connor cannot be blamed for my four points. The frees and seventies that I scored came from other areas of the pitch and I went out to take them. Had Clare got out of Munster in 1977 and 1978, I have no doubt that they would have won the All-Ireland in both years.'

John McMahon, however, feels that the Clare team was getting stale by the time July came around. 'I felt better in May than I did in July; I felt the edge was gone off us by July. It showed up in the replay with Kilkenny in June 1976. Waterford nearly beat us in the Munster championship just before that. 1977–78 were huge disappointments. Cork were a class outfit but we held their forwards to a few points. I'd agree with John Horgan's comments (about winning All-Irelands) provided the training didn't catch up with us.'

Mick Malone, who is now resident in Ennis, played at corner-forward on the 1978 Cork team. ' Clare hurling in the 1970s was good. They were unlucky in 1978 although I feel that we were under strength – Seánie O'Leary had to cry off and I wasn't fully fit – I lasted only forty minutes. Clare possibly should have won but we defended well against a strong wind in the second half. It looked at half-time like Clare were going to take it but Ring lifted us when our backs were to the wall. Possibly Clare did feel at half time that they had one hand on the Cup, but regardless of the advantage of the breeze or whatever, you still have to come out and play against the same players.'

For Ger Loughnane 'The most disappointing thing is that Clare didn't play anything near our full potential; we were way below form. The big showdown never materialised; it never got off the ground – 13 points to 11 points after seventy minutes of hurling!' Corner-forward Pat O'Connor says: 'The game was over before we knew it. It was like the Germans playing soccer; everything was controlled. There were no breaks, no mistakes. We were closed down and we couldn't cope with it. It was the most frustrating match I ever played in.'

I asked Justin McCarthy how he viewed the 1977–78 team, now that almost two decades have elapsed, and what did he consider were the reasons for their failure to win championship honours: 'They had tremendous spirit; the best team I was ever involved with, very close-knit and great to train; we did a lot of hurling practice. I was the coach and gave team talks; I was over the hurling side of things. I did have an influence, but at the end of the day I wasn't a selector. There was too much of a continuation from the league to the championship. There should have been a break and there should not have been as much physical training. It stemmed probably from a lack of success. They just needed to keep ticking over; a lot of the team were tired.

'We were very unlucky in 1977 when Jim Power was put off; it upset the rhythm of the team. That team was capable of beating Cork. We were better in 1978; they got a few long-range points and we had to work a lot harder for scores. We were good enough to win the All-Ireland, with four or five All-Stars and tremendous players like Jackie O'Gorman, as good a back as you'd get on any team, Johnny McMahon, Seamus Durack, Colm Honan, Noel Casey and the O'Connors. Maybe we needed an individual player to put the finishing touches to the team. It could have been someone like Pat Cronin; he probably would have got a point or two from nothing. We were missing a player of his calibre at the end of the day.

'We were a better second-half team, if you look at the league final against Kilkenny in 1978 for example. Cork knew we were a better second-half team. Clare usually took over in the first ten minutes of the second half, but a quarter of an hour passed in 1978 and nothing was happening. The opening quarter was disastrous; we were dormant. Cork realised what was going on and they picked up the pieces. Cork were under severe pressure but we never capitalised on it. After that traumatic defeat, the greatest hurler of all time, Christy Ring, came in to the dressing-room, shook my hand and said: "Hard luck Justin; ye were very close; it could have gone either way". And left.'

Colm Flynn has a different analysis of the possible reasons for the team's failure to Cork in 1978. 'We got a lot of unfair criticism after 1978. We were accused of pushing the team too hard over a long period of time; yet we did the same last year and we got the results. Things in 1977–78 were not as professional as they were in 1995. We didn't have the resources or the financial back-up, even the basic amenities. We had the nucleus of a fantastic side but we didn't have the full backing of the county board. Maybe it was bureaucracy.'

THE LAST HURRAH

Despite the overwhelming sense of disappointment that followed that Munster final defeat, Clare once more showed great character in maintaining their standard of hurling and qualifying for their fifth consecutive league semi-final. Newcomers Martin Meehan, Michael O'Connor (Parteen), Patsy Hehir and Seán Lynch were introduced. Seán Lynch, a talented hurler who had performed well at county level in minor and U–21, had been lost to hurling for a few years, but the recently-formed Banner GAA club brought him back into the game. His displays in the senior championship with Éire Óg–Dal's earned him a deserved call-up.

Clare gave excellent displays in the league with wins over Waterford, Wexford, Kilkenny, Limerick and Galway. The only point dropped was to resurgent Offaly in a highly-competitive game at Birr, with newcomers Leo Quinlan, Barry Smythe and Michael Noonan all doing well. Undoubtedly, the game of the league was Clare's final divisional game against Galway at Tulla. With four minutes left, the Tribesmen were leading 2–9 to 0–7 when Clooney's Michael Murphy was introduced. He caused havoc and was instrumental in setting up a blitz of late goals by Pat O'Connor, John Callinan and Noel Casey, thereby enabling Clare to snatch a late victory by 3–8 to 2–9. Many patrons in the huge crowd had already left and missed this extraordinary finish.

Michael Murphy looks back to that game, but maintains a modest view of his own achievements. 'I have good memories of Tulla; we were seldom beaten there. I played on Jimmy Cooney, the best hurler I ever played on. I wasn't doing too well and the selectors switched me to my favourite position at top of the left. I was lucky to get a couple of low balls and I laid on a goal for Pat O'Connor. People often say I won that match but I don't think so. I was lucky on the day to lay on a few passes.'

Clare and Tipperary clashed in the league semi-final before a crowd of 11,000 at Limerick. Tipperary came out on top by the minimum margin, 2–13 to 2–12. I did not think switching Brendan Gilligan from centre-forward to full-forward was good, especially as he had been going well on the forty on Noel O'Dwyer. Commenting on the outcome of the game Fr Harry Bohan said: 'I am very disappointed as this is a game we let slip'.

'Clare Full-Back Line Cut to Shreds' reported *The Clare News* following Clare's exit from the 1979 championship at the hands of Limerick some weeks later. Limerick ran Clare ragged in the first half and led by 2–12 to 0–6 at the interval, but a tremendous Clare fight-back saw them come within a point of Limerick. Clare scored 4–6 in the second half with Michael Moroney having a tremendous game at centre-field. Brendan Vaughan commented afterwards that the team looked 'mentally tired' and 'the subs need a chance'. County secretary, Michael McTigue, added: 'We gave them too much of an interval lead. Their full-forward line was lethal and Clare showed great determination to come back.' The referee Frank Murphy of Cork declared it a 'super game' and said that the standard was higher than the Cork *v* Tipperary clash a week earlier.

Clare team that beat Limerick at the Gaelic grounds, February 1979
Back row l/r: Noel Casey, Enda O'Connor, Seán Hehir, Michael Moroney, Jackie O'Gorman,
Brendan Gilligan, Barry Smythe, Jim Power, Ger Loughnane; Front row l/r: Seán Stack, John
Callinan, Johnny McMahon, Seamus Durack, Michael Murphy, Pat O'Connor

FAREWELL TO TULLA AND THE 1970S

This defeat marked a downward turning point for this great team that had given such pleasure and excitement to all followers of hurling. They had once again brought Clare to the top table of hurling counties and maintained their position for a number of years. Delivering two league titles to victory-starved but loyal Clare supporters, they were agonisingly close to championship honours. Cork continued to be the bogeymen, but have Cork produced a team of such quality since? Anyway, championship success was not to be, but this team must certainly have been one of those to loom large in Anthony Daly's mind when he delivered his great speech amidst the emotion of Clare's eventual triumph in the 1995 All-Ireland. To my mind, their most outstanding achievement was to play hurling of the highest quality in a Clare jersey. They proved that Clare had no need to have any feelings of inferiority on the playing field and reclaimed the county's hurling pride, thereby reestablishing a standard for other Clare teams to follow.

Marvellous memories remain of Tulla, Thurles, Nowlan Park, everywhere they played; Colm Honan going deep into defence to recover and making long runs down the field; his free-taking seen at its best in the league final of 1977 when he continually kept Clare in front. Also, we had the great duels between Noel Casey and Limerick's Pat Hartigan, the great attacking play of John Callinan, and the splendid half-back line of Loughnane, Hehir and Stack. Jimmy Smyth holds this team in high regard:

> They had quality forwards in Noel Casey and John Callinan; Jimmy McNamara was a great forward and the O'Connors were great men. This was a great team, unlucky to lose to Cork in 1978 when you consider that John Horgan scored four points that would beat any team. It could have gone either way. I'm certain that if Clare beat Cork in 1978 they would have won the All-Ireland; they combined well. If ever a team gave us value, it was this team that contested three successive league finals and two Munster finals. Even then they were criticised – they wouldn't hold a candle to the 1955 team etc.– we meet this attitude and it has a devastating effect on players. The 1976–78 team laid the ghosts of former failures.

Who did Gerald McCarthy see as Clare's stars at that time? 'Clare have in Seamus Durack an exceptional goalie. Seán Stack is a magnificent hurler in the mould of the real purists, classical in his play, and I say this having hurled against him. Ger Loughnane is another fine defender who revels in the cut and thrust of battle and has given great service to his county.'

John Callinan remembers 1976 to 1978 as great years for Clare. 'We were taken to the heart of the country. The media expended a lot of time and resources on us, expecting us to make the breakthrough. Expectations were raised and we started getting to finals more frequently. I feel we were unlucky to come up against a fine Cork team.' Seamus Durack won the Hurler of the Year award in 1978, as did his fellow Feakle man Ger Loughnane in 1977. In an interview with John O'Shaughnessy in *The Sunday Press*, Seamus made this comment: 'What makes it more exciting for me is that the old enemy, Cork, Munster and All-Ireland champions, were overlooked. They have a legion of talented hurlers, and for a Clareman to get an award for the second year running is really something.'

The man who is associated most strongly with this team is Fr Harry Bohan. 'Everyone acknowledges the contribution of Seán Hehir, Ger Loughnane and Seán Stack, that these three were as good a half-back line as ever played. But I would say, in addition, that other powerful influences were Jackie O'Gorman, Mick Moroney, Noel Casey and John McMahon. The fact that we had youth blended with experience made a huge contribution to the team. We had a successful run with the Clare team in that they won two national leagues and we played in two Munster finals. We went almost unbeaten and there was a hurling fever around the county because of the success of the team. That team were consistently good and had automatic discipline. They hated being beaten. I believed they were the best and had to be treated as such.'

Justin McCarthy concludes: 'Clare didn't get the credit they deserved in those years, primarily because Cork won three in a row; Clare were top notch. Fr Bohan didn't get the credit he deserved either. He was an organiser, a manager and co-ordinator. A strong character, he had charisma and played a huge part in building the fortunes of the Clare team. He gave me an opportunity to come to Clare when I was let go in Cork and was big enough to get someone in on the hurling side of it. He played a tremendous role. It was a great opportunity for me to get involved with Clare; it was a great experience and I have no regrets.'

FIVE ALL-IRELANDS

It was beyond our wildest dreams.

MARGARET O'TOOLE

Never before have we had so much skill.

KITTY McNICHOLAS

Camogie was first organised in 1904 when the Camogie Association was founded but went into decline during the turbulent years 1917–1923. It was popular in Clare during the 1920s but records are very sketchy. The game received a shot in the arm when the very popular county board secretary Mick Hennessy re-established camogie in Clare in 1932. Other officers elected included John Lee (president), Mary Donnellan (vice-president) and Martina Griffin (secretary). A county board was formed in 1934 and clubs came into existence in places like Kilshanny, Doolin and Ballynacally, plus hurling strongholds like Newmarket-on-Fergus, Tulla, Ennis and Clooney.

Clooney, trained by Paddy Carmody, were a dominant force in the 1930s. Some of their most notable players included Babs Clune, Chris Markham and Annie Conheady. Annie Conheady (later O'Loughlin) told me about those times. 'We were very strong in Clooney and we won the county championship two or three times before Kilshanny took it from us. Later there was a separation in Clooney and Creevagh formed a team; we beat them in a county final replay.'

The county teams met with little success, losing to Kerry at the Showgrounds in 1934 and to the all-conquering Cork team in 1935. Clare then withdrew until about 1944. In that year they created history by winning the Munster senior championship, beating Cork and later Waterford by 3–1 to 3–0. Chris Markham scored Clare's entire tally of 3–1 and the side also included Carmel Waterstone, Dympna Davis and the captain Theresa McNamara.

Clare took on Dublin in the All-Ireland semi-final and, though heavily defeated, Dympna Davis was able to see the humorous side of it. 'When we played Dublin in 1944, it was the biggest laugh of all time. Our skirts were too big and we couldn't run in them as the field was all muck and wet. When we hit the muck we couldn't get out of it; we stuck. Kay Coady was the star player of the Dublin team. They wore skirts twelve to fourteen inches above the knee; The mini was nothing to them!'

The 1944 All-Ireland semi-final was the highlight of Clare's achievement in camogie around this time. It went into decline in the late 1940s, mainly due to emigration, and it wasn't until 1958 that the game was revived following a meeting in Ennistymon. Several teams were formed including Liscannor, Coláiste Muire (Ennis), Spanish Point and Bodyke. Many friendlies were organised before a championship proper was played in 1959. The league trophy was sponsored by Egan's of Tuam, with O'Doherty's of Kilrush putting up the championship trophy.

ÉIRE ÓG V KILLANENA

Feakle had a strong team in the late 1950s which included Claire Harrington, Eva

Bane and Liz Howard. The Killanena club was formed in 1959 by Mrs Broderick, Patie Broderick and Fr Liam Murray. Celia Brady and Nancy Brady of Flagmount joined the side. The dominant teams at the time were Killanena and Coláiste Muire, with Killanena capturing both league and championship in 1959. The league final took three games before Killanena defeated Coláiste Muire. This Egan cup final, refereed by Peg Loughnane, is still talked about by enthusiasts of the game. Another notable team in the early 1960s was the North Clare amalgamation side Cliffs of Moher. Killanena retained their championship title in 1960, defeating Cliffs of Moher by 4–1 to 1–0. In 1964 Kitty Murphy (Killanena) and Chris Doyle were honoured with senior inter-provincial selection for Munster, winning Gael Linn medals.

Éire Óg were the dominant senior camogie club during the late 1960s and early 1970s. In 1970 they retained the championship when they beat Killanena at Tulla by 2–2 to 1–1. The game was played at a cracking pace, with Pauline Ryan and Catherine Glynn getting on top at centre-field and giving forwards plenty of possession. Catherine was in great form scoring all of Éire Óg's 2–2. After the game Fr O'Keefe, chairman of the camogie board, presented the cup to Liz Scanlan. Éire Óg retained the title in 1971 when they had a big win over Kilmaley at Cusack Park before a large attendance.

Shannon put up a brave bid in 1972 but failed to stop Éire Óg winning their fourth in a row. The final score of 5–8 to 3–1 did scant justice to Shannon who had opened very well with a goal from Jenny Downes, but were gradually worn down by the experienced Ennis team who ran out deserving winners. Éire Óg's prominent players during these very successful years included Catherine and Margaret Glynn, Mary Griffin, Stephanie McCarthy and Freda and Betty Ryan. Many of the successful Clare team of 1974 came from Shannon and Éire Óg, including Bridie McGirl, Rose Kelleher and Eleece Fitzgibbon (Shannon) and Theresa McDonagh, Pauline Ryan and Margaret O'Toole (Éire Óg).

1974 ALL-IRELAND JUNIOR CHAMPIONS
In 1964 Clare's fortunes improved greatly when they won a four-county tournament involving Cork, Limerick and Waterford. The formation of Éire Óg and Wolfe Tone's in the late 1960s improved standards and in 1974 county board treasurer Michael Brennan was appointed team trainer, ushering in a new era. Michael drew up a panel of twenty-five and, though defeated by Limerick in their opening league game, they improved greatly. They trounced Tipperary 13–2 to 2–0 and had a big margin to spare over Kerry.

The Munster final against Limerick attracted huge interest and was heavily featured in *The Clare Champion* at the time. It was played in the Fair Green, Ennis and Clare got off to a great start with a Maureen Davoren goal. Limerick fought back but trailed by three goals to two at the interval. An opportunist goal by Clare's Eleece Fitzgibbon proved the match-winner, 4–0 to 3–1. Clare shot many wides in the semi-final at Ballinasloe but overcame Galway 2–1 to 0–3 when Maureen Davoren scored a great second-half goal from twenty yards. Teresa Duane scored all three of Galway's points.

The 1974 All-Ireland against Dublin at Croke Park produced a high standard of play and some delightful ground hurling. Mary Dolan opened the scoring for Clare after two minutes with a goal, but Dublin quickly equalised with a goal by Maura Sutton. In the second half, Mary Mahon set off on a great solo run to set up top scorer Maura Davoren for a goal. In a tight game Mary Griffin scored the winning goal

History making Clare Camogie team, 1974 [Junior champions]
Front row l/r: Maureen Kelly, Teresa McDonagh, Mary Griffin, Bridie McGirl, Anne Marie
O'Loughlin, Maura McNicholas [mascot], Margaret O'Toole, Catherine Glynn, Rose Kelleher,
Geraldine Crowe, Pauline Ryan; Back row l/r: Kitty McNicholas, Anne Marie Russell, Maureen
Saunders, Martina O'Grady, Maureen Davoren, Eleece Fitzgibbon, Mary Dolan, Claire
Harrington, Mary Mahon, Theresa Daly, Michael Brennan [manager]

to leave the final score Clare 3–2, Dublin 3–0. In her acceptance speech, which was entirely in Irish, team captain Margaret O'Toole felt that the introduction of Mary Griffin won the match for Clare.

Margaret told me how she became interested in camogie. 'I got my first hurley from my father when I was four and this sparked my interest. Later I played Munster Colleges with Salesian Convent, Cahercon. In second year I wrote an essay saying that my biggest wish in life would be to captain Clare to an All-Ireland victory. The club in Ballynacally had gone into decline because of emigration, so Michael Brennan asked me to sign for Éire Óg in 1972. At that time, Shannon and Éire Óg were the dominant clubs and supplied most of the players. Claire Harrington, Anne Harrington and Anne-Marie O'Loughlin came back from Dublin and provided a big boost. We had some very dedicated people working behind the scenes, like Michael Brennan, Jim and Kitty McNicholas, Mary O'Halloran and Paddy Duggan; they had great interest. It was a great outlet for me and a great social scene.

'There is a huge commitment involved if you want to compete at the highest level; we trained three nights a week and some of us used to travel down from Dublin to matches. We lost several Munster club games by a point including a Munster final; these were bitterly disappointing defeats. I remember one night at the Fair Green when we lost a game. There was no net and the November darkness had descended. We were convinced that the ball had gone under the bar for a goal, but the white flag went up. I remember going back to Dublin totally distraught and very disappointed.

'We never expected anything like the reception we got having won the All-

Ireland; the roads were lined from Ballycasey Cross to Shannon. We were put up on the back of a lorry and brought to Shannon, Newmarket and Clarecastle. The square in Ennis was thronged; it was beyond our wildest dreams. A lot of time and effort went in to preparing for that All-Ireland but winning made everything worthwhile.'

1974 CLARE JUNIOR ALL-IRELAND WINNERS

Maureen Kelly
(Éire Óg)

Anne Marie O'Loughlin
(Dal gCais)

Rose Kelleher	Margaret O'Toole	Claire Harrington
(Shannon)	(Éire Óg)	(Celtic, Dublin)
Theresa McDonagh	Catherine McNicholas	Maureen Davoren
(Éire Óg)	(Éire Óg)	(Celtic, Dublin)
Mary Dolan	Mary Mahon	Pauline Ryan
(Shannon)	(Muskerry, Cork)	(Éire Óg)

Eleece Fitzgibbon
(Shannon)

Subs: Maureen Saunders (Éire Óg), Catherine Glynn (Éire Óg), Mary Griffin (Éire Óg), Theresa Daly (Shannon), Anne Marie Russell (Éire Óg), Bridie McGirl (Shannon), Geraldine Crowe (Éire Óg), Martina O'Grady (Éire Óg).

A very strong Éire Óg team, with Catherine McNicholas, Pauline Glynn, Anne-Marie Russell, Catherine Glynn and Theresa McDonagh, continued to dominate the club scene, winning the championship for the seventh consecutive time. Another important factor in the development of Clare camogie during the late 1970s was the inauguration of a very successful primary schools competition. As many as eighteen teams took part, with the Flan Garvey-coached Inagh team proving successful.

COLLEGE CAMOGIE
Well-known hurling and camogie coach Mary Hanly praises the contribution made by Sr Angela at Coláiste Muire. 'We reached the Munster Colleges final in 1969 but lost to St Al's of Cork by two points. We had a strong team which included Louise O'Connor, Betty McMahon and a sister of Brian Cody from Kilkenny. The team was put together by Sr Angela – she was fantastic'. Coaching at Coláiste Muire was later carried on by Kitty McNicholas.

Similar work by Colm Honan, Fr McNamara and Jim Cooney at St Patrick's Comprehensive School Shannon began to pay off when St Patrick's captured the junior title in 1978. Added to this, the Clare minors made history by winning the provincial championship. St Patrick's remained a strong force throughout this period, reaching several colleges' finals. In 1980 they lost to the eventual All-Ireland Champions, North Presentation, Cork but finally won the All-Ireland senior schools' title in 1982.

In the early 1980s Ennis Vocational School also became a major force in colleges competition, contesting a couple of deciders and eventually defeating Thomastown of Kilkenny at Banagher in the 1983 All-Ireland final. Ennis Vocational led by four points at half-time thanks to goals from Patricia Rynne, plus top-class displays by Jackie Moloney in goal, Mary Naughton, Marie Gormley, Bridie Roche and Monica Morgan.

A team under the guidance of Kitty McNicholas won the Munster U–18 title in 1978. Anne Gallery, Catherine O'Connell, Mary Howard and Claire Jones were amongst the stars of this team.

1981 ALL-IRELAND JUNIOR CHAMPIONS

After a lapse of seven years Clare regained the junior championship in 1981. Along the way they were held to a draw by Limerick in the Munster final at Shannon, Clare 1–1 to Limerick 0–4, with Claire Jones getting both of the Banner county's scores. A much-improved side defeated Limerick by 4–4 to 2–3 at Adare. Limerick looked in control, with goals by Agnes Sheehy, but Clare came back into the game. Mary Howard was in great form at centre-back and gave the forwards a plentiful supply of the ball. Goals from Carmel Wall (2) and Lourda Fox saw Clare to victory. Clare had the narrowest of victories over Kildare in the All-Ireland semi-final at Clane by 1–5 to 1–4. 'Lourda points Clare into another All-Ireland Final' was *The Clare Champion* headline the following week. Others to do well were Mary Carey in goal, Carmel Wall, Martina Beegan and Claire Jones.

Three members of the successful 1981 Camogie team pictured at St Senan's school, Shannon Caroline O'Meara, Claire Jones, Martina Beegan, with Margaret O'Toole, captain of the 1974 team, on the left

127

In the All-Ireland final against Antrim Clare got off to a great start with a goal in the opening minute. Veronica Casey sent a long clearance which was gathered by Lourda Fox, who drove a great shot to the net past Karen Coyles; Fox had an outstanding game with a personal tally of 2–1. Antrim came back strongly in the second half and reduced the defecit to two points but Clare finished strongly; this was a feature of their 1981 campaign.

The management and team had put in a huge effort under trainer Fr McNamara and mentor Kitty McNicholas, with over forty training sessions held over the season. At a reception held in Ennis for the victorious team, organised by Clare county council, Haulie Daly, Tadhg McNamara and Michael Guerin paid tribute to all concerned.

1986 All-Ireland Junior Champions

Clare won their second junior title of the decade in fine style, beating Limerick by nine points in a replay, then Cork and Roscommon to qualify for the final. This campaign drew up splendid performances from Patricia Ryan, Helen Cusack and Pauline O'Brien amongst others. In the final at Croke Park, inspirational performances from Catherine O'Loughlin and team captain Maura McNicholas led them to victory over a strong Kildare team by 1–13 to 3–4. An interesting feature of this game is that Maura McNicholas with 1–7 and Catherine O'Loughlin 0–6 were the only players to score for Clare. The New Ireland Cup was presented to Maura McNicholas. In her speech she paid tribute to the work done over the season by team coach Kevin 'Trixie' Twomey. In the senior final played afterwards, former Clare star Claire Jones won a senior medal with Kilkenny in their victory over Dublin.

In 1987 Catherine Molloy, Patricia O'Grady and Catherine O'Loughlin were honoured with selection on the Munster team, the latter receiving the *Cork Examiner* sports award for camogie. Other highlights included Anne O'Dwyer of Bodyke winning the skills competition at Feile na nGael and Kitty McNicholas refereeing

All-Ireland Junior champions, 1986
Pictured with Kitty McNicholas and Kevin 'Trixie' Twomey

the junior final between Armagh and Kildare. In 1990 Wolfe Tones swept the board at under-age level with star player Debbie McDonagh honoured with selection on the Clare team at U–16, minor, junior and senior levels.

INTERMEDIATE TITLES

The strength and interest in camogie at the moment is evident in the fact that the county has won two intermediate titles in the 1990s. The first of these came in 1991 when the Banner overcame Dublin at Ennis by 1-8 to 1-5. Clare were rocked early on by a Ruth Lyons goal but, inspired by Moira McMahon and Debbie McDonagh, they fought back to win the day. After the game, camogie board president Brídín Ní Mhaolagáin presented the Corn Úna Ní Phuirseál to the Clare captain Frances Phelan. At least seven survivors from 1993 featured in the successful 1995 team when Clare regained the title by beating Tipperary at Toomevara. Once again Clare came from six points down to snatch a victory. The marksmanship of Catherine O'Loughlin plus Patricia Moloney's goal and the skill of substitute Edel Arthur were the highlights of this game. A feature of these intermediate successes has been the large number of players from the Wolfe Tone's club.

Jim and Kitty McNicholas have been involved in camogie since they came to Clare twenty-five years ago, Jim from Mayo and Kitty from Galway. They spoke to me about how the game has developed during the years of their involvement. Kitty played at midfield on the All-Ireland winning team of 1974. 'We had huge crowds following us in the mid-1970s and we had a belief in ourselves. We went senior in 1975 and drew with Wexford, but they beat us in the replay; there's a big gap between junior and senior. Cork and Kilkenny were a couple of steps above us and we didn't have the pool to gather from as we had only eight clubs; today we have twenty-five.

'Never before have we had so much skill; now we have skill all over the team because they are starting earlier. There are lots of girls who want to play but there is a lack of personnel at the organisation end of things. However, the future is very bright from the point of view of the numbers playing. Recently three new clubs were formed in Parteen, Broadford and Meelick and we're working on clubs in Bridgetown and Ballynacally.'

1993 All-Ireland Intermediate Camogie champions

THE RISING TIDE
(1980–1987)

When we play for our county, we play for our club, and we don't let our club down.

TOMMY GUILFOYLE

There were no hayshakers.

ENDA O'CONNOR

Cusack Memorial Park re-opened on 29 June 1980. At this time there was a separate county hurling board and its chairman Brendan Vaughan was the main driving force behind the re-development scheme. 'Without him we'd still be in the Dark Ages,' says former board chairman John Hanly. 'I'd never have re-developed Cusack Park for the simple reason that I wasn't geared that way. I was pre-occupied with coaching. Brendan was the man for the job; he was a tireless worker and was stubborn in his attitude over the park.' Galway hurlers were invited to play Clare on re-opening day, with Clare winning by 2–15 to 0–13.

Brendan Vaughan gave me the background to the re-development scheme. 'I decided I'd take on Cusack Park as my particular project. The turf was soggy and the soil was bad, so we came to the conclusion that it wasn't viable to re-develop the park. The secretary Kieran Kennedy and I tried every possible site in Ennis but they all proved unsuitable. We had a site almost bought near the Showgrounds, but we decided against it at the last minute; it was a split decision.

'We then decided in 1977 to re-develop Cusack Park and take on the problem of drainage. We did a lot of fund-raising and the interest-free loan scheme (£100 from each investor), raised £120,000 – this was the backbone of the thing. Kieran Kennedy and I had a good committee, including the late Martin O'Loughlin, a link with the old Cusack Park 1936 committee. I stayed on as chairman until it was finished.'

ÉIRE ÓG v NEWMARKET

The 1980 county final between Éire Óg and Newmarket was probably the best final since 1973. Newmarket dominated the earlier exchanges but Pat Lynch was introduced at wing-forward at half time; this helped to sway the game towards Éire Óg as his speed was a vital factor. He had not been included in the starting line-up as he had just returned from the United States.

Colm Mahon was also on the Éire Óg team. 'Maybe if it hadn't been Newmarket it might not have been as good. Newmarket players like Gus Lohan and Paddy McNamara were all household names; they had done it all. Martin Nugent was outstanding with a personal tally of 3–3 from play. I didn't realise in 1980 what it meant to win a senior championship; I wasn't old enough to appreciate it. But it was great for the senior players like Joe Barry, Tony Roche and Paddy Kelly; they'd been around since 1975; the pressure was on them and, naturally, they rejoiced. Unfortunately, we couldn't represent Clare in the Munster club championship, because the Banner club had assisted us with players like Barry Smythe, Seán Lynch and Dermot Delaney.'

Seán Heaslip was another member of the Éire Óg team. 'Colm Flynn trained us. With a group of lads together who could hurl, combined with the experience of Colm's training, we were flying it. It was a good county final. Newmarket had beaten us in a tournament final a few weeks before and I'm sure they felt they could beat us again. We had a good backroom in Michael Hanrahan, Brother Cahill, Paddy Duggan and Vincent Loftus. Fr Bohan gave a great speech in the Forester's Club a few days earlier.'

In 1981, Colm Mahon was a spectator at the quarter-final of the county championship when the recently formed junior club, The Banner, gave Newmarket a fright. 'The worst thing we did was actually watch the game because Newmarket caught us in the semi-final. The Banner played great in that quarter-final and it was a pity that they didn't beat Newmarket. It would have been some clash, The Banner and Éire Óg, and would have recalled the great era of the town leagues.'

THE BANNER CLUB

The Banner club was formed in 1976 by a small dedicated group who felt that there was a need for a second club in Ennis. These included Tony Maher, Paddy Gilligan, Tony Blake, Seán 'Nobbers' Kelly and Frank O'Malley. Apart from competing at juvenile and adult level, they organised trips to London in 1979 and 1981 to play Clare-based London team Desmond's.

In 1979 the Banner defeated the London club in a high-scoring game by 7–6 to 4–13. The Desmond's team included former Clare hurler Mickey Burke (Whitegate), John and Michael Considine (Ennis), Malachy Hehir and Miko Cullinan from Dysart. For the Banner, Brenny Pyne, Haulie Russell, Pat O'Connor (Tubber) and Jackie Hynes excelled.

Tony Maher outlined for me why he became involved with the club's formation. 'The basic idea was to cater for youngsters who weren't getting games because there was only one club in Ennis. Naturally Éire Óg haven't the personnel to look after four or five teams simultaneously; we certainly weren't formed to upset Éire Óg or go against them. The ideal situation that I'd like to see in Ennis is a town board and about three minor clubs running at the same time. I can't see why we can't have at least seventy-five players coming out to play juvenile and minor hurling. The problem comes down to manpower. Ideally, to run a team, one would need at least five directly involved, with eight to ten others involved on the periphery.'

Michael Nihill, who had initially been involved with St John's, felt strongly about the need to give more players an opportunity to play: 'I remember being in Tulla in the mid-1970s at an under-age fixture between Éire Óg and Feakle. I looked across at the Éire Óg dugout and I saw that they had as many subs as they had on the field of play: I felt that this was not promoting hurling; these young fellows on the sideline were never going to get a game.

'At the next committee meeting I mentioned my thoughts on the structure of the GAA in Ennis and I argued that Ennis should be split into three areas with a town board. I just couldn't see the GAA being promoted for the GAA; I saw the GAA being promoted for Éire Óg, which wasn't my ideology. Any club that takes fifteen subs to a fixture is only antagonising people. The ironic thing is that Feakle won four U–21 crowns in a row a few years later. My philosophy of the GAA is – being small and having an identity is much more important than parading fifteen subs and going nowhere.'

Clare lost to Cork in the opening match of their 1979–80 league campaign. New blood was introduced to the panel, including Flan Quilligan, Martin Nugent and Donal Hassett, plus the recalled Tim Ryan and Noel Ryan. 1980 was the final year that Clare played the lion's share of their home league games at Tulla; their last games there included wins over an emergent Offaly team and Limerick. Sadly, due to incidents after the Clare *v* Offaly game, both counties were found guilty of misconduct and had to play all of their league games away for the 1980–81 season as a result.

Noel Ryan was selected at full-forward in the first round of the 1980 championship against Waterford. He proved to be a successful choice, scoring 2–2, but Clare failed to Limerick in the next round by 3–13 to 2–9, as the forward line flopped. In September 1980, Fr Harry Bohan was re-elected manager by a big majority.

Clare opened their 1980–81 league campaign with an away fixture at Castletowngeoghegan, where they had a narrow win over Westmeath. This campaign also included a trip to Casement Park in Belfast to play Antrim on 9 November. On this occasion, the team and a small number of supporters flew from Shannon and were well looked after before the game by the Antrim officials. Clare's only defeat in this campaign was at the hands of Kilkenny at Nowlan Park, so they qualified for a league quarter-final place but lost to Waterford in Thurles.

Many newcomers had been introduced to the team, including Gerry McInerney, Colm Mahon, Seán Heaslip and Michael Deasy. Seán Heaslip played at full-forward throughout the league campaign. 'I wasn't picked initially for the 1981 championship as I had lost confidence. Ger Loughnane proposed at a meeting that we change togs from white to blue for the championship; it would give the supporters an added buzz! On the way down, I was told that I was on as Seán Hehir was ill; so Martin Meehan went to the backs and I was given the centre-forward position.'

A new-look side, with Declan Coote and Tony Nugent at centre-field and Leo Quinlan at corner-forward, confounded the critics to turn the tables on Waterford, 3–14 to 2–14, and qualify for another tilt at Cork. In the semi-final, Clare gave one of their greatest performances in any championship, defeating Cork by 2–15 to 2–13. Declan Coote and Tony Nugent gave a great display at centre-field, where they dominated John Fenton and Pat Moylan, thereby giving a plentiful supply of the ball to the forwards who were in superb form. Seán Stack at centre-back also excelled.

For the subsequent clash with Limerick in the Munster final the Clare management placed their confidence in some of the more experienced players, such as Colm Honan and Pat O'Connor, who were introduced during the game. Colm Mahon feels that there may have been too much of an overlap between the hurling careers of those on the way up and those on the way back down from the peak of their abilities. 'At the time I thought that many of the younger players weren't given a fair chance. Michael Deasy for example was flying it.' James Shanahan supports this view. 'Michael Deasy played great stuff in several league campaigns, but I don't believe that he ever started a championship match. He'd be back the following year trying harder. You'd admire those guys a lot more than the guys that knew they'd be in.'

MINORS MAKE HISTORY

After accounting for Cork and Waterford, Clare had an historic win over Tipperary to capture their first ever Munster minor championship in 1981. Great work was put into the preparation of the team, with the selectors Seán Hehir, John Hanly and Paddy Duggan holding trials throughout the winter months. Val Donnellan, who missed the semi-final, returned for the final, replacing Martin Leamy. With the sides level 1–7 to 1–7 at the interval, Clare took the lead in the opening minutes of the second half with goals from Victor O'Loughlin and John Lynch. When Tipperary came back to level it, it took a series of excellent points from Val Donnellan to swing it Clare's way 3–13 to 3–11.

However, the All-Ireland semi-final in Croke Park proved to be another sad disappointment. Clare failed to produce their true form and fell to a very strong Galway side by 3–14 to 3–8. John Hanly feels that it was another lost opportunity. 'We threw away the semi-final against Galway. We got to Dublin late, but as well as this, their goal-keeper Tommy Coen made a series of great saves.'

Clare Minor team, Munster champions 1981
Back row l/r: Val Donnellan, Alan Cunningham, John O'Grady, Danny Chaplin, Michael Guilfoyle, Brian O'Connell, Brendan McNamara, Gerry Barry; Front row l/r: Tommy Neville, John Lynch, Eoin McMahon, Victor O'Loughlin, John Moroney, Julian Crimmins, Andrew Walsh

1981 MUNSTER FINAL

On the other side of the 1981 championship Limerick, the holders, defeated Tipperary to qualify for the Munster final against Clare. In the Munster final a quick Joe McKenna goal was cancelled out by a great goal from Noel Ryan at full-forward. However, Limerick prevailed on a score of 3–12 to 2–9, with Limerick's Joe McKenna clocking up a personal tally of 3–3. Many of the Clare players failed to play to form on the day, but the half-backs did well under extreme pressure. Barry Smythe was outstanding at corner-back, giving Eamon Cregan a roasting. Gerry McInerney, who scored a great goal from a penalty, was unlucky to be taken off and Noel Ryan put Leonard Enright under a lot of pressure.

Seán Stack feels that Clare had a good chance of winning that game. 'Tony Nugent and Declan Coote were playing marvellous hurling at centre-field. We fell behind three times, but when we fell behind for the fourth time it was the death knell. John Ryan played grand in the semi-final; it's very easy to talk in hindsight. I had a bad game at centre-back and my opponent John Flanagan did all the simple things well; he laid in on top of me. If I had played a better game, Joe McKenna might not have got the service inside either. That was one we were good enough to win.'

In the view of *The Clare Champion* reporter, 'It was unfair on John Ryan, as he wasn't experienced enough to hold McKenna. Smyth should have been moved to full-back or else Jim Power introduced. Limerick's close hurling had a detrimental effect on the Claremen.'

For John Callinan, '1981 was my biggest disappointment. The fact that we had beaten Cork made us feel that we had an obligation to win the Munster title, though Limerick were a good team in 1980 and 1981. We were conscious of how big it was to beat Cork. On a personal level I was playing my best hurling, but they got a lot of soft scores. It was a changed team since 1978. Barry Smythe, Leo Quinlan, Martin Meehan and Gerry McInerney had come from the successful St Flannan's teams of 1976 and 1979, but the county team seemed to disintegrate as quickly as it came together. That team had great potential and all of those players had good pedigree. As Enda O'Connor would say, "there were no hayshakers". 1982 was a very low period and Cork easily beat us in the championship. The problem with trying to make the breakthrough is when you come close to the plateau; if you don't succeed, you fall back below where you started. Hopefully, that's gone now.'

Clare Munster finalists, 5 July 1981
Back row l/r: Seán Stack, Ger Loughnane, Tony Nugent, Noel Ryan, Seán Hehir, John Ryan, Declan Coote, Enda O'Connor; Front row l/r: Barry Smythe, Gerry McInerney, Tommy Keane, Seamus Durack, Martin Meehan, Leo Quinlan, John Callinan

DUTCH TRIP

Prior to the 1982 championship the Clare and Wexford senior teams flew to Holland to play an exhibition game sponsored by Heineken. The Irish party was warmly received at Schipol airport by officials of the Amsterdam Hurley Club and there was an attendance of about 4,000 for the game. Colm Mahon was a member of the Clare contingent. 'The Dutch enjoyed it. We were wined and dined there and it was a great laugh. I enjoyed the Wexford lads and I've met some of them since, such as Jimmy Houlihan, Mick Jacob, George O'Connor and Martin and John Quigley.'

According to 'An Spailpín Fánach', writing in the *1982 GAA Yearbook*, 'There was a nice degree of pageantry about the whole event, including the dropping of three parachutists beaming greetings from blue skies on the well-manicured turf, which was ideal for hurling. Emulation is a nice form of flattery and, after the game, it was a revelation to see the young Dutch boys borrowing hurleys and having a go at the art of hurling, not too unsuccessfully either.'

1982–83 LEAGUE

Clare had a great run in the 1982–83 league. In fact, this campaign produced a series of great games, including a one-point win over Kilkenny at Cusack Park, 4–9 to 3–11. Among those who shone were James Shanahan and Pat Morey, who scored three goals from play. The game produced a thrilling climax and both sides received a standing ovation at Cusack Park. The following game against Cork at Páirc Uí Chaoimh was also an epic encounter, with Gerry McInerney scoring nine points and having one of his best games ever in the Clare colours. However, Cork prevailed on this occasion.

A late rally against Wexford saw Clare deny the Slaneysiders 3–7 to 0–15 in another excellent tie at Ennis. This earned Clare a divisional play-off against Wexford at Thurles a week later, with Wexford finishing a point ahead on this occasion.

OIREACHTAS VICTORIES

A new-look Clare defeated Offaly 1–14 to 2–7 to qualify for the final of the Oireachtas Cup against Limerick on 14 November 1982. It was Clare's first final appearance in the competition since losing to Kilkenny in 1967, and they overcame Limerick 3–9 to 2–9 at Ennis before a crowd of 12,000. Tony Nugent and James Shanahan were on top at centre-field, and recent newcomers Bernard Carroll, Michael Quaine and Kieran McNamara were also impressive.

'Brave Show as Limerick Lose' wrote Cormac Liddy in the *Limerick Leader*. 'When you shoot ten wides in the first half, you can hardly expect to succeed and that was what happened to Limerick in this thrilling Oireachtas hurling final at Cusack Park on Sunday, when Clare held on for a victory that was a little flattering.'

Clare retained the title on 6 November 1983, coming back from a six-point deficit at the interval to defeat Kilkenny 1–12 to 1–11. Goal-keeper Denis Corry, Seamus Fitzpatrick and Declan Coote were the most prominent contributors to Clare's victory on this occasion, with Coote giving a great display at centre-field. A Christy Heffernan goal from a penalty just before half-time put Kilkenny into a commanding 1–9 to 1–3 lead, but some great points from Seamus Fitzpatrick and an inspirational score from Tony Nugent brought Clare back into the game.

James Shanahan was introduced to the panel by selectors Fr McNamara, Kevin 'Trixie' Twomey and Robert Frost. He played on both Oireachtas-winning teams

Tony Nugent receives the Man of the Match award from John Morgan, as team captain John Minogue holds the Thomas Ashe trophy for the Oireachtas cup final, 1982

and became one of the most prominent players of the 1980s. He joined the team at the age of twenty-four. 'I didn't play earlier as my work took me to the United States a lot. I was also a bit wild; times were different then and there was more happening.'

John Minogue of Scariff was the popular choice for captain and remembers these Oireachtas finals. 'The Oireachtas was a major competition and Clare were playing well, getting to league quarter-finals and semi-finals. Seán Stack, Seán Hehir, Ger Loughnane, Pat and Enda O'Connor were great crowd-pullers. We played 1981 Munster champions Limerick in the 1982 final. About 12,000 attended.'

BREAKTHROUGH FOR SIXMILEBRIDGE

After many near-misses, Sixmilebridge won their first senior championship in 1977, beating neighbours Kilkishen 1–6 to 1–5 in the county final, with Michael White getting the winning point. Former Bridge hurler Seán Meehan saw the score in slow motion. 'Michael White's point was hanging in the air for what seemed like an eternity. I thought it would never go over.'

From there, Sixmilebridge reached the Munster club final at their first attempt, drawing with St Finbarr's 3–5 to 3–5 before losing to the Cork side in the replay. They regained the Clare championship at Tulla on 29 September, 1979 by beating the amalgamation side St Brendan's, a union of Kilmaley and St Joseph's, by 5–11 to 0–9. To be fair to St Brendan's, who included Martin Meehan, Joe Griffey, P. J. Purcell, Con Haugh and Tommy Keane, they did not do themselves justice in the final. Sixmilebridge were powered by Noel Casey, Pat Morey, Gerry McInerney, Flan McInerney and goal-keeper Mick O'Shea, and romped home to take their second senior title.

The drawn and replayed county finals of 1982 and 1983 between Éire Óg and Sixmilebridge were amongst the best in modern times. The drawn final of 1982, 2–11 to 2–11, produced some great scores. Noel Ryan's opening goal for Éire Óg from a Michael Chandler pass, some good points from John Lynch of Sixmilebridge and Éire Óg's Seán and Pat Lynch, plus a disallowed goal by P. J. Fitzpatrick of the Bridge, were amongst the highlights of the first half.

The second half saw some fine hurling served up with both sides enjoying dominant spells before Pat Lynch's superb goal brought the crowd to their feet. Lynch gained possession on the wing and weaved his way by a couple of tackles before cutting inside on a forty yard solo run through the middle, opening up the defence and sending a pile driver to the corner of the net. But a late goal from Peter Golden and a free pointed by Flan Quilligan gave Sixmilebridge a deserved draw. Pat Lynch was awarded man of the match.

The replay took place in a downpour on 26 September, 1982 and Sixmilebridge raced into a 2–4 to nil lead before a late first-half goal from Seán Lynch signalled an Éire Óg revival. Éire Óg came out for the second half a transformed side and, with fast ground hurling, wore down Sixmilebridge. A Pat Lynch goal, almost a replica of the one in the drawn game, signalled the end for the Bridge on a score of 3–8 to 2–9. Pete Barry of Éire Óg received the man of the match award and Tony Nugent accepted the Hamilton cup, reviving memories for the more senior followers, who recollected his father Matt lifting the same cup in 1958 as a member of the great St Joseph's team.

This comeback was probably the high point of this fine Éire Óg side which included several sets of brothers, Michael and Noel Ryan, Colm, Francie and Paschal Mahon, Seán and Pat Lynch, Martin and Tony Nugent, Seán and Francis Heaslip and Joe and Pete Barry.

Colm Mahon reckons that the tussles over the years between Éire Óg and Sixmilebridge produced good quality hurling, especially the county finals of 1982, 1983 and 1992 as well as the semi-final of 1990. 'I remember Pat Lynch's goal against the Bridge in the drawn final of 1982. It was one of the best goals ever scored in Cusack Park.' For Seán Heaslip, 'the Bridge seem to have something extra built in and Gerry McInerney has that bit extra.'

THE 'HONEYMOON' FINAL

As in 1982, the 1983 final also ended in a draw between Sixmilebridge and Éire Óg. Controversy raged over the fixture for the replay as some of the Sixmilebridge players had arranged holidays and at least two were due to go on honeymoon, so the club refused to play before 6 November. 'Éire Óg to be Awarded the Championship', headlined *The Clare Champion*. The county board awarded the title to Éire Óg, but Éire Óg chairman Michael Brennan announced that the Ennis club would not accept the cup in this way. The championship was declared null and void.

However, the game went ahead on the bank holiday Monday 31 October, with a sharper Sixmilebridge side making no mistake this time and taking their third senior title by 1–10 to 1–7 in a sporting game. Noel O'Gorman was awarded man of the match. Seán Stack says that he got tremendous satisfaction from the defeat of Éire Óg in the 1983 replay, but the attitude displayed by Éire Óg is also praised and acknowledged by Flan Quilligan. 'Éire Óg showed tremendous sportsmanship in 1983 when they refused to accept the cup for the famous honeymoon final.'

Sixmilebridge retained the senior championship in 1984, beating a luckless Clarecastle side by a point, before going on to take their first ever Munster club title.

Seán Stack with the Munster club trophy, 1984
L/r: Gerry Murray, Martin Murray, Danny Chaplin, Seán Stack, Paddy Meehan, John Chaplin, Noel O'Gorman

Along the way, they beat St Finbarr's of Cork by 2–10 to 1–7 and Patrickswell by 4–10 to 2–6 in the final itself. Seán Stack holds that Sixmilebridge team in high regard. 'It's not that we had the best individual hurlers in 1984, but as a team we were very hard to beat. We had workers and solid guys who were committed to each other. Pat Chaplin, P. J. Fitzpatrick and Tommy Morey were good forwards and we had a few exceptional players. The biggest break we got was to draw St Finbarr's at Páirc Uí Chaoimh. If we played them in Sixmilebridge, we may not have been as effective; we played with total abandon.'

CLARECASTLE
Gerard O'Loughlin began playing senior hurling with Clarecastle in 1984. 'We reached the county final in 1984. Our team was very well prepared, but we lost to

Action from the 1983 county final replay
James Keogh [SMB] is blocked down by Michael Chandler [ÉO] with Seán Lynch in support.
Frannie Heaslip is in the background

Sixmilebridge by a point, though we had led by five points with a few minutes to go. It was typical Clarecastle at the time. The preparation in 1984 was down to two men, Michael Slattery and Paddy "Jack" Moloney. Michael Slattery was involved throughout those years and it was he got the interest going around this time.

'The decade prior to that had been lean enough for us. We won the Clare cup in 1983 after three great games with Tubber. That Clarecastle team had great skill and a great level of fitness'. Team-mate Tommy Howard agrees with this. 'The Clarecastle team of 1984 (county final) gave the best exhibition of hurling by a Clarecastle team during my years with the club.'

The centenary county final of 1984 was due to be played in Carron, the birth-place of Michael Cusack, but the arrangement fell through and the finalists of 1986, Clarecastle and O'Callaghan's Mills agreed unanimously to play the 1986 final there. The attendance of only 3,500 was low for a final. Clarecastle led by eight points to four at half time, but O'Callaghan's Mills fought back strongly in the early part of the second half in a tense struggle.

Clarecastle were mindful of the fact that they had lost a lot of finals in recent years, notably 1973 and 1984, but a George Power goal five minutes from time gave them breathing space. This was followed by a last-minute goal by Victor O'Lough-lin to give the Magpies the championship by 2–11 to 0–7. Victor's brother Gerard recalls: 'The pitch was tight and, as we had many young players like Paddy Quinn, Pat Tuohy and Ken Morrissey, who liked the open spaces, it didn't really suit us, though 2–11 to 0–7 was rather flattering.'

Full–back Anthony Scanlon accepted the Hamilton Cup on behalf of Clarecastle.

The late Aidan Tuttle speaking to three long-serving Clarecastle players after the 1986 county final
L/r: Dermot FitzGerald, Paschal Russell, Paul Higgins

It was a great day for the manager Paddy Moloney, selectors Oliver Plunkett and Paul Higgins and players such as Paschal Russell and Dermot Fitzgerald who had seen a lot of disappointments in the Clarecastle colours since their last championship success in 1970. They followed up with tremendous wins over Mount Sion (Waterford) and St Brendan's (Ardfert) in the Munster club championship, but failed to a Noel O'Dwyer-inspired Borrisoleigh side by 1–13 to 1–9 in the final.

Clarecastle retained the championship at Cusack Park in 1987 before a huge attendance, beating the emerging Feakle team by 0–15 to 0–11. On the way to the decider, Clarecastle had to stave off a marathon session with the 1985 winners Kilmaley before winning out 3–12 to 2–10.

KILMALEY

Kilmaley made a historic breakthrough in 1985 by becoming the first team promoted from intermediate ranks to win the senior championship in over a quarter of a century. Their achievement is all the greater considering that they defeated the then Munster club champions Sixmilebridge in a semi-final replay. Many felt that Kilmaley had lost their chance the first day, but they accounted for a very strong and experienced Éire Óg side in the final.

Kilmaley were probably underestimated, though I don't know why considering that their team included many of the defeated St Brendan's finalists of 1979, including Martin D'Arcy, Paddy Hill, Gerry Pyne, Johnsey Mungovan and Joe Griffey. They also had leading inter-county players in Tommy Keane, Martin Meehan and Seamus Fitzpatrick. The success of the side originated with a successful juvenile team of the early seventies, whom I saw play a very attractive brand of hurling. I was also familiar with some of these players through their involvement with colleges hurling in the local CBS and Vocational School, including Tom McGann, Joe Griffey, Gerry O'Connor and Paddy Hill.

CLARECASTLE V TUBBER
The Clare cup final of 1983 was a memorable affair involving Clarecastle and Tubber. One hundred and eighty minutes of tremendous hurling was played before the Magpies won *The Clare Champion* cup by 2–12 to 2–9. These three games threw up some of the most skilful and wholehearted hurling seen in Clare for many years. The second game was played at Cusack Park on 13 November 1983. It was a classic, with Pascal Russell, Haulie Russell, Tommy Howard and Barney Lynch outstanding for Clarecastle and Noel Earley, Noel O'Grady, Don O'Loughlin and Pat O'Connor giving all for the North Clare side.

NEAR MISSES
Clare fell at the hands of Tipperary in the 1983 championship, losing a closely-fought tie at the Gaelic Grounds by 2–11 to 1–11. The sides were level on six occasions but the winners finished strongly, scoring three points in the final seven minutes. A wonderful effort from Enda O'Connor went unrewarded in the dying moments as the Tipperary goal-keeper John Sheedy brought off a great save. Nicholas English caused numerous problems for Clare. It was Tipperary's first victory in the senior championship since 1973 and signalled the beginning of a new era for them.

The Ford centenary (open draw) championship was introduced in 1984 and Clare reached the quarter final against Cork at Thurles on 6 May. Jim O'Sullivan of *The Cork Examiner* takes up the story:

> There was never any real doubt about the outcome of the Ford Cup at a deserted Semple Stadium yesterday, for the reason that the winners Cork were invariably the most competent side. By no means was their display over-impressive, but by comparison with Clare's it had more to recommend it. Tomás Mulcahy was called in at centre-forward; he had the distinction of having more successes against Seán Stack than any Cork player over the last few seasons.

However, Clare's form improved greatly and they had a one-point victory over Waterford in the first round of the Munster championship, 0–15 to 2–8, to qualify for a tussle with Tipperary at Thurles. Tipperary overran Clare in the first twenty minutes and led by nine points to one after twenty-six minutes, mainly due to the brilliance of Nicky English, who scored a series of magnificent points. Suddenly, Clare came to life and had the better of the last ten minutes after English had been curbed by Stack.

This great second half fight-back also included two goals from Gerry McInerney, one from a penalty after Kieran McNamara was brought down. This put Clare ahead 2–11 to 0–15 with time running out. The referee awarded another penalty, this time to Tipperary after a Clare defender fouled the ball. It was saved by Seán Stack but Liam Maher, coming in from the corner, connected beautifully with the rebound to put his team into the Munster final on a final score of 1–15 to 2–11.

John Minogue remembers 1984 and 1985 as unlucky years. 'In 1984, Liam Maher got a last-second goal from a rebound after Ger Loughnane went off injured. Tipperary should have won the Munster championship title afterwards. In 1985, Nicholas English got a last-minute point at Cusack Park to draw 1–8 to 1–8. We were playing very well and we reached the national league final of 1984–85, beating Kilkenny in a quarter-final replay and Galway in the semi-final. Gerry McInerney was injured in the game against Kilkenny and it knocked him out of hurling for a long time. He was flying, our leading forward at the time. Limerick beat us well in the league final at Thurles; Pat McCarthy at full-forward and Shane Fitzgibbon scored about 3–6 between them.'

Paddy Hickey wrote in the *Evening Herald*: 'The Clare crowd in the official attendance of 20,700 were stunned into silence.' Clare manager Fr Michael McNamara added: 'We never recovered from the early Limerick goals. Limerick played inspired hurling and, unfortunately for us, they improved as the game went on. Two weeks later, Tipperary beat Clare in the Ford open draw by 3–13 to 1–12 at the Gaelic Grounds.

Clare showed a huge improvement when they took on Tipperary in the 1985 championship at Cusack Park before 21,305. John Callinan excelled at wing-back, curbing Nicky English. Clare were well on top but their finishing let them down. A goal by Enda O'Connor was disallowed and a free awarded instead. Val Donnellan's blistering shot from the free was deflected over the bar. Tommy Guilfoyle went on to score a fine goal early in the second half from a ground shot and the game eventually ended in a 1–8 to 1–8 draw.

Once again Denis Corry excelled in goal, but a sad feature of the game was the conduct of a small group of Tipperary supporters who persisted in throwing smoke-bombs around his goal area. Aidan Tuttle, a local GAA commentator at the time, remarked on the fact that this kind of behaviour was being introduced by Tipperary followers 'who boast of being the cradle of the GAA'. In the replay, Clare were beaten in all sectors and lost 5–14 to 4–6. Tipperary's Gerry Stapleton and Ian Conroy got on top early on. It was Clare's heaviest defeat in many years.

1986 MUNSTER FINAL – A WEEKEND IN KILLARNEY

Clare got back to form in the 1986 championship. They were outplayed by Limerick in the first twenty minutes of the first round, but went on to give one of their finest displays for some time, beating the Shannonsiders 2–14 to 0–14. Goal-keeper Eoin McMahon, John Moroney and Tommy Keane were magnificent; Seamus Durack felt that a crucial save by Eoin McMahon turned the match. Cormac Liddy, reporting for the *Limerick Chronicle*, was not happy with Limerick's performance. 'My immediate reaction at the final whistle was one of anger at the result. All the sweet flowing play of the first quarter was by then only a memory as Clare were totally on top in the second half.'

The Clare mentors made some shrewd moves, including the introduction of Val Donnellan, as the Feakle man scored some glorious points. In an interview with Aidan Tuttle after the game, John Callinan remarked: 'Val Donnellan's hands are amongst the best in the country. He can put a ball over; he doesn't need sight of the goal.' Ger Loughnane was also in a positive frame of mind. 'There was a time when I wanted to opt out. I came back and found a great family atmosphere and I wanted to be part of it. We have great strength in depth; Micheál Glynn would get on any county team.'

Tipperary lined out in Cusack Park on 22 June without their star player Nicky English, who was replaced by Liam Stokes. For Clare Micheál Glynn replaced Ger Loughnane. In the early minutes, Éire Óg's Pat Lynch had a great goal chance, but his shot struck the crossbar. Shortly afterwards, however, disaster struck for him, as he had to be taken off with a broken ankle. Then Tipperary got on top and were

Action from the drawn 1985 championship at Ennis
Michael Doyle [T] is tackled by John Minogue and John Callinan. Tom Howard is on the right

Action from the Clare–Tipperary championship tie
James Shanahan in typical pose with Micheál Glynn in support. The Tipperary players are Donie
O'Connell and Nicky English

cruising to victory 1–10 to 0–6 after fifty-three minutes against a lethargic Clare side when their goal-keeper Tony Shepperd was penalised for over-carrying the ball after he had saved a shot from Syl Dolan. Jackie O'Gorman instructed Gerry Mc-Inerney to shoot for a goal; McInerney duly obliged and the game was transformed. Cyril Lyons and Tommy Guilfoyle added points before the latter goaled from a Syl Dolan pass. Then Guilfoyle and Seamus Fitzpatrick wrapped it up with two more points against a shell-shocked Tipperary.

Aidan Tuttle interviewed several players and mentors after the game. For Fr Harry Bohan, 'It was very sweet to come back the way we did. While we're thrilled, we're still only in the Munster final. Seán Stack and I have been involved in many Munster finals and we have to go the whole way this time. The training has been excellent and we have great strength in the panel; we have the subs capable of coming on and turning it on.'

His fellow Feakle man, Tommy Guilfoyle, was passionate as ever in his comments. 'Hurling is our life in Feakle. We love the game and it's a bonus for us to play for Clare. When we play for our county, we play for our club and we don't let our club down.' Seán Stack thought that it was 'a strange game' and that the referee's decision to award the twenty-one yard free was the turning point in the game. 'It's decisions like that which bring winning teams back into it. How often have we seen Cork coming back in similar situations?'

The overall consensus after this game was that Clare had a 'rub of the green' on this occasion. 'Fortunate Clare Dash Tipperary's Dream' was the heading in *The Cork Examiner*. Tipperary captain and goal-keeper Tony Shepperd felt that the decision to penalise him for over-carrying was harsh and Clare captain, Tommy Keane, also acknowledged that Clare got the breaks in the second half.

Unusually, the 1986 Munster final against Cork was held in Killarney. There was a tremendous atmosphere in the town throughout the weekend between Cork and Clare supporters, and the banter lasted long into the night at the Danny Mann, the Gleneagle and other hostelries. Both sets of supporters were eagerly anticipating the following day's clash and Clare's supporters were in a buoyant mood, though their hopes were tempered by the memory of previous Munster final defeats at the hands of Cork.

The proceedings opened with the U–16 provincial final between East Clare and Mid Tipperary. Clare were inspired by Davy Fitzgerald in goal and overcame their opponents to win provincial honours for the second year running. Two goals from Whitegate's Kenneth Doyle separated the teams at half-time. The first was a spectacular effort when he connected with a P. J. O'Connell cross to score. Geoffrey Flynn and Ian Mulready in defence plus Ger Rodgers, Kevin Sammon and Damian Considine were others to shine for Clare.

The senior game opened with a dream start. James Shanahan and Cyril Lyons playing strongly at centre-field taking control, with Cyril Lyons scoring a point, which was soon followed by a superb Gerry McInerney goal. Having taken a pass from Seamus Fitzpatrick, he broke through the Cork defence to send a pile driver to the corner of the net; it was the dream start that Clare needed. Cork fought back strongly, but Tommy Guilfoyle hit a superb individual goal on the stroke of half time, when he fielded, turned the full-back, and drove a bullet-like shot to the net past Ger Cunningham; this gave Clare a four-point cushion at the interval, 2–7 to 0–9.

Unfortunately, things went wrong yet again in the second half and Clare were narrowly beaten in the end by 2–18 to 3–12. 'Tony O'Sullivan was the difference,'

Two hurling purists leave the pitch at Cusack park [1981]
Jimmy Barry-Murphy and Seán Stack

wrote Michael Ellard in *The Cork Examiner*, 'scoring three good points and setting up John Fitzgibbon for a goal.' John Minogue considers that Clare were very unlucky in Killarney. 'Tommy Guilfoyle had a brilliant game; if he got enough ball that day, we'd have beaten Cork.'

This opinion is echoed by Jimmy Barry-Murphy. 'That's one we definitely got away with. We struggled and Clare should have won it; I got a handy goal. Tommy Guilfoyle had a great game at full-forward for Clare'.

In spite of the defeat, however, the spirit in the Clare camp was more one of 'beaten but unbowed' on this occasion rather than outright despair as Aidan Tuttle's post-match interviews show. Firstly, a very disappointed Tommy Keane: 'Cork got scores at vital stages and Jimmy Barry-Murphy's goal changed the game. It's very heartening that we came back; other teams would have folded. We were very unlucky that we didn't get a score to level it; a score would have given us the initiative. The panel are young, nine players new to Munster finals.'

Selector Jackie O'Gorman also emphasised the youth of the team. 'We got a bunch of young guys of 21 and 22 who were unheard of and came through the strong side of the Munster championship. We're going to be involved next year, so we might as well be positive.' Fr Harry Bohan's mood was also one of hope tinged with regret. 'We have to be disappointed. We were there, so close, but there is hope. We beat Limerick and Tipperary, so we have to be as good as any of them. They showed great character today. Maybe they made a few mistakes, but so did Cork.'

This mood is also reflected in comments made afterwards by Seamus Durack to *The Clare Champion*. 'A bit of craft and a few mistakes beat us on the day. The two points scored by Cork in the opening minutes of the second half were the crucial scores; we were in control and should have cleared the ball. Cork regained their rhythm and we lost ours. While I'm sad with the result, I'm happy with the attitude, approach and commitment of the team. They gave us 100% always and I warmly compliment them on that. Everything that could be done was done.'

A Low Ebb

Despite yet another Munster final defeat, Clare regained their composure and performed well in the league, winning six of their seven divisional games to contest the league final. These included a win over Cork, 1–12 to 1–7, their first since the 1981 championship. In the final against Galway, however, Joe Cooney gave an exhibition of what he was capable of, scoring 2–6. Good performances from John Russell, John Moroney and Mike Guilfoyle just weren't enough to bring the league title back to the Banner. This narrow two-point defeat by Galway, 3–12 to 3–10, and their subsequent defeat in the first round of the 1987 championship to Tipperary, signalled the final whistle for many of Clare's long-serving players.

The first championship game against Tipperary was a draw, when a late Gerry McInerney equaliser had given Clare what turned out to be false hope. A long ball from Micheál Glynn to Cyril Lyons, who passed to Leo Quinlan, who in turn linked with Mike Guilfoyle, set up Gerry McInerney for a cracking goal. It was just a pity that we were three points down and not two as it might have spared us the pain of the subsequent replay.

Gerard O'Loughlin of Clarecastle, more commonly known these days as 'The Sparrow', made his championship debut that year. 'They ran us off the pitch in the replay at Killarney. The drawn game was played on a glorious day but we played badly; I remember Colm Flynn saying to me that we could never be as bad again!'

Fellow Clarecastle man John Callinan's last day in the Clare jersey, following a career that spanned almost two decades, is not one of his most cherished memories. 'We fell asunder in the replay in 1987. We had played Tipperary earlier in the league semi-final in Cork and beaten them. Six weeks later, they had a huge change in personnel and five or six players never saw a Tipperary jersey again. It was the last throw of the dice for Michael "Babs" Keating and it worked for him.

'Preparing well for the league final and being beaten by a puck of a ball had a bigger adverse impact than it should have. The confidence of the team evaporated. We played Tipperary the first day expecting to win and we got a lucky draw. We seemed to follow near victories with disasters, but that's something that I hope we have overcome. The 1987 game against Tipperary was my last one for Clare. I can't analyse what happened; it was a bad way to go out.'

James Shanahan feels that the league final of 1987 marked a downward turning-point for this team. 'I feel that Martin McKeogh got a raw deal; he was a brilliant coach and he knew the players. I dropped out of the panel but Fr Walsh approached me in 1990 to come back. Though I have a keen interest in horse-riding, shooting and fishing, I missed hurling so I jumped at the offer.'

Under–21

Clare reached their first U–21 decider of the 1980s in 1983 against Cork. They fielded a strong team which was very similar in personnel to the successful minor team of two years earlier, featuring Gerry Barry, Danny Chaplin, Tommy and Mike Guilfoyle in the line-up. The first run of the final at Kilmallock ended in a draw, 2–11 to 2–11. 'Daring Donnellan guides Clare to Replay' ran *The Clare Champion* headline.

In the replay, Cork got off to a flying start, scoring 1–5 without reply, and led by ten points coming up to the interval. A magnificent fight-back by Clare, with some great points from Tommy Guilfoyle, Val Donnellan and Danny Chaplin, had

Clare on level terms twelve minutes into the second half, before pulling away to qualify for a showdown with Tipperary at Cusack Park on 27 July.

A Tipperary side powered by Nicholas English at centre-back, Willie Peters at full-forward and Colm Bonner, decisively beat Clare 2–17 to 3–8, pulling away in the final quarter. Val Donnellan, who scored seven points from centre-field, was responsible for keeping Clare in the game for so long. John Moroney at corner-back and Tommy Howard also played well on a disappointing evening. Tipperary and Clare clashed again in 1984, this time in the first round at Thurles. The game ended level but Tipperary once again won the replay in Ennis.

The 1985 Clare U–21 team was regarded by many as one of the strongest to represent Clare for many years and featured Victor O'Loughlin, Jim McInerney, Gerard O'Loughlin, John Russell, etc. They qualified for another Munster final showdown with Tipperary in Thurles having defeated Limerick and Cork. Clare led Tipperary for part of the game, but surrendered a five-point lead at the interval to lose by two points. Tipperary's Michael Scully had a great hour, contributing 1–10 of his side's tally, which was 1–16 to Clare's 4–5. Highest scorers for Clare were Tommy Guilfoyle (2–0) and Danny Chaplin (2–2).

1986 seemed to be the final straw at U–21 level. In the semi-final, Clare accounted for Cork by five points, 2–13 to 1–11, and were held to a draw in the final against Limerick in the Gaelic Grounds before a crowd of 10,000, with Limerick's Pat Reale scoring the equalising point thirty seconds from the end. The following is an extract from an article by Pádraig MacMathúna entitled *The Painful Wait Continues:*

> The lead-up to the equalising point was unusual … The referee stopped play and threw in the ball on the twenty-one yard line; from the clash Limerick scored. However, on the run of play, Clare were fortunate to have got a second chance. Poor finishing, plus great defensive play by John Lee, Seán McCarthy and Gerard O'Loughlin, saved Clare. In the replay a week later at Cusack Park, Clare were well and truly beaten.

Cork put paid to Clare's chances in the early stages of the 1987 and 1988 championship. However, despite the disappointments of losing three Munster finals in 1983, 1985 and 1986, this very attractive grade of hurling produced a host of senior county players, such as Mike and Tommy Guilfoyle, Victor and Gerard O'Loughlin, John Lee, Seán McCarthy, Kieran O'Neill, John Moroney, John Chaplin, Declan McInerney and many more.

Ex-Clare hurler and manager of the 1988 U–21 side Tony Kelly gave his views to West Coast Radio in 1988. 'Seán Hehir, the manager of the senior team, will be able to analyse what is happening at U–21 level and should see that there are quality players coming through to senior ranks. Of course, senior is a different level; the game is faster and a lot more strength is needed.'

Munster council representative Liam McInerney was also interviewed on the same programme. 'Hurling is tremendous at primary school and post-primary level. St Flannan's record is outstanding at colleges' hurling. It's a pity hurling at Ennis CBS isn't what it was; it should be fostered better as it was once a great fortress of hurling. I remember Fr Tim Tuohy who was a curate in Newmarket many years ago; he thought that what Clare lack is the killer instinct. We had teams on the rack at U–21 level in 1972, 1974, 1976, 1985 and 1986. A couple of years ago, we drew with Limerick in the U–21 when we should have put them away, and they made a show of us in the replay at Ennis.'

St Flannan's eighteen-year wait for Harty cup honours ended on a glorious spring afternoon in 1976 when they had two points to spare over De La Salle, Waterford in the Harty final, 2–9 to 3–4. Leo Quinlan became the first St Flannan's player to lift the coveted trophy since Pádraig Kennedy in 1958.

Barry Smythe gave a great display at centre-back that day and was well supported by future Clare stars Martin Meehan, Barney Lynch and P. J. Deasy. John Callinan was a St Flannan's student from 1967 to 1972. 'Fr Seamus Gardiner and Fr Willie Walsh did tremendous work. We had a great bunch of players in 1971 and 1972. Fr Gardiner and Fr Walsh learned how to lose them with us, and in so doing learned how to win them later.'

Bishop Willie Walsh spoke to me about his years with St Flannan's. 'We contested four finals from 1962 to 1972 but lost them all. The 1971 semi-final game against Ennis CBS was very tense. It was very finely balanced going into the final quarter. Suddenly our team, facing defeat, began to hurl. The build-up for the semi-final was so big that we failed to rise to the occasion in the final. After we made the breakthrough in 1976 it seemed easier to win. Up to 1976, if a game was finely-balanced going into the last quarter, we tended to lose it, whereas after 1976 we tended to win in similar circumstances because the players had the conviction. From 1976 to 1987 I was involved with Fr Seamus Gardiner and later Fr Hugh O'Dowd. We won five Harty cups and that good tradition has been carried on by John Minogue, Michael McInerney, Con Woods, Tim Kelly, Peter Quinn and Eamon Giblin; they are still working hard with the teams.'

In a recent piece written for the quarterly publication *The Banner*, Fr Seamus Gardiner recalled his years of involvement with St Flannan's teams. 'I began training Harty cup teams in 1969 with Fr Willie Walsh, now our bishop. No doubt, the greatest thrill I got from training was winning the Dr Harty cup in 1976; eighteen years is a long time for a college used to the successes of the 1940s and 1950s.

'Past students constantly asked in those years: "What has gone wrong with Flannan's?" Certainly, the change of training methods helped. At that time, the national hurling courses were held each summer in Gormanstown. Fr Tommy Maher of St Kieran's was one of the coaches. When I described to him the type of training that we had been doing he said: "Too much physical. These are young lads; you have them four or five evenings a week. All the training should be done with a sliotar – skill – skill – skill". We went on to win the All-Ireland that year.'

In fact the famed Ennis college contested four Munster colleges' finals in a row, losing to St Colman's, Fermoy in 1977 and to Templemore CBS in 1978 before winning the title again in 1979. St Flannan's, fielding an all-Clare side, built up an interval lead of 1–10 to 1–1 before going on to win 2–11 to 1–3 against Cork's North Monastery. The St Flannan's stars on that occasion were Gerry McInerney, John Moroney, Tommy Howard, Tommy Neville and Brendan McNamara.

They went on to beat Presentation College, Birr in the All-Ireland Colleges competition by 3–15 to 2–3. For Fr Gardiner, this was a high-point in terms of pure hurling. 'We played some of the best hurling we have ever played. Jimmy Smyth thought it was the best performance he had ever seen from a Flannan's team. Great praise indeed, and for an all-Clare team, the first one to win the title for the college. A remarkable change from the teams of the 1940s and 1950s.'

St Flannan's regained the All-Ireland again in 1982, with a 2–9 to 0–10 win over St Peter's of Wexford in a replay. This side included Jim McInerney, John Russell, Eoin McMahon and Niall Romer and was captained by Peter Leyden of Clarecastle.

More Harty cups were won in 1983, 1987, 1989 and 1990. Clare FM GAA commentator Matthew McMahon regards the final of 1987 with Midleton as the best he saw. 'Anthony Daly was captain. That was the greatest performance I have ever seen from a team wearing the St Flannan's jersey. Oliver Mescall, Joe O'Gorman, Ivor Slattery and Pat Healy were all in it. I think Fr Willie Walsh said to Aidan Tuttle that Midleton had beaten St Flannan's in all competitions up to the Harty cup. He said: "They have them all but we have the one that matters". It was an awesome second half; they played the greatest ground hurling that I have ever seen that day in Kilmallock.' The final score was St Flannan's 3–12, Midleton CBS 2–6.

ALL-CLARE HARTY CUP FINAL

The 1989 Harty cup final was an all-Clare encounter between St Flannan's and St Patrick's Comprehensive School, Shannon. It was played on 12 March in atrocious conditions at Cusack Park before an official attendance of 7,000. A physically stronger St Flannan's won their fourteenth Munster senior title with a 0–9 to 0–5 victory. St Flannan's held the upper hand at centre-field where Stephen Sheedy and Liam Meaney got on top.

This tie produced a high standard of hurling despite the conditions. Ciaran O'Neill, who was forced to retire after only a few minutes, was a huge loss to the Shannon side. St Flannan's goal-keeper David Fitzgerald gave a wonderful display and saved a certain goal from Paul O'Rourke late in the game. Others to shine for St Flannan's were the Clooney pair Pat Markham and Ray O'Halloran, and Tony McEnery, Andrew Whelan and James O'Connor. For St Patrick's, John McPhilips gave a towering display at full-back; others to play well were Paul Lee, Seán Power, Paul Keary and Gary McGettrick. Many of the players who featured that day were members of the Clare team that contested the All-Ireland minor final later that year.

Brian Lohan, who was one of the subs for St Patrick's in the 1989 Harty final, recalls learning his hurling at St Tola's primary school under the guidance of Brian Torpey. He also praises the contribution made by Gerry Arkins at St Patrick's, who organised the class leagues and organised hurling and camogie Monday to Friday after school.

Fr Seamus Gardiner's stewardship of St Flannan's hurling spanned a couple of decades. So, how does he feel having spent that long coaching Clare's most successful hurling teams of that period? 'Twenty years is a long time, and as one looks back, the years crowd into one another, the disappointment of the lean years don't hurt as much. Almost forgotten too are the hours of training, often in appalling conditions, the worries about injuries, the disputes over venues, dates and referees, the driving home of players after training. I've no doubt, if we never won a Harty cup, one might question the time and energy, but one victory changes all that and the great feeling of satisfaction afterwards keeps one going.'

ST JOSEPH'S, TULLA

St Joseph's secondary school, Tulla, was established as an all-girls school in 1950 and remained so until the late 1960s when it became co-educational. By the late seventies the school had established a reputation for hurling, winning the Munster colleges C competition in 1980. This side included Flan Harrison, Donal Vaughan, Michael Bolton and Eddie Conheady. Promotion to the colleges B competition brought further success, with a win over Scariff in a replay and victory over Doon CBS in the 1981 Munster final.

In the All-Ireland semi-final Tulla beat Athenry before going on to take the All-

Ireland crown with a hard-earned victory over St Vincent's. Vincent's took command in the early part of the second half, but a strong finish by Tulla won the day. Tommy Guilfoyle scored three goals and Michael 'Larry' McNamara scored a goal. Clare county minor Val Donnellan was a big loss as a result of an injury but Seamus Cusack was an able replacement. Others who featured on the day included Tony Nelson and John Tuohy of Feakle and Andrew Walsh of O'Callaghan's Mills.

In 1981–82 St Joseph's participated in the Harty cup competition, becoming the smallest school ever to participate in the A competition. They put up a creditable performance in the first round before bowing out to Cork's Coláiste Chríost Rí. Their trainer was John Stack.

VOCATIONAL SCHOOLS

Clare had early successes in the Munster Vocational Schools competition which was inaugurated in 1958, winning provincial honours in 1958 and 1959. Some of the players who featured in these victories went on to play senior for Clare, such as Paddy McNamara, Pat Cronin, Chris Hanrahan and Liam Danagher.

Throughout the 1960s and most of the 1970s the All-Ireland series was dominated by North Tipperary and Kilkenny. Clare had useful sides in the early 1970s, with players such as Tom McGann, Tom Harvey and Gerry O'Connor, but failed to make any major breakthrough. Clare did reach the provincial final in 1978 but failed to North Tipperary by 5–5 to 3–5.

In the early rounds of the 1979 competition Clare beat Limerick by 3–12 to 2–6 and Cork by 3–6 to 0–6, thus qualifying to meet the 'specialists' in the competition, Kilkenny. The 'Cats' were in fact competing in their fifth consecutive final, having won in 1975, 1976 and 1977, as well as having been the defeated finalists in 1978.

Clare went in to the game as complete underdogs but led by 1–6 to 0–2 at half-time, before withstanding a late rally to hold out for a draw; the final score was 1–8 to 1–8. Paul Callinan, Noel McNamara, James O'Donoghue and Joe Mullins in goal stood out.

In the replay at Gardiner Park, Borrisokane, Clare got off to a great start and led by 3–1 to 0–2 at the half-time stage. John Crowe had a great game scoring three goals, with Martin Enright getting the fourth. Despite a strong Kilkenny rally Clare held out 4–5 to 1–8. Once again Paul Callinan and Seán Lyons were on top at centre-field, with John McNamara and Paschal Mahon also shining.

Ennis Vocational School took the All-Ireland schools title, defeating Banagher in the final 2–5 to 0–5, with P. J. Lyons and Edmund Kelly getting the goals. With St Flannan's lifting the All-Ireland colleges title it was a memorable year for Clare at college level. Seán Lyons (Éire Óg) was on the 1978–1979 team and gave me his recollections of the period and some interesting comments on the status of vocational schools hurling: 'After coming close in 1978 we felt we had a good chance in 1979 as many of the 1978 panel were still available. Seán Stack, who taught at Scariff, and Kevin Marren put a lot of work into it; I remember training in the snow in Tulla. We had a fine side; John Lynch and James O'Donoghue later played senior for the county.

'The standard of vocational schools hurling is high but it doesn't get the same recognition as colleges. To win an All-Ireland medal is tremendous, yet our success went almost unnoticed. It's a pity our success of 1979 wasn't built on; maybe the All-Ireland senior success of 1995 will bring it on again. I feel that we were influenced by the success of the Clare team of 1976–1979. It was a tremendous achievement considering that we had only two schools to pick from, Scariff and Ennis.'

Clare All-Ireland Vocational Schools champions, 1979
Back row l/r: John Lynch, John McNamara, Paschal Mahon, Pat Malone, Pat Giblin, Noel
McNamara, Paul Callinan [capt.], John O'Grady, Joe Mullins; Front row l/w: Jarlath Duggan,
Martin Enright, John Dillon, John Crowe, Seán Lyons, James O'Donoghue. Missing from photo-
graph are Eamon Nelson, P. J. Lyons, Michael O'Loughlin, Ger Kennedy

CLARE COLLEGES COMPETITIONS

At present, a great deal of effort is being put into the promotion of secondary school hurling within the county. One of the driving forces behind this is Mary Hanly, vice-principal of St Caiman's community school in Shannon, who is a passionate believer in the development of a more broadly-based pool of hurling talent and believes in aiming high: 'I decided in 1994 to get involved with hurling in St Caiman's because I want to see them win the Harty cup. We just can't stand back and let St Flannan's dominate; that's no good for Clare hurling. In the four or five years prior to 1984, I'd say we only had three matches in Clare; that's no way to develop the game.

'We decided to get all the schools together and we started the Clare Colleges post-primary schools competition four years ago. Brendan Vaughan was county board chairman; he's a man who listens to your ideas. I went in as chairman and brought in Alan Cunningham and Louis Mulqueen. We played eighty-one hurling and camogie matches in our first year. John Minogue of St Flannan's is now chairman for two years; then Scariff will take over for a two-year cycle. Games, fixtures and referees are organised by the schools in charge for those two years.'

THE ROAD TO CROKE PARK (1988–1995)

*I'd seen them the morning of the All-Ireland in the hotel. I was hugely impressed by Ger Loughnane,
his whole attitude, the way he handled the players; they were a credit to their county.*

JIMMY BARRY-MURPHY

The general state of Clare hurling at the beginning of 1988 gave little indication of
what progress would be made in a few short years. The fortunes of the county
senior team went into a decline after the 1987 championship replay defeat to Tipperary. The narrow defeat to Cork in the Munster final of 1986 seemed to have had
a demoralising effect on the players.

Clare overcame Waterford at Thurles 3–12 to 3–10 in the opening round of the
senior championship in 1988, but failed badly to Cork 3–22 to 2–9 in the semi-final.
This trend continued over the next couple of years and they lost to Waterford 5–13
to 1–10 in 1989 and to Limerick 2–16 to 1–5 in 1990. Speaking of this era, Gerard
'Sparrow' O'Loughlin had this to say: 'A lot of the senior players, Ger Loughnane,
Seán Stack and Martin Meehan retired. These were dismal years from 1987 to 1990.
You couldn't blame anyone at the top – a big percentage of it had to do with the attitude of the players themselves. We trained hard but we didn't believe we could
win. The big difference between now and then is that the panic button doesn't set
in if we go four or five points down. Heads don't go down.'

John Minogue's thoughts on this era bear out those of Gerard O'Loughlin. 'It
was a time when a lot of players didn't want to play for Clare. If you look at the
panels at the time, a lot of them were coming back for the championship and not
playing during the league and many of the old guard were gone. We had a new
group who needed help and leadership.'

The 1989 team was managed by Seán Hehir with selectors Fr Michael Mc-
Namara and John Hanly. They were strong enough on paper but received a drub-
bing from Waterford. The team included John Moroney, Martin Nugent, Cyril
Lyons, John Russell and newcomer Liam Doyle. Clare suffered a similar fate in 1990
under manager Tony Kelly when they had one of their biggest home defeats, going
out tamely to Limerick by 2–16 to 1–5. This was something of a transition team with
newcomers David Fitzgerald (just out of minor ranks), Anthony Daly and Victor
O'Loughlin, plus seasoned veterans James Shanahan, John Minogue and Gerry
McInerney.

Anthony Daly made his championship debut in 1990, although he had been a
sub on the 1989 team, and comes from a distinguished hurling background: 'John
Hanly was a huge influence on us in Clarecastle; he showed us the finer points of
hurling during our school days. John Callinan was also a big influence on us as the
only regular Clarecastle player on the county team for many years. My family were
also influential, though my father Pat Joe died when I was only eight. I didn't know

much about him but I did know that he played full-back for Clarecastle and that in itself carried some reputation. My uncle Haulie was captain of the Clare team that won the 1946 league and my uncle John was in goal. It was a great honour for me to captain Munster to the Railway Cup victory in 1996 as Haulie had represented Munster in 1949.'

MINOR MUNSTER TITLE

However, things are never as bad as they seem and the 1989 minor team brought the supporters a lot of joy, reaching the All-Ireland U–18 final for the first time ever by defeating Cork 7–8 to 0–7, Kerry 3–13 to 1–4, and Limerick by a solitary point 2–13 to 2–12 in a thrilling Munster final at Páirc Uí Chaoimh. They then accounted for a strong Galway team 1–15 to 0–16 at Croke Park in a pulsating semi-final. This side was put together by Gus Lohan, John Nihill, Michael 'Danno' Doyle, P. J. Kennedy and trainer Mike McNamara. The team included Paul Lee (captain), Pat Markham, Seán Power, Paul O'Rourke, Conor Clancy and the late Pádraig Mc-Namara.

The Clare Minors, captained by Paul Lee, came to Croke Park in a confident mood. They had scored a massive 13–49 in four games, with leading scorers Pádraig McNamara (4–6), Paul Keary (2–9), Conor Clancy (2–8) and Pat Minogue (1–8) in great scoring form. On the big day they played a very attractive brand of hurling but squandered many scoring chances and generally tended to overdo it. Offaly, with future senior stars Johnny Dooley, Hubert Rigney, John Troy and Brian Whelehan, captured the *Irish Press* Cup for the third time in four years. The final score was 2–16 to 1–12.

LEN GAYNOR

Len Gaynor was appointed team manager in October, 1990; he spoke about his appointment. 'I was approached by members of the Clare county board to get involved but I wasn't really interested; it wasn't on my agenda to step outside my

Enda O'Connor, Tim Crowe and Len Gaynor [manager], Limerick 1993

own county. Then I considered it and I thought why not. Morale was low and we had to gather it up. I believe in comradeship, unity of purpose, unity of mind.'

John Minogue recalls Len Gaynor's appointment. 'Len made a huge contribution, though I was only with him for four months. He had great enthusiasm for the game and got on well with the players. He knew how players reacted and got good turnouts for training in Crusheen during the winter months. He put pride back into it and stuck with it. Many of the present Clare team played under Gaynor.

'Another thing that helped a lot was the fact that the Clare footballers began to have success, winning the All-Ireland B championship in 1991 and later the Munster championship in 1992 against Kerry. Furthermore, Seamus Clancy got an All-Star'. Brendan Vaughan also credits the success of the football team of 1991–92 which produced players like Frankie Griffin, Francis McInerney, David Keane and Martin Daly. 'John Maughan lifted the county; we could conceivably have won the All-Ireland.'

Anthony Daly says: 'Len Gaynor made a huge impression on us immediately. His vision was a Munster championship. He spoke of winning a Munster championship rather than just putting pride back into the jersey. We were unlucky to lose to Limerick in his first year in charge.' Broadford's James Shanahan also feels that Gaynor's contribution was crucial. 'He was a super coach, a players' man; he looked after the simple things. He was a complete Clareman when he was with us.'

Under Len Gaynor's management, Clare opened their 1990–91 league campaign with a share of the spoils against Waterford at Cusack Park. Many new players including Seán McCarthy, Declan McInerney and Pat O'Rourke were introduced during this campaign.They had a number of defeats by very narrow margins and only managed to win one game, the final league tie against Dublin in Croke Park. Two Pat Minogue goals and seven points from Cyril Lyons swung the game for Clare. In the 1991 championship a very young Clare team lost narrowly to Limerick by 0–21 to 1–15.

FEAKLE

Feakle contested two senior county finals in 1987 and 1988, winning the latter. The members of this team came from the very successful minor and U–21 teams of the early 1980s. Feakle had the distinction of winning four U–21 championships in a row, one of the highlights being an excellent final against Sixmilebridge. Powered by the Guilfoyles and Val Donnellan, they won a memorable game by 3–19 to 5–8.

Feakle reached their second senior final in a row on 11 September 1988 when they faced Ruan in the decider. They trailed a strong Ruan team at half time by seven points to six. Ruan had Cyril Lyons at centre-back, the late John Moroney and Jimmy Courtney, with Donal Hassett and Mike Daffy operating on the full-forward line. Feakle began to take over early in the second half, with Michael Guilfoyle rampant at corner-forward, Val Donnellan at centre-forward and a strong full-back line marshalled by Ger Loughnane and Paul Callinan. Feakle ran out comfortable winners 1–17 to 1–10 to take their first senior championship since 1944; it was the first senior championship title to go to East Clare since 1975; it was also the first senior title to come to the parish since 1964 when a team inspired by Dermot Sheedy, Jimmy Conroy (ex-Whitegate), Oliver Lynch, John Anglim and others defeated a gallant Tubber side by 3–9 to 2–10 to take the Clare Cup title.

THE HURLEY MAKER

Jimmy Conway of Larch Hill was one of Ireland's best known hurley-makers. He supplied hurleys to some of the most famous hurlers throughout the land, turning out about 3,500 per year by hand. His workshop contained many patterns of sticks to suit the individual tastes of his many customers. Each fellow had his own style; for example, Naoise Jordan favoured a small light stick. According to John Mc-Mahon of Newmarket, 'He was the best; he knew exactly what you wanted'. Jimmy usually relied on ash which grew in Ballygriffey his neighbouring townland. Sadly he passed away in the summer of 1989.

ÉIRE ÓG

The final of 1990 between Éire Óg and O'Callaghan's Mills was very disappointing, but Éire Óg had a great run afterwards in the Munster club championship. In the first round against Roanmore (Waterford), they trailed by seven points at the interval but fought back well to win 2–16 to 1–14, with Pete Barry and Declan Coote prominent. In the next round, Éire Óg and Na Piarsaigh served up tremendous fare in their first ever clash in the club championship.

Na Piarsaigh won their first ever Cork senior championship in 1990. Cork inter-county hurler Tony O'Sullivan, who played with the Rebels from 1982 to1994, gave me some insight to their success. 'We had tremendous success at juvenile level and didn't actually lose a game from juvenile until we reached U–21 level. The players from those years are basically the nucleus of our present senior team. We didn't make the breakthrough at senior level earlier because the Glen, the Rockies, the Barrs and Midleton were very strong; we had to wait until players matured.'

In the game against Na Piarsaigh, Éire Óg's Barry Smythe, Seán McCarthy and Tomás Corbett gave tremendous defensive performances. A fine goal from Pete Barry before half time and a tremendous goal from a twenty-one yard free in the second half by his brother Gerry were crucial scores. A wonderful point by Tony McEnery from close to the corner flag helped Éire Óg to a 2–5 to 0–9 victory.

'McCarthy and Smythe excel as Éire Óg make History' was *The Clare Champion* headline. This victory was all the more noteworthy as John Russell, Colm Mahon and Francis Corey were injured during the game. Jim Hanafin, Leonard Forde and Christy Connery were outstanding for the Cork champions. *The Cork Examiner* had the following to say about the game:

> Displaying greater determination, Éire Óg caused a major surprise when they scored a fully-merited victory over Cork champions Na Piarsaigh in a tremendous Munster club semi-final at Cusack Park, Ennis. This was a magnificent game with many outstanding passages of play but in the end the newly-crowned Cork champions were unable to break down a teak-tough Éire Óg defence to get the vital scores and the Ennismen deservedly qualified for a final meeting with Patrickswell.

Patrickswell had overcome Holycross–Ballycahill in the other semi-final by 0–13 to 0–9. Some bad feeling crept into the final ever before a ball was struck. Ciaran Carey of Patrickswell had been suspended and this resulted in controversy over his eligibility to play against Éire Óg.

A very experienced Patrickswell side opened well with points from Gary Kirby. Éire Óg got on top during the second quarter but were guilty of poor finishing. They had the winning of the game during this spell but let it slip. The final score of 0–6 to 0–8 is indicative of the tension that prevailed throughout the game in ideal conditions at Cusack Park. Éire Óg didn't play their usual open game and, with the exception of Colm Mahon and Tomás Corbett, the team in general disappointed.

For Seán Heaslip, 'the games with Roanmore (Waterford) and Na Piarsaigh

(Cork) made up for the poor county final; the Roanmore game was the most satisfying game I ever played in. Seán McCarthy had a blinder against Na Piarsaigh, but we flopped in the Munster club final against Patrickswell, losing by eight points to six. Victory in the final would have been the best thing to happen to us, especially the more senior players like Colm Mahon, Barry Smythe, Declan Coote and myself.'

1992 CHAMPIONSHIP

After a modest run in the league of 1991–92 Clare and Waterford clashed in the first round of the Munster championship at Thurles. Clare got off to a fine start when Fergus Tuohy flicked an opportunist goal to the net after a Gerard O'Loughlin effort had come off the upright. Clare were forced to make a number of changes due to a accident to Tommy Guilfoyle. Cyril Lyons had a great opening quarter scoring 2–3 in all and Corofin's Seán O'Loughlin came in at centre-forward, with a bit of re-shuffling going on elsewhere. O'Loughlin came on to the senior panel during the league of 1991–92. He was called up after a great individual performance in Corofin's intermediate championship win over St Joseph's. Other notable members of that Corofin team included Michael Ryan and former inter-county players Gerry Halpin and John Malone.

However, Waterford fought back with goals from John Meaney and Shane Aherne and accurate point-scoring by Kieran Delahunty to earn a deserved draw, Clare 3–10 to Waterford 2–13. Waterford dominated the first half of the replay at the same venue on 31 May, but led by only twelve points to nine at the interval. According to John Murphy writing in *The Cork Examiner*, the score 'made a mockery of their dominance throughout most of the opening thirty-five minutes when they ran Clare ragged at times'.

Clare came back however to level the game, with Cyril Lyons in scoring form and the half-back line of Seán McCarthy, Jim McInerney and John Chaplin also coming more into the game. Then John Meaney of Mount Sion flashed over two late points for the Waterford men to put Clare out of the 1992 championship.

1993 CHAMPIONSHIP

Clare's display in the 1992–93 league was a dismal one with defeats to Wexford, Cork and Galway, before a fine Jim McInerney-inspired Clare defeated Waterford by 4–8 to 0–15 at Cappoquin to earn a play-off with Cork at Thurles. This turned out to be one of Clare's most inept performances for some time, losing a lack-lustre match by 1–17 to 0–10. However, in the run-up to the championship, Clare and Kilkenny served up excellent fare in an Aer Rianta challenge at Cusack Park before an attendance of about one hundred people, with Kilkenny winning the trophy by a narrow margin. The few spectators in attendance were not too surprised at Clare's tremendous performance against a confident Limerick in the championship the following week.

Anthony Daly remembers a rousing speech in the Clare dressing-room from selector Enda O'Connor before the game. Clare tore into Limerick from the word go, displaying tremendous hunger from players like Stephen Sheedy, Eoin Cleary and Pat Markham. An unfortunate injury to Clarecastle's Alan Neville in the very early exchanges saw the arrival of Gerard O'Loughlin on to the pitch. O'Loughlin proceeded to give one of his best performances in the Clare jersey, scoring at will. Added to this, Cyril Lyons was bang on form. Between them, Lyons and O'Loughlin scored 3–9.

Limerick didn't seem to know what hit them in those early minutes, with John

Moroney and newcomers Brian Lohan and Pat Markham doing well. Clare built up a huge interval lead but, true to form, Limerick fought back gallantly, only to be denied time and again by excellent points from O'Loughlin. The final score of 3–16 to 3–12 did scant justice to Clare's superiority. Afterwards team manager Len Gaynor remarked to *The Clare Champion*: 'We knew our performance against Cork in the league was below par and we were embarrassed after that game, but that wasn't our true form. The players did all we asked of them and we got the result.'

Rank outsiders Clare took on Cork the newly-crowned league champions at Limerick's Gaelic Grounds in the semi-final of the championship; the game was played in a constant downpour. Clare played with a new-found confidence throughout the field and had the better of the early exchanges. A goal from an over-head pull by Cyril Lyons was disallowed but they never let Cork play with the con-fidence they displayed to overcome Wexford at the third attempt in the epic league final of 1993.

Clare wasted chances, particularly in the second half, although they were re-ceiving good quality passes from the half-back line of Pat Markham, John Chaplin and John Russell. In the terrible weather conditions, the most decisive factor was Clare's greater hunger for victory; Anthony Daly in particular stood out. *The Cork Examiner*'s Jim O'Sullivan had this to say: 'On the Clare side nobody personified it better than their inspiring captain Anthony Daly. More than that, Daly gave an ex-hibition of full-back play the like of which has not been seen since possibly the best days of former Cork captain Martin O'Doherty in the late 1970s and before him Limerick's great Pat Hartigan.' A late goal by Fergus Tuohy, after Jim McInerney had brought a great save from Ger Cunningham, gave Clare victory by 2–7 to 0–10.

In the subsequent Munster final at the Gaelic Grounds, Clare left their best form well behind them. An early point by Tipperary's Anthony Cross was cancelled out by a magnificent John O'Connell sideline point. Tipperary then got on top with points from Pat Fox, John Leahy, Aidan and Declan Ryan, before Declan Carr kick-ed a goal past David Fitzgerald. Tipperary led by 2–13 to 1–6 at half time, with Jim McInerney getting the Clare goal. Four fine points from James O'Connor was one of the few highlights from Clare's point of view.

In what was an ideal day for hurling, this game was as good as over after twen-ty minutes, and a sense of complete anti-climax and disappointment pervaded the entire stadium. Clare appeared to be suffering from stage-fright and their perfor-mance bore little or no resemblance to their games against Limerick and Cork. It was not a good day for Len Gaynor, despite the success of his native county. 'We got off the ground in 1993; beating Limerick and Cork, we sailed into the Munster final and got blasted out of it. I was worried coming back in 1994 but the players came out of that defeat well'.

When I spoke to Gerard O'Loughlin recently about his memories of the 1993 Munster final he said: 'We were tuned in but we had no answer to them; we were swept off the field. Again it was a learning process – getting used to 40,000 people. It was a day you'd like to forget.' Anthony Daly also remembers it as a sharp les-son. 'We weren't focused properly; some of us were overcome by the occasion ever before the throw-in. We were having a cup of tea in the Greenhills Hotel, Ennis Road, Limerick before the game and well-wishers were coming up to shake hands. Personally, Anthony Crosse's face should have been etched on my mind. The 1993 Munster final hammering was, in hindsight, the best thing to happen; it showed us how ruthless you need to be. We were totally geared up for the return game in 1994 and beat them by four points.' Pa Howard likened the manner of Clare's 1993 defeat to the defeat by Limerick in the 1955 Munster decider, a view which he said was shared by his neighbour George Taaffe when they raked over the embers on the morning after the 1993 final.

JUNIOR SUCCESS 1993

The Clare junior team of 1992 were most unlucky not to win the Munster championship when they failed narrowly to Cork in the provincial decider. The 1992–93 team was trained by Tony Considine, Mike McNamara and P. J. Kennedy. They opened their campaign against Limerick at Cusack Park in an entertaining game which produced a high standard of hurling. Limerick, with the wind behind them, led by 1–8 to 2–3 at the interval, but an immaculately-struck Val Donnellan semi-penalty after the re-start put Clare on the road to victory. Donnellan struck a personal 3–2 in Clare's 4–7 to 1–10 win. This was followed by a 1–9 to 0–9 win over Cork, with a tremendous centre-back display by Terry Kennedy, who scored two long-range points, with Brendan McNamara getting the all-important goal.

Clare faced Waterford in the Munster junior final. Clare goal-keeper Noel Considine takes up the story. 'Waterford had a mixture of seasoned and talented young players like Brenner and Fives. They were good but we withstood early pressure. Then just before half time Brendan McNamara got a goal and it took off from there. Val Donnellan got some great points. We were asked to play the All-Ireland final in Croke Park as a curtain-raiser to the Leinster final replay. We loved the idea of going to Croke Park before 40,000; it was a great platform. We travelled up the day before. The preparation was excellent – Mike McNamara is meticulous, Tony Considine a great organiser and P. J. Kennedy a great man on the sideline, very shrewd. The atmosphere in the hotel was great. The players were close; they gelled together and it was relaxed.'

I consider the All-Ireland performance by the Clare juniors to be one of the best team performances I have ever seen from any Clare team. From the throw-in. they played with tremendous confidence. Kilkenny goal-keeper James McGarry made a great save from Ger Rogers but Val Donnellan flicked the rebound to the net. Donnellan's second goal is one of the best I've ever seen. While standing close to the end-line, he connected beautifully on a long-range free to drive the ball to the corner of the net. Clare then raced into an early lead of 2–4 to 0–1, with the backs and goal-keeper giving a marvellous exhibition. The team spirit in the dressing-room at half time was epitomised by Noel Considine's throwaway remark to Val Donnellan: 'That was a great goal Val, but I'd have stopped it'.

Kilkenny fought back in the second half and created a lot of chances but were forced to shoot for goals to no avail. Dual star Kieran O'Neill scored a spectacular third goal towards the end of the game putting it beyond Kilkenny's reach, 3–10 to 0–8. The team's strength down the middle – Francis Corey, Terry Kennedy and Damien Considine – plus a great understanding among the backs, and tremendous players like Liam Doyle, Seán Power and Brian Quinn, all contributed to Clare's victory. Niall Romer of Kilmaley accepted the cup on behalf of an exceptionally well-drilled team.

Tony Considine told me how his involvement with the junior team came about. 'McNamara brought me in as coach/trainer to the junior team in 1992. We were very unlucky to lose the provincial final to Cork. Previously I'd been involved as a player with my own club Cratloe, and later as a coach with Inagh, Kilnamona and Kilfenora (football). In 1992 I got involved with Broadford, a great hurling parish.

Niall Romer holds the All-Ireland Junior Cup aloft at Croke Park [1993] with Barney Lynch

The Team

Noel Considine
(Clarecastle)

Liam Doyle	Francis Corey	Barney Lynch
(Bodyke)	(Éire Óg)	(Clarecastle)

Seán Power	Terry Kennedy	Niall Romer
(Wolfe Tones)	(Kilmaley)	(Kilmaley)

Damian Considine   Christy Chaplin
(Cratloe)   (Sixmilebridge)

Paul O'Rourke	Ciaran O'Neill	Brian Quinn
(Wolfe Tones)	(St Joseph's)	(Tulla)

Val Donnellan	Brendan McNamara	Ger Rogers
(Feakle)	(O'Callaghan's Mills)	(Scariff)

Subs who played Colin Lynch (Éire Óg) and John McKenna (Ogonnelloe)

'The 1993 junior team were fantastic mentally. I remember the Munster final; this was a big thing because our seniors had been annihilated in the Munster senior final the previous Sunday. We travelled to Thurles to play Waterford on the Wednesday evening; we didn't have much support because the supporters were burned out. We beat Waterford and qualified for the All-Ireland final with Kilkenny. They asked us to go to Croke Park and we were delighted to do so. It was the place to play it. There was a greater buzz when the lads heard it was to be played in Croke Park. They wanted to do well; they wanted to perform. We knew then we were capable of winning.'

1993–94 LEAGUE AND CHAMPIONSHIP

Brian Lohan considers Clare's 1–10 to 0–6 victory over Kilkenny in round five of the 1993–94 league at Nowlan Park to be the turning-point in this present Clare team. 'The fifteen played the full hour in the same positions, no switch made, no subs – a brilliant performance. We got a great ovation from the small Clare crowd, especially in the circumstances, as we had been beaten by Dublin in the previous round at Croke Park by 2–11 to 1–12. It was the first time I was conscious of an ovation coming off a hurling field.' Clare reached the semi-final of the league, losing to a physically stronger Galway side by 1–13 to 0–10 at the Gaelic Grounds.

According to Anthony Daly, Clare were eager to salvage their reputation in the 1994 championship and were presented with an ideal opportunity to do so when drawn against Tipperary in the first round. The first half of that encounter was a close, tense affair with James O'Connor scoring some good points to keep Clare in touch. The half time score was 0–7 to 0–5 in favour of Tipperary. The game came to life in the second half when Tommy Guilfoyle scored two great goals. Tipperary fought back in characteristic style with Pat Fox and Michael Cleary trying hard for the equalising scores, but Fergus Tuohy clinched the issue for Clare with a point which gave them a four-point winning margin.

In a glorious day at Austin Stack Park, Tralee, Clare overcame Kerry in the semi-final by 2–16 to 1–8, with Andrew Whelan and Jim McInerney to the fore. Expectations were high for the Munster final against Limerick at Thurles. However, a devastating display by an in-form Limerick, particularly in the second half, denied Clare in what was one of our blackest days in recent years. Andrew Whelan was unlucky not to goal in the first half when he was hooked. Cyril Lyons did well when he was introduced in the final quarter, setting up a goal for Tommy Guilfoyle and scoring one himself. The full-back line of Anthony Daly, Brian Lohan and Liam Doyle excelled. 'Limerick Inflict a Deep Cut in the Clare Psyche' was the headline in *The Irish Times*.

Bishop Willie Walsh was a selector in 1994. 'To beat Tipperary was an enormous achievement. In some ways, we put so much into the Tipperary game that we exhausted all our efforts and we never rose for the Munster final. Nevertheless, progress was made.'

James O'Connor confirms this viewpoint. 'Right from the start of the year all the talk was about Tipperary and revenge for 1993. We had a meeting before the league started and the 29 May game against Tipperary was all that was spoken about. When we beat Tipperary, we were on a huge high; it was our All-Ireland. Mentally, we couldn't get up there again. 1994 was much more disappointing than 1993, especially to collapse the way we did, because expectations were much higher.'

Liam Doyle in control, pursued by T. J. Ryan [Limerick]

161

1994–95 League

The 1994–95 league campaign opened with Ger Loughnane now at the helm, ably supported by Tony Considine and Mike McNamara. In their opening game Clare defeated Kilkenny by 0–14 to 0–9 at Sixmilebridge before accounting for Galway 3–12 to 1–10 at Athenry, with Jim McInerney scoring two goals in a late flourish. Clare had notched up six straight wins when they overcame Tipperary at Ennis, 2–9 to 0–10, in a fine game. Commenting afterwards, Ger Loughnane said: 'It was the most satisfying victory in the league to date.'

Clare and Waterford clashed in the league semi-final at Thurles with the Bannermen winning by 2–14 to 0–8. A feature of this game was the tremendous display by Eamon Taaffe, who contributed seven great points, and a fine centre-field display by the Clarecastle pair Ken Morrissey and Stephen Sheedy. Many Clare and Waterford supporters were justifiably angry at the lack of proper stewarding which caused many patrons to miss up to fifteen minutes of the opening half. In the other semi-final Kilkenny overcame Offaly by 4–8 to 0–14.

The league final was held at Thurles on 7 May. An exceptional display by Kilkenny saw them overcome Clare by 2–12 to 0–9. Clare were well in the game until Eamon Morrissey and Denis Byrne struck with two magnificent goals to lead 2–4 to 0–7 at the interval. Kilkenny dominated in most positions in the second half, but the Clare backs shone, particularly Seán McMahon with four great points. Brian Lohan and Liam Doyle gave their usual top-class performances and Stephen Sheedy at centre-field did well in an otherwise disappointing game from Clare's point of view. One positive feature however was the never-say-die attitude displayed by the Clare team in general on this occasion. There was no sign of a collapse at any stage despite Kilkenny's dominance and they battled on to the end.

Ger Loughnane's comment to the media 'We're going to win the Munster championship' was what the Clare supporters needed to hear on their radios returning home from Thurles. It matched the spirit demonstrated by the team on the pitch. Jimmy Barry-Murphy gave his match analysis in *The Irish Times* the following day. 'Brilliant Kilkenny have set the standard. An unbelievable performance from Kilkenny. They scored two classic corner-forward goals. They played well within themselves early on and then cut loose. Clare have a lot going for them and shouldn't judge themselves on this display. Their backs are good but against Kilkenny, if you don't take your chances early on, you dig a hole for yourself.'

1995 Munster Final

After the disappointment of the league final defeat, Clare opened their championship campaign against Cork at the Gaelic Grounds. Clare started well with some good points early on from Fergal Hegarty, but it was Cork who led 2–4 to 0–7 thanks to a couple of fine opportunist goals. Clare went further behind early in the second half when Cork began to dominate, but a tremendous fight-back by Clare saw Gerard O'Loughlin score an inspirational goal. Clare's determination to win was epitomised by Seán McMahon's courageous decision to stay on the pitch after he had suffered a broken collar bone.

The game ended in drama and confusion. Cork's Alan Browne scored a goal in the last minute to give his team a two-point lead. It looked as if Cork had once more snatched victory. Even Clare FM's Matthew McMahon lamented 'It's all over, it's all over!' The ball was pucked back upfield and the injured Seán McMahon courageously won a line ball which was expertly struck by Fergus Tuohy and flicked to the net by second-half substitute Ollie Baker. It felt as if Clare had done to Cork

162

what they had so often done to us. However, there was yet more drama to come as a last-gasp attempt by Alan Browne to equalise came off the upright and fell into the path of fellow Corkman Kevin Murray, but a brilliant interception by Frank Lohan saved the day.This was truly a team performance, with every member playing his part. Though the hurling wasn't always classical it was a pity it was witnessed by only 14,500 people.

So Clare were heading towards their third Munster final in a row. Their opponents Limerick had beaten them decisively just twelve months earlier and, in the opinion of many, had one hand on the McCarthy cup in the 1994 All-Ireland final before it was dramatically snatched away from them by Offaly. Limerick were such firm favourites to win the 1995 Munster final that the main focus of attention in newspaper articles, etc. before the game was the prospect of a re-match between Offaly and Limerick in the All-Ireland. Clare generally kept a fairly low profile.

Sunday 9 July was Munster final day and the streets of Thurles were awash with colour, particularly the green and white of Limerick, whose followers were in a celebratory mood and who out-numbered wearers of the saffron and blue by about two to one. Over the years Clare had been famous for the loyalty of its supporters in spite of many setbacks, but it seemed as if the possibility of a third Munster final defeat in a row was more than many Clare hearts could bear. It was also a glorious, hot day and people might be due some forgiveness for heading west to the beaches rather than east to the cauldron that was Semple Stadium!

Mike Galligan opened the scoring for Limerick after two minutes and P. J. O'Connell replied for Clare before Gerard O'Loughlin and Pat Heffernan exchanged points. Limerick had opened up a five-point to three lead after twenty-five minutes when Stephen McNamara prised open the Limerick defence with a great solo run and passed to Conor Clancy who was fouled in the square. The resulting penalty was driven expertly to the net by an injured David Fitzgerald who limped up to take it but raced back to his own goal afterwards without showing any signs of pain!

The second half seemed to belong totally to Clare who had opened up a three-point lead by the forty-first minute. With approximately twenty minutes to go, Clare hit a purple patch and a series of superb points were scored by an in form P. J. O'Connell, James O'Connor and Seán McMahon. The Clare forwards showed tremendous understanding throughout and, with about ten minutes to go, the game was totally beyond Limerick's reach.

For Cyril Lyons, it was his fourth appearance in a Munster final and certainly the most memorable. 'Winning the Munster championship in 1995 was the highlight of the year. I remarked to Anthony Daly on the difference between the photographs of him receiving the Munster Cup and the McCarthy Cup – you can seen the sense of elation at having finally won a Munster championship. We never knew what it was like to lose an All-Ireland because we weren't there, but we lost so many Munster finals. Journeys to and from Thurles had been ones of great expectation going and of great disappointment coming home.'

James O'Connor had only been on the senior panel since 1993 but had still managed to experience two consecutive Munster final defeats. 'Going back to my days on the minor and U–21 teams, the Munster championship was all we talked about. Even in our preparations at the beginning of the season, it was the Munster championship, the fact that it hadn't been won and so many great Clare teams had come so close. There was so much satisfaction because it was such an achievement; it was like a huge hunger being satisfied.

'We went to the Anner Hotel after the match. There were very few people there and we got on the bus in our own time. We had a bus journey from Thurles right back home with just the people who mattered, the players, the management and a few girlfriends. We had time to ourselves which we never got after the All-Ireland final. The bus journey home was fantastic.'

Semple Stadium 1995 washed away the memory of all previous Munster final defeats such was the magnificence of Clare's victory. Euphoric scenes were witnessed afterwards at Anthony Daly's acceptance speech and at the homecoming that evening through Newmarket and Clarecastle to Ennis. On the following evening there was a civic reception in O'Connell Square, where Bishop Willie Walsh, Bishop Edward Darling, Peter Considine, chairman of the county council, and many others paid tribute to the team who were afterwards introduced individually to the adoring masses.

This was the breakthrough that Clare had been dreaming about for so many years and the entire county went into a party mood which was to last all through a long, hot summer. It seemed that every man, woman and child now wanted a ticket for the semi-final against neighbours Galway so that they could see their heroes dash on to the turf of Croke Park.

Anthony Daly with the Munster Cup addresses the masses

OFF TO CROKE PARK

'It was a big relief to come out of Munster and we were able to express ourselves against Galway,' remarked Stephen McNamara, who got two wonderful scores in the All-Ireland semi-final. His first, a kicked goal, had come from a lob by Fergus

Tuohy, with McNamara running out before his man, gathering it and kicking to the net. Stephen McNamara is a grand-nephew of Johnny 'Joker' Coote (a member of the Dalcassian hurling team of the 1920s) and a grandson of former Limerick great Jackie Power. He told me of the influence that the former Ahane and Limerick hurler had on him. 'I heard all the stories from him about the great hurlers Jimmy Langton, Jack Lynch, Christy Ring, the Mackeys and later Matt Nugent and Jimmy Smyth. My interest in hurling took off from there.'

Clare led by 2–6 to 0–7 at half time, having hit a brilliant spell after the fifteenth minute when Gerard O'Loughlin scored a fine goal after a great long ball from Fergal Hegarty. O'Loughlin, finding himself inside the defence, expertly fired a low shot to the net. However good this goal was, it paled beside his second goal two minutes into the second half, a marvellous piece of teamwork involving a passing movement from Fergus Tuohy to Hegarty, who knocked it back to Daly, who passed to Conor Clancy, who passed to Tuohy again, and finally to O'Loughlin, who drove it expertly to the net – without doubt one of the finest build-ups and finishes witnessed in Croke Park for some time. Galway replied with a good opportunist goal and hung on to the end but marvellous defensive play from all six backs, capped by an unyielding display at full-back by Brian Lohan, plus some magnificent long-range points from James O'Connor, Liam Doyle and P. J. O'Connell put Clare through to the All-Ireland final.

In the run-up to the All-Ireland, the county decked itself in its best finery, with the residents of Clarecastle taking first prize for their extraordinary efforts. The village was presented in a blaze of saffron and blue intermingled with the local magpie black and white. It seemed that anything resembling the Clare colours was utilised for bunting. Car number plates, and even cars themselves, were painted saffron and blue by fanatical Bannermen!

The scramble for semi-final tickets paled by comparison with the angst that was generated for the final as people laid siege to Cusack Park and jammed county board secretary Pat Fitzgerald's telephone line in search of that elusive ticket. Club memberships mushroomed, appeals were made to the generosity of other counties, and all kinds of long-term promises were entered into to see them right if their turn should come to grace Croke Park some day.

The supporters of Clare and Offaly brought tremendous colour to Dublin on the eve of the All-Ireland final, giving the capital a Mardi Gras-type atmosphere as huge Clare crowds took over the city. On the night before the big match Dublin taxi driver and former Dublin hurler Martin Morris told me about his many tussles with Clare players during the 1970s in Tulla and elsewhere, and also credited the fantastic contribution made to Dublin hurling by Michael Slattery during the years 1978–1980 when be coached them.

On the morning of the big match the team flew from Shannon to Dublin after spending the night before in a semi-deserted county. Supporters made the usual last-gasp attempts to secure that vital ticket or swop one with displaced Offaly supporters, who were designated to occupy Hill 16, before everybody headed towards the great event. With the exception of Hill 16, it seemed as if the rest of Croke Park was sporting the colours of the Banner County.

Cork scored an easy victory over a young Kilkenny team in the minor game. Then the Artane Boys Band gave their traditional performance, which included a rendition of the Perez Prado tune 'Guaglione' (the Guinness advertisement tune) before the Cork team of 1970, led by Paddy Barry of St Vincent's, were honoured and introduced to the crowd. After the arrival of An Taoiseach John Bruton, GAA

Clare's management team, 1995
L/r: Mike McNamara, Ger Loughnane, Tony Considine

president Jack Boothman made the customary introduction of the teams to An tUachtarán, Mrs Mary Robinson.

In a last-minute comment on RTE Limerick hurler Ger Hegarty tipped Clare to win, as he felt they had come from the harder side of the draw and had class players in Gerard O'Loughlin, Brian Lohan and Liam Doyle, describing the latter as the outstanding player of the year. The teams posed before a bank of photographers and, just before referee Dickie Murphy threw in the ball, a minute's silence was observed to recall the tragedy of the great famine of 1845–47. It had the added effect of providing a striking contrast to the clamour and excitement which lay ahead.

Offaly got off to a good start with two points from Daithí Regan and Billy Dooley before a number of spirited Clare attacks put the Offaly defence under fierce pressure. From my position in the Nally Stand I had a birds-eye view of the hard but fair exchanges in the Offaly goalmouth as Kevin Kinahan and Martin Hanamy withstood fierce pressure. Clare centre-back Seán McMahon settled Clare with two fine points before Ollie Baker scored another point from a sideline cut reminiscent of the great Michael Moroney of Crusheen, the sideline specialist of the 1970s.

Offaly were ahead 0–6 to 0–5 when Michael Duignan hit a speculative shot towards the Clare goal after a run along the left wing. It seemed as if it would pose no problem for Davy Fitzgerald who attempted to tap it down onto his hand with the hurley. However, the greasy ball slithered off his stick and into the net. This could have been a hammer-blow to Clare's morale but it was cancelled out soon afterwards by two fine points from Gerard O'Loughlin and Fergal Hegarty on the stroke of half time, leaving Clare only two points in arrears 1–6 to 0–7.

Six minutes into the second half Seán McMahon narrowed the gap to the minimum. A great point from Fergie Tuohy levelled matters, ushering in a stalemate situation for several minutes, before Johnny Pilkington scored an opportunist goal for Offaly. However, the magnificent play of the Clare backs didn't allow Offaly to

Gerard O'Loughlin scores a vital point in the 1995 All-Ireland final

build on this three-point lead and this was to prove vital. Both sides missed valuable chances before Eamon Taaffe's wonderful goal, when he snapped on a rebound which seemed to come off the crossbar from an Anthony Daly long-range free. Taaffe had only come in a few minutes earlier, forced out of the starting line-up due to injury. He was about to be taken off again when fortune ensured his place in Clare hurling folklore. Taaffe is one of a select group of notable Tubber hurlers to have represented Clare over the years – Tom Burnell, Matt Nugent, Donal O'Grady, George Taaffe, brothers Michael, Enda and Pat O'Connor and Johnny Lee all spring to mind.

Offaly came back immediately to level the match before inspirational play from Ollie Baker who shouldered Brian Whelehan over the end-line to concede a sixty-five. With two minutes to go, Anthony Daly played a captain's part in accepting responsibility as free-taker. He stood over the ball for some moments as an injured player was attended to and the tension around was almost unbearable. As he lifted the ball the hopes of all Clare supporters lifted with it and a deafening cheer greeted his effort as the ball sailed over the bar.

Offaly once more came back with another assault on the Clare goal and were unlucky to strike the upright before Frank Lohan cleared. The final score in the game was a point by James O'Connor from a free after Kevin Kinahan pulled both ways under pressure from Cyril Lyons. As Offaly goal-keeper David Hughes pucked out the ball, the referee blew the final whistle and Croke Park erupted to ecstatic scenes, with thousands of Clare supporters rushing out on the pitch to greet their heroes, both players and mentors alike.

In spite of appeals from GAA president Jack Boothman, it seemed an age before Anthony Daly got through the crowd of well-wishers. Anthony's magnificent speech was one of the finest acceptance speeches ever heard on All-Ireland final day. He spoke to me about this recently. 'The night before the match Sparrow and

Frank and Brian Lohan, with Johnny Dooley of Offaly

myself were relaxing in the Clare Inn jacuzzi – the whole of Clare was gone to Dublin. I mentioned to Sparrow that I hadn't any words prepared for the following day and he said: "The only thing you have to worry about tomorrow is Johnny Dooley; forget your speechin. The speech was spontaneous. I was aware that Clare had produced better teams in the past and I wanted them to share in the glory.'"

A Uachtarán, a Uachtarán Cumann Luthchleas Gael, tá an-áthas orm an Corn Liam MacCárthaigh seo a ghlacadh ar son foireann Iomána Chondae an Chláir. There's been a missing person in Clare for 81 long years. Today that person has been found alive and well and that person's name is Liam McCarthy. In that long period the people of Clare and those who wore the saffron and blue suffered much. We have listened to many jibes and been told to stick to our traditional music. We love our traditional music but we also love our hurling. 1995 will go down in history as the greatest year in Clare GAA. 1995 was no accident. Many people are due many thanks so today could become a reality. I'm thinking first and foremost of many Clare teams down the years. Many of those Clare teams were better than this one but they were never as fortunate as this team. Now we accept the Liam McCarthy Cup on behalf of all those teams who wore the Clare saffron and blue.

The county board and our sponsor Pat O'Donnell deserve special mention. Our medical people Dr Pádraig Quinn, Dr Conor Fanning, Colm Flynn, Ursula Loughnane and Joe Horan. But, mostly, tribute is due to three great men; to our selector and mentor from Cratloe Tony Considine; to a man who drove us to hell and back in Shannon and Crusheen and everywhere we trained the great Scariff publican Mike McNamara. And finally to Ger Loughnane, a man whose obsession might become reality, gave every last drop of sweat and blood – the great Ger Loughnane.

It's going to be one hell of a week. We look forward to seeing you in Ennis tomorrow night. Finally we say to Offaly: many years you have been our inspiration. We looked at your success story and said why can't we achieve that. We thank you sincerely for a great struggle and we know that Offaly hurling is strong and you'll be back. Three cheers for Offaly! Come on the Banner!

Anthony Daly with the Liam McCarthy Cup
Also included from left are Brendan Vaughan, Dr Patrick Hillary and Jack Boothman

Ger Loughnane's comments on RTE summed up the Clare spirit: 'Twelve months ago we were in the depths of despair but we weren't going to surrender out there today.'

Before going in to Semple Stadium for the Munster final I met a confident John Hanly who said: 'This is our year'. After the All-Ireland I asked him why he was so confident. 'I felt after the Cork match that we had that edge of luck and I also felt the Clare players were different from previous times. They had fight in them and they had the physical strength to do it. I was confident we could beat Galway. I had only one reservation about the All-Ireland and I said it to Ger Loughnane and Mike McNamara; could they maintain the level of fitness over such a long period of time? Happily they did and we ran Offaly into the ground; they had nothing left.'

Such was the wish for Clare to succeed that every county except gallant Offaly seemed to get behind them. John Horgan told me: 'We were hoarse shouting for Clare. The six Clare backs and their goal-keeper were magnificent; they laid the foundation for victory. Frank Lohan at corner-back played excellently, maybe it's because I have an affinity for corner-back play. They were great going back and well able to clear left and right. Seán McMahon's two points settled Clare and I liked Ollie Baker at centre field.'

Cyril Lyons played his first senior match with Clare in the league in 1982, having been on the panel briefly in 1978. 'Growing up, it was a dream and an ambition to play in an All-Ireland final and to be lucky enough to be part of it. As I grew older and wiser with years, I thought that it was a distant dream; we were struggling. I had given up hope of being part of it myself, but certainly not of Clare winning an All-Ireland.

'It took a huge amount of effort to win the All-Ireland. We trained for twelve months; we began training at Ballyline the night after Offaly beat Limerick in the 1994 All-Ireland and we didn't stop for twelve months'. Following Clare's defeat of Tipperary in the 1994–95 league, Cyril had described the team to Dermot Crowe in The Star as 'the best Clare team for years and there are a lot of young players who haven't reached their true potential yet'. As someone who had first-hand knowledge of different Clare line-ups over the years, I asked him what the basis for this comment was.

'Players took responsibility on the field and weren't looking to someone else. What impressed me was that the lads who took responsibility were very young. They also impressed me as a group. Once they had a year's hurling behind them they were men; they grew up quickly. They trained hard, gave their best in games and had a very responsible attitude'.

THE TEAM

David Fitzgerald
(Sixmilebridge)

Michael O'Halloran
(Sixmilebridge)

Brian Lohan
(Wolfe Tones)

Frank Lohan
(Wolfe Tones)

Liam Doyle
(Bodyke)

Seán McMahon
(St Joseph's, Doora/Barefield)

Anthony Daly
(Clarecastle)

James O'Connor
(St Joseph's, Doora/Barefield)

Ollie Baker
(St Joseph's, Doora/Barefield)

Fergus Tuohy
(Clarecastle)

P J. O'Connell
(O'Callaghan's Mills)

Fergal Hegarty
(Kilnamona)

Stephen McNamara
(Éire Óg)

Conor Clancy
(Kilmaley)

Ger O'Loughlin
(Clarecastle)

Subs: Stephen O'Hara (Tulla), Alan Neville (Clarecastle), John Chaplin (Sixmilebridge), Cyril Lyons (Ruan), Ken Morrissey (Clarecastle), Christy Chaplin (Sixmilebridge), Jim McInerney (Tulla), Ger Moroney (O'Callaghan's Mills), Brian Quinn (Tulla). Un-named sub Eamon Taaffe was introduced after fifty minutes, Cyril Lyons after sixty and Alan Neville after sixty-six minutes.

It took a couple of days for celebrating Bannermen to make their way back across the Shannon, cheered all the way by flag-waving well-wishers from every county. The team arrived back to Shannon the following evening and took several hours to make the journey from the airport to a massive reception in Ennis, after lengthy stop-overs in Shannon, Newmarket and Clarecastle. Everyone then went into action for an all-night party.

With the celebrations still in full swing, the rest of Ireland played Clare in a charity match in aid of GOAL at Cusack Park a few days after the All-Ireland. Over 16,000 turned up to witness a light-hearted and highly entertaining spectacle, with players freed from the tensions of competitive hurling allowed to express themselves. The game produced seven goals, including five for Clare, with Cyril Lyons getting two and Alan Neville, Eamon Taaffe and Jim McInerney scoring one each. For the rest of Ireland Michael Galligan and Michael Cleary excelled.

After the supporters left.
Two former Clare greats at Croke Park. – Naoise Jordan [Whitegate] and Johnny McCarthy [Ennis]

All-Ireland Senior Champions, 1995
Back row l/r: Brian Lohan, Michael O'Halloran, Frank Lohan, Conor Clancy, Davy Fitzgerald, Seán McMahon, Gerard O'Loughlin; Front row l/r: Liam Doyle, P. J. O'Connell, Ollie Baker, Anthony Daly, James O'Connor, Fergal Hegarty, Fergus Tuohy, Stephen McNamara

Michael Arthur summed up his feelings about Clare's great year. 'We will never forget 1995 – the three wise men – Ger Loughnane, Tony Considine and Mike McNamara. I will always remember and salute the players who won the Munster and All-Ireland trophies, Davy Fitzgerald, the Lohan brothers, Sparrow O'Loughlin, Seán McMahon, Anthony Daly and, for his great scores in the All-Ireland final, Fergus Tuohy.'

Clare star of the 1950s Mick Leahy later wrote about the game in terms which summed up the feelings of Clare people everywhere. 'I have spent most of my adult life outside Clare. I have seen victorious Cork teams in open-topped buses carry the McCarthy cup from Glanmire Station over the Lee and into Patrick Street I have seen Kilkenny teams carry the same cup through the streets of their city. I have seen my old friends Tim Flood, the Rackards, Ned Wheeler and company carry the same cup through the narrow streets of New Ross. Was it any wonder that I thanked God for letting me live long enough to witness the scenes in Ennis when Anthony Daly and the Clare team brought the McCarthy cup home.'

Members of the Clare team pictured at Guinness' the morning after the All-Ireland
L/r: Ger Moroney, Michael O'Halloran, Cyril Lyons, John Chaplin, Ollie Baker, Colin Storm,
Guinness official, P. J. O'Connell, Kenny Morrissey, Christy Chaplin, Eamon Taaffe, Jim McInerney

ALL-IRELAND CHAMPIONS

An All-Ireland title with your club is every player's dream

GERRY MCINERNEY

We have a fount of talent and it will be a pity if it's not utilised

COLM FLYNN

During the autumn of 1995 the entire county basked in the afterglow of Clare's unexpectedly sudden rise to the pinnacle of hurling achievement. Supporters were by now emotionally and financially drained after a summer which put even Italia '90 in the shade and there was a fairly quick return to life's normal routines – like attending to those cows much beloved by the sports media! Pubs even reported a down-turn in trade between the All-Ireland and Christmas, so it would seem that supporters were either exhausted, or else they had started to save up in anticipation of 1996.

For the team however, it was time to celebrate and an extensive round of social engagements began. Particular priority was given to visiting all the schools in the county with the McCarthy Cup. This was strongly promoted by manager Ger Loughnane as an ideal opportunity to further encourage school-children's interest in hurling. It was also in keeping with the patient attitude which the team had displayed throughout the year when faced with hordes of young autograph hunters, and tremendous credit must be given to all of them for their generosity in the face of what must have seemed at times to be a never-ending duty.

Then of course there were the usual round of civic and club functions throughout the county. The Banner population overseas were also included, with visits to London, Chicago and New York. As with any group of people, some team members were more enthusiastic than others about attending such a multitude of events, but every effort was made to respond to invitations by sending team representatives.

Several team members received additional honours in the shape of All-Star award – Anthony Daly, David Fitzgerald, Brian Lohan, Liam Doyle, Seán McMahon, Ollie Baker, James O'Connor and Gerard O'Loughlin. For the first time ever, the All-Stars were picked by their fellow hurlers and this gave the awards an additional value. Manager Ger Loughnane received both Manager of the Year and Person of the Year Awards as confirmation of the widespread recognition which he had already received as the prime architect of Clare's success.

In January the team went on a well-deserved holiday to Thailand. The destination chosen did not fall within the usual All-Ireland winner's itinerary and once more displayed that we like to do things differently in the Banner County. It would seem in any event that a good time was had by all and the only news flash which made it back from the Far East was that P. J. O'Connell had cut his hair!

1995–96 League

In the context of the above, the 1995–96 league campaign was slow to inspire effort and enthusiasm in a team which had gone through over twelve months of relentless training and preparation up to the All-Ireland. Clare travelled to Tralee for their opening game of the 1995–96 league.Having provided the Bannermen with a guard of honour coming on to the pitch, the home side gave an exhibition of brilliant first-touch hurling to bring the All-Ireland Champions very firmly back down to earth, with Seán O'Sullivan and Tony Maunsell outstanding for The Kingdom. Their display put me in mind of Clare back through the years when they entertained the All-Ireland Champions at Cusack Park or Tulla. It was also great to see the scores of young Kerry lads surrounding the Clare players and looking for autographs before the game.

Clare only managed a 50% record in the league but produced some great flashes of hurling, notably Ronan O'Hara's point-scoring display against Offaly, Fergal Hegarty's tremendous gem of a goal at Cusack Park against Waterford and Barry Murphy's brace against Tipperary in Thurles (unlucky not to get a third). Brian Quinn's display at corner-back against Galway was reminiscent of Tommy Keane at his best and the tremendous team display against Cork at Páirc Uí Chaoimh is best described by Cork manager Jimmy Barry-Murphy. 'I couldn't believe how good Clare were when we played them in the park. Clare were exceptional, very impressive, very strong'. Clare's win over Cork was not enough to earn them a play-off in the league but they secured their position in division one for the 1996–97 season.

Sixmilebridge: All-Ireland Champions

After the disappointment of losing the Munster club finals of 1989 to Ballybrown, 1992 to Kilmallock and 1993 to Toomevara, Sixmilebridge came back in fine style to capture their second Munster club title. The 1989 and 1992 titles had been let slip when Sixmilebridge seemed in control but they were well beaten by Toomevara in 1993, 0–15 to 0–7, though Eamon Healy was very unlucky not to score a couple of goals in the closing minutes, with Jody Grace making a couple of top-class saves. After this defeat it looked all over for the Bridge at this level for at least a few years.

There was no shortage of excitement on their road to victory. A superb Scariff team were most unlucky not to beat them in the county final, with Ger Rodgers (Clare club player of the year), Barry Murphy, Mark McKenna and John Minogue in great form. Leading by two points in the dying moments, an effort at a point from the Bridge's Gerry McInerney came off the upright and was finished to the net by David Chaplin, thereby denying Scariff in the dying moments.

Scariff selector Fr Brendan Moloney spoke to me about the difficulties for rural clubs posed by a decline in population and pointed out that they seldom benefit from inward population movement like their urban counterparts. An exception in the case of Scariff are the Murphy families who are of Kilmihil origin. Brothers Derek and Enda and their cousin Barry are a great addition to the local club, with Barry also featuring prominently on the Clare U–21 and senior teams. Fr Moloney went on to say that Scariff have good players coming through in Alfie Rodgers and Darren McNamara, while Terence Fahy and Brian Minogue are featuring strongly for Whitegate. Hopefully this marks the beginning of a new era in these traditional East Clare strongholds.

Sixmilebridge overcame Waterford's Ballygunner (conquerors of Na Piarsaigh Cork) at Walsh Park in the Munster Club semi-final. The game was finely balanced until the Bridge's Noel Earley and Flan Quilligan stepped up a gear to orchestrate a win by 5–11 to 2–10. The story of the provincial win was similar with the 'Bridge pulling away in the second half against Éire Óg, Nenagh. This was exhibition stuff, with Martin Conlon, John Chaplin and Declan McInerney scoring points at will after Noel Earley got on top at centre-field. The switch of Gerry McInerney from corner to centre-forward was vital.

In the All-Ireland semi-final a very strong and experienced Sarsfield's side were hanging in there entering the last quarter, when once more McInerney came to the forty and began spraying the ball around. Again the Bridge finished very strongly with Danny Chaplin proving a most effective target-man at full-forward and scoring a great goal to leave his team well on top at the end, 5–11 to 1–12.

So the men from The Banner were off once more to Croke Park, this time for the All-Ireland Club final. This annual St Patrick's Day event has produced some great games in both hurling and football over the past few years and the clash between Sixmilebridge and their opponents Dunloy of Antrim was eagerly awaited. The Antrim champions had been defeated in the previous year's final and it was anticipated that this experience would forge them into determined opponents for the men from the Bridge. On their journey to Croke Park, Dunloy had easily disposed of the Kilkenny and Leinster champions Glenmore.

A wonderful early goal from Danny Chaplin, showing great wrist-work, provided an early taste of Sixmilebridge's style. Dunloy fought back gamely but found themselves two goals down at half time. In the second half the Bridge completely dominated, with Kevin 'Socks' McInerney and Michael O'Halloran inspirational in defence. The introduction of Niall Gilligan was also a great move as he created havoc in the Dunloy defence. In the end the Bridge won comfortably 5–10 to 2–6 to lift Clare's first ever All-Ireland Club title in the most appropriate of seasons.

Injured team captain Ian Mulready had come on in the dying moments of the game and accepted the Tom Moore Cup on behalf of his team. It was a just reward for a club who have been our representatives on many occasions in recent years. It was also an especially sweet victory for senior players like Flan Quilligan, Gerry McInerney, Danny Chaplin, Noel Earley and Noel O'Gorman. It was also a dream come true for the late Anthony Cusack, who told me after the provincial final that 'the Bridge club in the early 1930s played in the worst grade of junior'. They had indeed come a long way.

Sixmilebridge veteran Gerry McInerney spent ten years on the county team from 1981–1990 and was a star of many games. He proved in 1996 that he was still one of the best forwards around, scoring a total of 8–28 in the 'Bridge's eight club games during the 1995–96 season, a fine tally by any standards. Before the final he spoke to Seán McGoldrick of the *Sunday World*. 'It's something exceptional to be playing for your club in an All-Ireland; it's like representing your family. The lads you are playing alongside are your brothers, relations, school friends and next-door neighbours'.

1996 CHAMPIONSHIP

Clare's first game of the 1996 championship was the Munster semi-final against Limerick at the Gaelic Grounds. In their first-round game, Limerick had already crushed Cork at Páirc Uí Chaoimh and had given notice that they were going to be a serious threat to the All-Ireland champions.

The run-up to the game generated tremendous excitement and a packed Gaelic Grounds (43,534) waited in nervous anticipation under the blistering sun. Clare opened well and scored two early points, the first from Gerard O'Loughlin after he whipped on a long ball from Fergal Hegarty. By the eleventh minute, Limerick had fought back to equalise, and the first half went on to produce some excellent bouts of play and old-style first-time hurling, with the sides level on several occasions.

The first quarter of the second half saw Clare produce their best hurling when they raced into a 0–14 to 1–8 lead with points from Eamon Taaffe, James O'Connor and Fergus Tuohy. Taaffe had been introduced for the second half and was set up for a great goal chance by another substitute Ronan O'Hara shortly after his introduction. The ball seemed destined for the net but came off Declan Nash for a sixty-five which was pointed by Seán McMahon.

An injury to Ollie Baker in the fifty-third minute seemed to unsettle Clare's rhythm. Limerick seemed to gather themselves during this stoppage and dug in, not allowing the Clare forwards any room, with Mark Foley of Limerick excelling. Two points from Limerick substitute Barry Foley and one from their star marksman Gary Kirby (1–7) levelled the match. Then, in what Anthony Daly later described as 'one of the worst moments of my life', Limerick's Ciaran Carey made a brilliant solo run from his own half-back line to drive the ball over the bar and snatch an injury-time victory for Limerick.

From the point of view of drama and excitement, the game could hardly have been surpassed but, in spite of a great performance, Clare's defence of their titles was overcome by a resilient Limerick. It was little consolation that James O'Connor and Fergus Tuohy scored some great points or that Fergal Hegarty gave a great performance at centre-field. The solid full-back line of Michael O'Halloran, Brian Lohan and Frank Lohan also soaked up extreme pressure, with Brian Lohan receiving RTE's man-of-the-match award.

RTE match analyst Cyril Farrell described the second half as fantastic. 'Clare took the initiative of bringing in their subs, while Tom Ryan threw caution to the wind and the switches worked. Clare were great champions and they will be disappointed to lose a game they felt they could have won'. That was certainly how James O'Connor felt. 'It was a game we should have won. A million and one things happen in a game of hurling; you can point to any one of them and say that was the turning-point. But I would agree that Ollie's injury was a factor; that break in the game didn't help'.

U–21

Clare's U–21 hopes were also dashed when they were decisively beaten by Cork in the Munster final. Clare had barely survived the previous round after their huge 3–15 to 0–11 lead over Waterford had been whittled back to a single point. However, this game had given cause for greater hopes in the final, with some outstanding displays. A feature of the game had been two superb goals for Clare, the first from Martin Conlon, after senior player Barry Murphy dummied his opponent and allowed Conlon inside to finish the ball to the net. The second goal, scored by Murphy himself, was definitely worth the admission fee, after he linked up with David Forde in a lovely one-two before crashing the ball to the roof of the net from thirty yards. Others prominent players in that game were defenders John Kenirons and Richard Woods in defence, with Niall Gilligan excelling in the forwards.

Unfortunately, the next game proved to be a different story and Clare suffered one of their biggest defeat ever in an U–21 Munster final when they failed to Cork by twelve points, 3–16 to 2–7 at Semple Stadium. Clare were well in the game at half time, although they trailed by 0–9 to 1–4. On the restart, Clare's most polished forward on the day, Niall Gilligan, put Clare ahead with a great goal, but Cork immediately hit back for a goal. After that Clare had no answer to Cork, or more particularly Cork corner-forward Joe Deane, who clocked up a personal tally of 2–4. Two inspirational line balls from Kevin Egan certainly added to Clare's woes.

The Bannermen certainly looked out of sorts in the second half, with senior stars Eamon Taaffe and Barry Murphy held in check. On the whole, the Clare team disappointed, with only Enda Murphy, Pat Hayes, Richard Woods, Brian Minogue and Niall Gilligan doing well.

END GAME

When it came to winning major competitions, 'Poor Clare' has often ended up as the bridesmaid. The 1995 All-Ireland win certainly liberated us from a long sentence when it began to look like we might become permanently institutionalised! The passion which always fired Clare hurling once more came to the fore and, in combination with some great skill and courage, cleared a pathway to success.

The county's relatively low placings on the Munster Championship or All–Ireland rolls of honour have sometimes concealed the fact that Clare is a county with a proud hurling tradition. This may have ebbed and flowed over the years, but any analysis of other counties will show that this has happened to the best of them. The fact that we are in a strong hurling province has meant that it has been difficult to achieve championship honours, particularly when the arrival of a talented team has often co-incided with great eras for our neighbouring counties. So why were we successful in 1995 and what might the future hold for Clare hurling? Three people who have long associations with Clare hurling, Colm Flynn, Fr Harry Bohan and Bishop Willie Walsh, point to some of the factors which have led to success and cast their minds to the future. The longest-serving member in Clare's present backroom is team physio Colm Flynn, also a well-known figure in the boxing world. He got involved with the 1995 team having been absent for a number of years, although not absent from hurling. 'I was asked to get involved by Ger Loughnane in 1995. Prior to that I'd seen professionalism at its best within the Galway camp under Cyril Farrell. There was a tremendous buzz and the whole of the Galway county board were behind you. Ger Loughnane was the catalyst in 1995; he made it happen and was just what Clare needed.

'One cannot go on indefinitely; there's a lot of hard work and we have a lot of other commitments. You can give a commitment to a county hurling team to the detriment of other things; it's a huge sacrifice; things can pass you by. The highs are great, but the lows when they come, one can do without them. It's no joyride, dark nights in Crusheen and a terrible expenditure of one's time. Mike McNamara has given tremendous service. We have a fount of talent and it will be a pity if it's not utilised. I think that there's another championship in this team. There should be a spin-off from 1995'.

Bishop Willie Walsh has also been a long-time servant of Clare hurling, from his days with St Flannan's to his involvement with the county team. '1995 represented a dream come through in the sense that I've been involved with Clare hurling over the past twenty-five years, mostly with St Flannan's. From 1986 on I've been involved with minors, U–21 and seniors in latter years. I was delighted for the players, mentors and supporters, especially for the supporters. Time and again they went full of hope to Munster finals and came home disappointed, but somehow having won a match or two the following year, the supporters gathered and returned again.

'The county board chairman Brendan Vaughan pushed the idea of bringing somebody from outside the county to manage the senior hurling team. Len Gaynor had a major influence in transforming the team and the attitude of the players. I think that Len's outstanding achievement was not actually his coaching but his player management, his respect for players. He insisted that the players be treated well by the county board and the board responded extremely well – the players then responded. I was involved with Len and Tony Kelly first, then with Len and Ger Loughnane. After that Ger and I departed the scene and Enda O'Connor and Tim Crowe came in.

'I regard Ger Loughnane as the best hurling coach I have come across; his training sessions were marvellous. The players worked extremely hard and they enjoyed the sessions. Ger's emphasis on hurling and improving the quality and speed of hurling showed last year. He brought with him Michael McNamara and Tony Considine, both of whom had been involved with winning Clare teams. They brought that confidence of having won; as a team of three they did an excellent job.

'However, I wouldn't give all the credit to management. Going back to the late 1980s, a lot of work was done quietly at Féile na nGael, which I would regard as a very significant event in the uplifting of Clare hurling. Many of the lads involved in the present senior team emerged from the good work being done at under-age level in the late 1980s, coming through the minors of 1989 and the U–21s of 1992. If I were to issue a warning at the moment, I would say that's where we need to be looking. Are we maintaining the standards at that level? If we're not, we'll pay the price early next century'.

As regards the general development of hurling, Mick Malone and Fr Harry Bohan aired some views on the general development of hurling. Firstly, Mick Malone: 'The GAA is lacking a professional PR system. In any company, they identify the product and they market it. We have the product in hurling but we're not marketing it; we may have to go more professional in our approach. Colleges hurling is neglected; third level is neglected.

'I think that the education system will have to change in so far as anyone that's good at any type of sport should be allowed to pursue it, be examined on it and allotted points on it. The pressures that are generated within the walls of a college are great. If sport is overlooked, I think you'll get a generation of sociological misfits from the lack of not realising the safety valve of sport. It should be recognised more and the GAA should step in to give grants to players for colleges hurling'.

Fr Harry Bohan feels that constant regeneration is important at all levels within the GAA if sport is to thrive and interest is to be maintained. 'There seems to be two GAA's, one in administration and the other on the field. The GAA is a voluntary organisation and, with the best will in the world, people can only give a certain amount at top level for a period of time. This means that, in effect, there should be a good healthy turnover of personnel at officer level. Even if they were the best and most skilled administrators in the world, you do need a turnover to ensure that the vision, dynamism and excitement of the GAA is kept before the people at all times. Just as you have a turnover of players, you need a turnover of officers at board level. I think that's a fundamental problem within the county and at national level'.

So what do the players think? Cyril Lyons echoes the views of Bishop Walsh. 'Years slip by quickly. Different years bring different problems and it's important that Clare win at least two All-Ireland titles before the turn of the century. The players are young and they're good enough'.

James O'Connor sees a bright future for hurling in general. 'Hurling at the moment is up there on a pedestal and the coverage in the papers is excellent. The high profile is incredible in *The Examiner* and *The Irish Times*; Seán Moran in the *Times* and Jim O'Sullivan in *The Examiner* are great writers'. And how does he see Clare making it back to the headlines?

'We need to find a couple of new players to give the thing an impetus. Tipperary will have new players coming through and Cork won't be down for long either. I also think it's important that the players themselves put the work in. There's certainly no reason why we can't be there or thereabout next year. Ger Loughnane is the best coach; he's streets ahead of everyone else. His pride and passion for Clare hurling outstrips everybody's. I don't think anybody else in Clare was capable of doing what Ger Loughnane did. It's vital that the present backroom team stay on next year'.

A last word to Anthony Daly: 'There's a great team-spirit instilled in the present county side; the players are close. We have tremendous young players down the middle. Certainly the future looks bright'.

The thoughts and feelings of hurling people have been an essential element of this book. In 1934, Cumann Dal gCais (Ennis Dalcassians) published a booklet on the history of Clare GAA clubs to commemorate the organisation's fiftieth anniversary and I will end with the passionate cry of one anonymous contributor:

> Like the Atlantic charging with violent fury against the cliffs of Corca Baiscin to be flung back in a seething mass of spray and foam and smoke, the mighty giants of our race, with strength, speed, brain and eye, sway to and fro in the great contest, rhythmic in movement and eager for the prize, but unconquered in defeat. The games are symbolic of our story; they bind our scattered race with an eternal sympathy and they shall endure for ever.

Up the Banner!

'I said we were going to do it!' – Ger Loughnane

WHO'S WHO

Arthur, Michael: Newmarket. All-round sportsman, also played rugby and soccer. Member of the all-powerful Newmarket team of the late 1960s. Played for Clare from 1966–1970.

Barry-Murphy, Jimmy: St Finbarr's, Cork. Dual star for Cork. Holder of six All-Ireland medals including one for football.

Bohan, Fr Harry: Feakle. Manager of the Clare team during the 1970s. Played senior hurling for Feakle during the late 1950s.

Brennan, Pat: Ennis. Played senior hurling with Éire Óg during the 1960s.

Callinan, John: Clarecastle. Long-serving Clare hurler. Made debut at seventeen in 1972 and retired from county seniors in 1987.

Carroll, Des: Scariff. Long-serving Scariff and Clare hurler. Almost constant on Clare team from 1945–1955. Captained Clare for two seasons.

Connellan, David: Ennis. Wing-back on Ennis CBS Harty Cup teams of 1970 and 1971.

Considine, Noel: Clarecastle. Played in goal for Clare at junior and senior level. Custodian with 1993 junior team. Now with Éire Óg.

Considine, Tony: Cratloe. Selector of All-Ireland winning Clare junior team of 1993 and senior team of 1995.

Corry, Jimmy: Sixmilebridge. Former club secretary and team mentor.

Cronin, Pat: Newmarket. Highly-rated Newmarket and Clare forward of the 1960s.

Cullinan, Jimmy: Newmarket. Long-serving club and county hurler. A constant part of the Clare team for 1961–1976. Great ball-player.

Curtis P. J.: Broadcaster, record producer and author.

Cusack, Anthony: Sixmilebridge. Founder member and chairman of club. Died in 1996.

Custy, Frank: Ruan. Goal-keeper during a great spell for Ruan (1959–1962). Played on a few occasions for the county team.

Custy, Seán: Ruan. Member of Clare team from 1960–1962. A constant member of the New York teams during the late1960s. Brother of Frank.

Daly, Anthony: Clarecastle. Member of Clare team since 1989. Inspirational captain since 1992. Member of a distinguished sporting family.

Danagher, Liam: Newmarket. Stylish Clare mid-fielder of the 1960s.

Danaher, Pat: Tulla. A member of the successful senior amalgamation Brian Boru's in 1975. Also played for Clare.

Dilger, Bernie: Ennis. Also known as 'Champ'. Éire Óg and Clare wing-back of the late 1950s. One of four brothers to play for Clare, Michael 'Gruggy', Massie and George.

Donoghue, John: Kilnamona. County board delegate from 1940 to 1954.

Doyle, John Joe: Newmarket. Highly-rated Clare corner-back during the period 1928–1938. Captained Clare in the 1932 All-Ireland final.

Doyle, Ned: Whitegate. Represented Clare at junior and senior level, mostly at wing-back. Father of present Clare wing-back, Liam Doyle. Now lives in Bodyke.

Flynn, Colm: Ennis. Trainer of Clare team 1966–1967. Physio during 1970s and current physio. Also has been involved with Galway.

Gallagher, Michael: Kilkishen. Clare FM sports reporter and hurling enthusiast.

Gaynor, Len: Tipperary wing-back 1964–1974. Managed Clare 1991–1994.

Gilligan, Esther: Gowran, Co. Kilkenny and Ennis. Long-time follower of Kilkenny and Clare. Mother of hurlers Noel, Paddy and Brendan.

Guilfoyle, Tommy: Feakle. Talented Clare full-forward c. 1984–1994, injury curtailed his career. Brother of Mike, another inter-county player during these years.

Guinnane, Michael: Clarecastle. Also known as 'Tolly'. Well known Clare hurler c. 1946–56. Brother of hurlers Peter and Christy 'Wax'.

Hanly, John: Clarecastle. Has coached many teams at all levels. Former county board chairman.

Hanly, Mary: Newmarket. Prominent camogie and hurling coach at secondary schools level. Trained Newmarket senior hurlers in 1992.

Harvey, Tom: Inagh. County board official and prominent member of Inagh GAA club.

Heaslip, Seán: Ennis (Éire Óg). Long-serving club hurler. Represented Clare 1980–81 and 1987.

Hogan, Jack: Newmarket and Feakle. Clare hurler of late 1940s.

Horgan, John: Cork (Blackrock). Member of the Cork team of 1970–81.

Howard, Pa: Tubber. Archivist and longtime supporter.

Hurley, Joe: Ruan. Club secretary during 1940s.

Hynes, Flan: Ennis. Long involvement with club hurling. Played for Ennis Faugh's and also won two senior medals with St Joseph's. He also played for Avondhu in Cork.

Kelly, Tony: (Éire Óg) Clare senior hurler 1974–76. Manager of county team in 1990.

Leahy, Mick: Ruan. Clare team member c. 1950–56. Also played club hurling in Limerick, Wexford and Kilkenny.

Lohan, Brian: Shannon (Wolfe Tone's). Clare full-back. Players' Player of the Year award in 1995. Brother of Clare corner-back Frank and son of former Galway and Clare hurler Gus.

Loughnane, Ger: Feakle and Shannon (Wolfe Tone's). Wing-back of the 1970s and 1980s – regular from 1973 to 1987. Manager of 1995 All-Ireland winners.

Loftus, Vincent: (Éire Óg) Clare corner-back 1964–1974. His brothers Paddy and Des also played for Clare.

Lyons, Cyril: Ruan. Has played with the county since 1982. Most senior member of the 1995 squad.

Lyons, Seán: Ennis. Member of All-Ireland winning Clare Vocational Schools' team of 1979.

McCarthy, John: Ennis (Éire Óg). Regular member of Clare team 1960–1965.

McCarthy, Justin: Passage, Co. Cork. Played with Cork 1965–75. Clare coach 1976–79.

McInerney, John: Clarecastle. Long-serving, popular, Clarecastle official.

McKeogh, Martin: Killaloe (Smith–O'Brien's). Played in several positions with Clare from 1972–79. Injury curtailed his career.

McMahon, Johnny: Newmarket. Member of Clare team throughout 1970s. Two All-Star awards at corner-back.

McMahon, Matthew: Clare FM GAA commentator.

McNamara, Joe: Newmarket. A brother of Patrick 'The Hound' McNamara who played on 1932 team. Lifelong follower of Clare hurling.

McNamara, Paddy: Newmarket. Forceful Clare forward of the 1960s. Holder of a record thirteen county championship medals.

McNamara, Stephen: Ennis (Éire Óg). Member of All-Ireland winning team. Dual player at senior level.

McNicholas, Kitty: Galway and Ennis. Prime mover in Clare camogie, both as player and mentor since coming to Clare in 1972.

Maher, Tony: Ennis (Rovers). Colleges star with Ennis CBS 1960–61. Founder member of Banner club.

Mahon, Colm: Ennis (Éire Óg). Gave tremendous service to his club. Played for Clare 1981–82.

Mahony, Jimmy: The late Jimmy Mahony of old Mill Street [Ennis] and New York was an authority on the social, political and sporting history of Ennis during the early decades of the twentieth century.

Malone, Mick: Cork (Muskerry). Played with Cork c. 1970–1980. Part of three in a row team.

Malone, Tom: Miltown Malbay (Clonbony). Long-serving supporter and promoter of hurling in West Clare.

Meehan, Seán: Sixmilebridge. Club player from c. 1950–63. Played for Clare at all levels.

Minogue, John: Scariff. Regular on Clare team c. 1982–90. Captain for a number of years.

Moloney, Fr Brendan: Scariff. Dean of St Flannan's College.

Moloney, Johnny: Scariff. Long-serving selector with Clare teams during 1940s.

Murphy, Michael: Clooney. Member of Clare team 1976–79. U–21 selector 1996.

Nihill, Michael: Ennis. One of the founders of the Clare supporters club.

Nugent Matt: Tubber and St Joseph's. Regarded by fellow players as one of the all-time greats of hurling. Played for Clare 1946–1963. Regular on Munster team. [RIP] Father of hurlers Michael, Martin and Tony.

O'Brien, Paschal: Ennis (Éire Óg). Popular Clare goal-keeper 1965–71.

O'Connell, Christy: Barefield. Long-time follower of Clare teams, especially from 1928–1932.

O'Connor, James: Barefield (St Joseph's). On county team since 1993. Vital member of the 1995 team.

O'Connor, Pat: Tubber. Member of county team c. 1976–82. His brothers, Enda and Michael, also played for Clare.

Ó hEithir, Pádraig: Miltown-Malbay, Oileán Inis Mór, and Ennis. Teacher for many years on Inis Mór. Father of the late Breandán Ó hEithir, well-known television presenter and author (including *Over the Bar).*

O'Loughlin, Gerard: Clarecastle. Better known as 'Sparrow'. Talented Clarecastle and Clare forward since 1987.

O'Shea, Pat 'Whack': Sixmilebridge. Club hurler of the 1960s. Brother of Mick who played for Clare.

O'Toole, Margaret: Ballynacally. Played for Éire Óg and Clare in the 1970s. She captained Clare to their first ever All-Ireland camogie title in 1974.

O'Sullivan, Tony: Cork (Na Piarsaigh). Member of Cork team 1982–94. Current selector.

Purcell, Flan: Feakle. Highly-regarded Clare centre-back of the 1930s.

Pyne, Noel: Member of well-known Ennis sporting family. Richard and Noel played for Clare while Derry and Brendan played for Éire Óg.

Quinn, Jimmy: Clarecastle. Represented Ennis CBS in college hurling 1962–64. Played senior for Clarecastle. Jimmy is probably better known in equestrian circles.

Quilligan, Flan: Sixmilebridge. Club player from 1977 to 1996. All-Ireland club medal winner. Clare senior during early 1980s.

Shanahan, James: Broadford. Clare centre-field player 1982–90.

Sheedy, Kieran: Feakle. Writer and broadcaster. Author of *Feakle* and *The Clare Elections.* Brother of Clare hurler Dermot Sheedy 1955–64.

Sheridan, Michael 'Aoner': Ennis (Dalcassians). Clare hurler of the 1930s.

Small, Eugene: Ardnacrusha. Clare goal-keeper 1948–54.

Smyth, Jimmy: Ruan. Played for Clare from 1948 to 1967. Free-scoring forward. On Munster Railway Cup teams for twelve seasons. Won eight medals – a record for a Clareman. Regarded by contemporaries and writers as one of the greatest forwards of all times.

Stack, Seán: Sixmilebridge. Stylish Clare centre-back from 1974–87.

Vaughan, Brendan: Clooney. Long-serving member of Clare county board. Former chairman.

Walsh, Jimmy: Bodyke. Also Brian Boru's. Gave many fine displays in goal for Clare. Sub to Seamus Durack for some years.

Walsh, Willie: Bishop of Killaloe. Long-serving coach in St Flannan's College. Also former Clare selector.

White, Paddy: Ennis. Involved with Ennis Rovers and Éire Óg for many years. Son of Mickie White, Clare hurler of the 1930s.

Wiley, Colm: Bodyke. Captained Brian Boru's to senior championship success in 1975. Played for many years in London. Played for Clare.

ROLL OF HONOUR
COUNTY CHAMPIONSHIP RESULTS

Year	Winner	Score	Runner-up	Score
1887	Smith O'Brien's-Garranboy	0–3	Ogonelloe	0–1
1888	Ogonelloe	3–1	Tulla	0–1
1889	Tulla	2–3	Feakle	0–6
1890	Ennis Faughs		Feakle	
1891–1895		no championship		
1896	Tulla	3–5	O'Callaghan's Mills	2–6
1897	Tulla	3–8	O'Callaghan's Mills	1–8
1898	Carrahan	awarded	Tulla	
1899	Tulla	1–9	Ennis Faughs	1–1
1900	Carrahan			
1901		no official championship		
1902	Kilnamona	1–17	Barefield	2–2
1903	Kilnamona	4–14	Thomond's	Nil
1904	O'Callaghan's Mills	2–4	Tulla	0–4
1905	Tulla	2–11	Carrahan	0–1
1906	O'Callaghan's Mills	5–10	Kilnamona	0–1
1907	Scariff	4–12	O'Callaghan's Mills	5–5
1908	Kilnamona	0–11	O'Callaghan's Mills	0–10
1909	Fireball's (O'C. Mills)		St Patrick's (O'C. Mills)	1–2
1910	O'Callaghan's Mills	5–0	Tulla	3–2
1911	Ennis Hurling Club	3–1	O'Callaghan's Mills	1–2
1912	Newmarket	3–3	O'Callaghan's Mills	3–1
1913	Tulla			
1914	Ennis Dalcassians	3–1	Newmarket	1–0
1915	Ennis Dalcassians	3–4	Newmarket	2–4
1916	Newmarket	8–2	Ennis	2–2
1917	Scariff	5–2	Feakle	5–0
1918	O'Callaghan's Mills	7–2	Scariff	4–5
1919	Clonlara		Scariff	
1920	Ennis [declared null and void]	2–4	O'Callaghan's Mills	1–1
1921		no county board		
1922		championship undecided		
1923	Kilkishen	awarded	Feakle	
1924	Ennis Dalcassians	7–2	Newmarket	3–2
1925	Newmarket		Tulla	
1926	Newmarket	3–5	O'Callaghan's Mills	2–3
1927	Newmarket		Ennis Dalcassians	
1928	Ennis/Clarecastle	4–1	Newmarket	0–3
1929	Ennis Dalcassians	awarded	Newmarket	
1930	Newmarket		Ennis	
1931	Newmarket	3–4	Ennis	1–3
1932	Kilkishen	6–5	Newmarket	1–1
1933	Tulla	7–1	Newmarket	2–1
1934	Ennis Dalcassians	4–2	Clooney	3–1
1935	Feakle	6–1	Newmarket	2–3
1936	Newmarket	6–2	Clarecastle	2–3
1937	O'Callaghan's Mills	5–2	Clarecastle	2–2
1938	Feakle	4–6	Kilkishen	1–5

Year				
1939	Feakle	4–6	Clarecastle	3–4
1940	Feakle	3–4	Clooney	2–3
1941	Ennis	5–2	Clooney	2–1
1942	Clooney	3–6	Scariff	3–5
1943	Clarecastle	4–3	Scariff	4–2
1944	Feakle	9–3	Clooney	0–4
1945	Clarecastle	4–7	Broadford	2–2
1946	Scariff	3–3	Feakle	2–5
1947	Bodyke	5–8	Clarecastle	3–5
1948	Ruan	6–4	Clarecastle	5–7
	Ruan (replay)	6–3	Clarecastle	3–5
1949	Clarecastle	4–8	Ruan	3–3
1950	Whitegate	5–1	Ruan	3–1
1951	Ruan	3–6	St Joseph's	2–2
1952	Scariff	4–6	Sixmilebridge	2–0
1953	Scariff	5–2	Newmarket	2–7
1954	St Joseph's	3–6	O'Callaghan's Mills	2–2
1955	Newmarket	3–9	Éire Óg	3–3
1956	Éire Óg	4–5	Clarecastle	2–8
1957	Éire Óg	5–9	Whitegate	2–3
1958	St Joseph's	3–6	Feakle	2–2
1959	Ruan	2–6	Éire Óg	0–4
1960	Ruan	6–9	Scariff	3–10
1961	Whitegate	5–7	Newmarket	3–9
1962	Ruan	3–4	Sixmilebridge	1–10
	Ruan (replay)	3–9	Sixmilebridge	2–8
1963	Newmarket	6–10	Whitegate	3–7
1964	Newmarket	8–12	Clarecastle	5–7
1965	Newmarket	2–6	Éire Óg	1–6
1966	Éire Óg	2–8	Whitegate	1–4
1967	Newmarket	3–10	Clarecastle	2–4
1968	Newmarket	2–8	Clarecastle	1–9
1969	Newmarket	3–5	Clarecastle	2–8
	Newmarket (replay)	9–13	Clarecastle	3–6
1970	Clarecastle (replay)	1–7	Crusheen	0–5
1971	Newmarket	3–9	Clarecastle	2–12
	Newmarket (replay)	2–7	Clarecastle	1–7
1972	Newmarket	7–8	St Senan's	3–5
1973	Newmarket	7–10	Clarecastle	4–16
1974	Newmarket	1–6	Crusheen	2–2
1975	Brian Boru's	4–7	Éire Óg	2–9
1976	Newmarket	1–11	Sixmilebridge	1–5
1977	Sixmilebridge	1–6	Kilkishen	1–5
1978	Newmarket	3–10	Clarecastle	2–8
1979	Sixmilebridge	5–11	St Brendan's	0–9
1980	Éire Óg-Dal gCais	3–10	Newmarket	1–9
1981	Newmarket	3–8	Tubber	1–10
1982	Éire Óg	2–11	Sixmilebridge	2–11
	Éire Óg (replay)	3–8	Sixmilebridge	2–9
1983	Sixmilebridge	1–10	Éire Óg	3–4
	Sixmilebridge (replay)	1–10	Éire Óg	1–7
1984	Sixmilebridge	3–7	Clarecastle	1–12
1985	Kilmaley	0–10	Éire Óg	0–8
1986	Clarecastle	2–11	O'Callaghan's Mills	0–7
1987	Clarecastle	0–15	Feakle	0–11

1988	Feakle	1–17	Ruan	1–10
1989	Sixmilebridge	3–14	Clarecastle	1–11
1990	Éire Óg	1–5	O'Callaghan's Mills	1–3
1991	Clarecastle	0–14	Scariff	1–5
1992	Sixmilebridge	1–11	Éire Óg	1–10
1993	Sixmilebridge	3–8	O'Callaghan's Mills	2–6
1994	Clarecastle	1–8	St Joseph's	0–8
1995	Sixmilebridge	2–10	Scariff	0–15
1996	Wolfe Tone's (Shannon)	1–11	Clarecastle	0–8

CLARE CHAMPION CUP

More commonly known as The Clare Cup, this was presented to the GAA by Mr Sarsfield Maguire of *The Clare Champion* in 1928 for a senior league competition.

1928	Ennis–Clarecastle	3–3	Newmarket	1–4
1929	Ennis Dalcassians	awarded – game unfinished		
1930	Newmarket	4–7	Ennis Dalcassians	2–4
1931	Newmarket	5–5	Ennis	3–6
1932	Newmarket	8–3	Kilkishen	2–0
1933	Newmarket (replay)	2–6	Tulla	1–6
1934	Clooney	4–4	Clonlara	4–2
1935	Newmarket	7–6	O'Callaghan's Mills	1–1
1936	Newmarket	2–4	Feakle	1–6
1937	Ennis Dalcassians	walkover	O'Callaghan's Mills	
1938	Feakle	6–2	Tulla	3–2
1939	Tulla (replay)	5–5	Newmarket	5–3
1940	Feakle	6–5	Clooney	0–4
1941	Clooney	5–2	Bodyke	2–3
1942	Scariff	4–4	Clooney	3–3
1943	Clarecastle	4–6	23rd Battalion	3–2
1944	23rd Battalion	2–5	Clooney	2–4
1945	Clarecastle	4–4	Tulla	4–1
1946	Clarecastle	4–5	Tulla	4–1
1947	Newmarket	walkover	Feakle	
1948	Newmarket	5–3	Bodyke	4–1
1949	Newmarket	2–8	Ruan	3–3
1950	Scariff	5–7	Newmarket	3–4
1951	Broadford	awarded	Whitegate	
1952	Newmarket	5–3	Clarecastle	2–5
1953	St Joseph's	3–7	Newmarket	2–3
1954	Sixmilebridge	4–6	Newmarket	2–6
1955	Éire Óg	4–6	Feakle	2–3
1956	Sixmilebridge	2–13	Ruan	2–4
1957	St Joseph's	5–5	Whitegate	2–5
1958	Whitegate	3–3	St Joseph's	1–5
1959	Éire Óg (replay)	6–5	Clarecastle	4–6
1960	Whitegate	6–8	Scariff	2–1
1961	Ruan	5–6	St Joseph's	1–2
1962	Newmarket	3–4	Sixmilebridge	1–9
1963	Newmarket	8–5	St Joseph's	0–6
1964	Feakle	3–9	Tubber	2–10
1965	Crusheen	5–4	Éire Óg	4–6
1966	Newmarket	5–12	Feakle	2–4

1967	Newmarket	7–14	Crusheen	1–3
1968	Newmarket	7–13	Clarecastle	6–1
1969	Newmarket	5–8	Éire Óg	3–4
1970	Crusheen	2–6	Clarecastle	0–5
1971	Newmarket	8–5	Éire Óg	1–5
1972	Newmarket	5–6	Crusheen	3–1
1973	Newmarket	3–5	Éire Óg	1–5
1974	Newmarket	5–14	Brian Boru's	3–8
1975	Sixmilebridge	1–9	Feakle	0–11
1976	Sixmilebridge	2–9	Newmarket	1–4
1977	Brian Boru's	2–8	Sixmilebridge	2–5
1978	Sixmilebridge	3–9	Crusheen	3–8
1979	Sixmilebridge	on points system		
1980	Sixmilebridge	2–8	Tubber	2–5
1981	Kilmaley	1–14	Tubber	3–1
1982	Sixmilebridge	3–9	Feakle	1–13
1983	Clarecastle	3–6	Tubber	2–9
	Clarecastle	3–9	Tubber	3–9
	Clarecastle	2–12	Tubber	2–9
1984	Clarecastle	2–14	Feakle	1–10
1985	Tubber	2–13	Éire Óg	0–16
1986	Tulla	3–7	Sixmilebridge	4–3
1987	Feakle	2–10	Éire Óg	2–7
1988	Feakle	2–15	Broadford	1–7
1989	Sixmilebridge	3–13	Feakle	0–10
1990	O'Callaghan's Mills	0–15	Clarecastle	0–11
1991	O'Callaghan's Mills	2–8	Scariff	1–6
1992	Clarecastle	3–5	O'Callaghan's Mills	0–10
1993	O'Callaghan's Mills	1–11	Sixmilebridge	1–11
	O'Callaghan's Mills	2–10	Sixmilebridge	2–6
1994	Scariff	2–12	Clarecastle	3–4

ACKNOWLEDGMENTS

BIBLIOGRAPHY:
The G.A.A. by Marcus de Búrca; *Ballads of Clare* by Seán P. Ó Cillín; *Christy Ring* by Val Dorgan; *A Lifetime in Hurling, The Clash of the Ash* and *A Century of Gaelic Games* by Raymond Smith; *Giants of the Ash* by Brendan Fullam; *Feakle* by Kieran Sheedy; *Seán Óg* by Seán Óg Ó Ceallacháin; *The Kilkenny G.A.A. Story* by Tom Ryall; *Camán* by Art Ó Maolfabhail; *Scéal na hIomána* le Bráthair Ó Caithnia; *The Banner* published by Claremen and Women's Association New York; *Munster G.A.A. History* by Jim Cronin; *The Begrudger's Guide to Irish Politics* and *Over the Bar* by Breandán Ó hEithir; *History of the Irish Brigade in the Service of France* by John Cornelius O'Callaghan; White's *History of Clare.*

CLUB HISTORIES:
The Claret and Gold (Tulla); *Treasured Memories* (O'Callaghan's Mills and Kilkishen); *A Proud Past* (Newmarket-on-Fergus); *Images and Memories* (Quin/Clooney/Maghera/Dangan); *The Clash of the Ash in Ruan; Éire Óg 1952–1967; Ennis Rovers; Cumann Dal gCais; The G.A.A. in Clarecastle* by Joseph Power; *History of the G.A.A. in Whitegate and Mountshannon* by Patrick Madden; *History of Smith O'Brien's G.A.A. Club* by Seán Kierse; *History of Kilnamona; History of Scariff (The Crooked Ash); Clare Association Yearbook 1995; Christian Brothers Ennis 1927–1937; Christian Brothers Ennis 1827–1977; St. Flannan's College 1881–1981.*

ARTICLES:
'The Golden Age of Clooney Hurling' by Jimmy Smyth; 'A Magpie View' by John Hanly; 'The Passing Years' by Monsignor Michael Hamilton; 'A House Divided' by Noel Pyne; 'The Day Ennis Split in Two' by Marie Barrett; 'Fifteen C.B.S. Heroes Capture Harty Cup' by Bobby Burke; 'Paradise Revisited' by Arthur Ford; 'Camán' by Vigilant; 'Down Memory Lane' by Michael Henchy; 'The Best Years of My Life' by Jimmy Conroy; 'What's in a Name' by Pádraig Puirséal; 'The Colleges Front' by Peadar O'Brien; 'Clonlara's Seán Clancy Remembers' by Brendan Vaughan; 'The Ghosts of Past Defeats laid to rest' by Mick Leahy; 'The Clareman who taught hurling to the French' by Leo Bowes; 'Schools Manuscript Collection – Hurling in Clonlara' by Josie Moloney and Kitty Galvin; 'The Painful Wait Continues' by Pádraig Mac Mathúna.

NEWSPAPERS/PHOTOGRAPHS/RADIO/VIDEO:
The Clare Champion; The Clare County Express; The Banner; The Cork Examiner; The Irish Times; Irish Independent; Irish Press; Evening Press; Nenagh Guardian; Limerick Leader; Munster G.A.A. History; Our Games Annual 1958; Seán Stack interviewed by Joe Ó Muircheartaigh of Clare FM; 'Fifty Years of Ruan Hurling' by Brooks Studios; Michael Arthur; Pat Brennan; Seán Custy; Esther Gilligan; Seán Lyons; John McCarthy; John McInerney; Kitty McNicholas; Christy McNamara; Margaret O'Toole; Seán Meehan; Michael Nihill; Joe Pender; Flan Purcell; Aoner Sheridan; Aidan Sweeney; Michael Mulcaire.

THANKS TO: Mary Arthur, Johnny Barry, Paschal Brooks, Denis Canty, Martin Casey, Joe Carmody, Michael Corley, Gay Cooke, Peter Considine, Paddy Crowe, Martin Crowe, Elizabeth Crimmins, Breda Cullinan, Stephen Chapman, Maureen Comber, Tony Cusack, Michael Dinan, Seán Dinan, Geraldine Dinan, Kenneth Doyle, Paddy Duggan (RIP), Michael Donnellan, Kevin Doherty, John Dunne, Haulie Daly (RIP), Mary Duggan, Val Donnellan, Donal Hassett, Jimmy Hassett, Liam Harvey, Nuala Hogan, Brian Hynes, Liam Hynes, Bridget Edwards, Donal Fitzpatrick, Pat Fox, Ann Gallagher, Colman Garrihy, Ann Glynn, Michael Griffin, Jane Guthrie, Liz McGonagle, Dympna McNamara, Pakie McNamara, (RIP), Jackie Hynes, Liam McInerney, Colm McDonagh, Cora McNulty, Audrey McMahon, Ann McMahon, Maura McNicholas, Pádraig MacMathúna, Frank Malone, Róisín McMahon, Vinnie McMahon, Patrick McMahon, Anne McBride, Agnes McBride, Mary McGrath, Gerry Moroney, Maureen Nihill, John Nevin, David O'Loughlin, Tony O'Gorman, Ciarán Ó

Murchadha, Niamh Ní Mhurchadha, Donal O'Grady, Ann O'Donnell, Paddy O'Donoghue, Angela O'Sullivan, Michael O'Gorman (RIP), Frances O'Gorman, Mick O'Halloran, Sarah O'Halloran, Patrick 'Duckle' O'Loughlin, Annie O'Loughlin, Máiréad Ní hEithir, Liam Ó Muirthile, Joe Pender, Geraldine Pender, Marion Petty, Edith Pieperhoff, Birdie Purcell, Matt Purcell, Kieran Hennessy, Peter Keane, Michael Keane, Michael Kilmartin, Josie Kerin, Tony Kelly, Fr Gerry Kenny, Jack Keane, Marie Kinney, Gerry Kennedy, Albert Keating, Charlie Lynch, Francis Lynch, Seán Lynch (RIP), Michael Leahy, Billy Loughnane, Cathy Kelleher, Liam Kelleher, Brian Kelleher, John Looney, Aidan Looney, Jimmy Mahony (RIP), Joe Molony, John Moroney (RIP), Betty Murphy, Eoin Marren, D. J. Meehan, Paddy Quinn (RIP), Jimmy Quinn, Pete Robins, Mary Robins, Liam Ryan, Jimmy Reale, Brendan Ryan, Sinéad Spellissy, Donal Twomey, Aidan Tuttle (RIP), Vincent Sheridan, Marian Small, Mary Sugrue, Marian Shanahan, Brídí Vaughan, Michael Varden, Nora Wallace, Maura Walzer, Patsi Wycherley.

Visit County Clare

Carved out by nature.

A SPORTING PARADISE

You'll find more sporting facilities, more fun, more entertainment and more holiday adventures in Clare. Top-class golf courses, a wealth of fish-filled lakes, rivers and streams. The Atlantic for seafishing, snorkelling and diving and the pot-holing challenge of the Burren's underworld.

SCENIC BEAUTY

Clare has natural beauty - the magnificent Cliffs of Moher; the famous Burren with its lunar landscapes and rare flora; and superb gardens and forest parks.

THE MAJESTIC SHANNON

A river of exceptional beauty with placid lakes and many tributaries. Rent a cruiser and relax into a voyage of discovery, or partake in a variety of watersports including sailing, fishing, skiing and swimming on Lough Derg.

ENTERTAINMENT

Clare offers variety: traditional Irish music, pub sing-songs; theatre and variety; fun-filled festivals; discos and cinemas. Enjoy yourself!

BEACHES

Golden sandy beaches and clear seas at the resorts of Kilkee, Spanish Point, Lahinch and Ballyvaughan... make Clare a paradise for children and adults alike.

EXPLORE THE PAST

Clare is rich in reminders of our ancient past. Visit the mediaeval castles of Bunratty and Knappogue, ancient abbeys; Megalithic tombs; Bronze Age settlements and a recreated 19th century village at Bunratty Folk Park.

MEDIAEVAL FESTIVITY

The mediaeval castles of Bunratty and Knappogue are renowned for sumptuous banquets and merriment. Singers, musicians and storytellers provide the superb entertainment.

COUNTY CLARE

This is only a taste of the pleasures in store for you. Add in excellent restaurants and a variety of quality accommodation and you'll know why we say "You're spoiled for choice in Clare". But isn't that what you want on a holiday?